Some Degree
of Power

SOME DEGREE
OF POWER

FROM HIRED HAND
TO UNION CRAFTSMAN
IN THE PREINDUSTRIAL
AMERICAN PRINTING TRADES,
1778–1815

Mark A. Lause

THE UNIVERSITY OF ARKANSAS PRESS
FAYETTEVILLE   1991

95 94 93 92 91 5 4 3 2 1

Designer: Brenda J. Zodrow
Typeface: Trump Mediaeval

The paper used in this publication meets the minimum
requirements of the American National Standard for Permanence of
Paper for Printed Library Materials Z39.48-1984. ∞

Library of Congress Cataloging-in-Publication Data

Lause, Mark A.
    Some degree of power : from hired hand to union craftsman in the
  preindustrial American printing trades, 1778–1815 / by Mark A. Lause.
        p.   cm.
    Includes bibliographical references and index.
    ISBN 1-55728-185-8 (alk. paper)
    1. Trade-unions—Printing industry—United States—History. 2. Printing
  industry—United States—History—18th century. 3. Printing industry—
  United States—History—19th century. 4. Printers—United States—
  Directories.   I. Title.
  Z243.U6L38   1991
  331.88'116862'0973—dc20   90-38565
                                                                      CIP

Contents

Illustrations

Tables

Acknowledgments

This study grew over the years from the efforts of numerous people. I am most indebted to Professor Leo Schelbert of the University of Illinois at Chicago, who directed this piece as a dissertation. Professor Elizabeth Balanoff of Roosevelt University earlier had supervised this project as a master's thesis and continued to support it. I am also grateful to the department of history at the University of Illinois at Chicago for an assistantship, which enabled me to pursue graduate work while introducing me to the joys of teaching and the intricacies of academic life.

The Newberry Library's collections on printing and local history have fed my own curiosity for almost twenty years. Over the course of this project, the interlibrary loan services at the University of Illinois at Chicago, Roosevelt University, the University of Missouri at St. Louis, and the University of Cincinnati opened the resources of distant institutions and research centers. The special collections section of the Milton S. Eisenhower Library of Johns Hopkins University graciously provided copies of the extant minutes of the early typographical societies for my use, and the State Library of New York, the Library of Congress, and the Brown University Library also copied rare pamphlets for me. My research also took me to various institutions, including the American Antiquarian Society, New York Historical Society, New York City Public Library, the Historical Society of Wisconsin, and the libraries of Columbia University, Queens College, and Princeton Universities.

At the other end of this process, editor Sandra Frierson and other readers at the University of Arkansas Press played a vital role in preparing the manuscript for a broader audience. I am greatly indebted to the staffs of these institutions for their assistance. For permission to reprint John Sartain's "allegory" from the official International Typographical Union history by George A. Tracy, I am indebted to Thomas W. Kopek secretary-treasurer of what is now the Printing, Publishing and Media Workers Sector of the Communications Workers of America. So, too, the use of illustrations from George Stevens' book on the New York City local is thanks to the kind cooperation of the New York Commissioner of Labor.

In my pursuit of these forgotten founders of the American labor movement, I have also enjoyed the indispensible moral support of various individuals beyond the academic community, including members of labor organizations. Particularly supportive was the late Henry Rosemont, a retired member of the Chicago Typographical Union and a tireless researcher into the history of unionism in the industry. Such interest sustained and periodically revitalized my own enthusiasm for the project.

An all-consuming labor of this sort also requires the sacrifices of friends and family. They share the prolonged privations of graduate school, a dismal job market, and the periodic, uninvited ghostly visitations of a preoccupied researcher's subjects. I was especially fortunate in that these burdens have been so well accepted, particularly by my wife, Katherine Allen, who has supported this project in every sense.

To all these people and institutions, I am grateful. The strengths of this study are greatly due to their guidance, assistance, and support, while its weaknesses are my own.

Some Degree
of Power

The Art Preservative

*The Eighteenth-Century
Anglo-American Printing Trades*

O urs is the Heaven-descended art.
      To give fair knowledge birth,
To mend the human heart,
And civilize the earth.
    —Samuel Woodworth,
    "The Art of Printing," 1810

The most prominent figure in the early American printing trades also became for many the symbol of an industrious,
enlightened, and optimistic New World civilization. Early in
his career, Benjamin Franklin had written that "so vast is the
territory [of America] . . . that it will require many ages to settle
it fully. No man continues long a labourer for others, but gets
a plantation of his own. No man continues long a journeyman
to a trade but goes among these new settlers and sets up for
himself."[1] No doubt Franklin had drawn such conclusions from
his own experience as an artisan.

Recent scholarship has clarified much about the experiences
of those early American "meckanicks," a coherent social group
that embraced masters who generally owned their own shops,

as well as the employed journeymen and bound apprentices. Skills and status set these craftsmen apart from the unskilled day laborers of either the agricultural hinterlands or the urban waterfronts whose activities remained largely circumscribed by custom and law. So, too, some skilled workmen, like butchers and bakers, operated within the framework of municipal licensing and regulation, in contrast with the unregulated "free" trades like shoemakers, tailors, house carpenters, or printers. Experience very different from Franklin's would move the hired men of these unregulated urban crafts, especially in Franklin's own craft, to secure some power over the conditions of their lives and labors.

Several considerations inform our understanding of the postrevolutionary conditions that shaped the lot of those hired printers who soon began to make their own history. The craft's rapid development during the colonial and Revolutionary years, with its increasing numbers of workmen and shops and publishing capacity, remained within the framework of a system of small-scale production, even in the most important offices. From the face-to-face human relations in those shops grew a distinctively artisan pattern of life and labor. The values and practices that grew out of such conditions formed a peculiarly ideological subculture and a sense of mission unique to the "art preservative."

I

Colonial printers like Franklin enjoyed a level of opportunity premised on the rapid expansion of their craft in the New World. The steady growth of its output provides an important measure of the rapidity of its expansion, within which two centers, Philadelphia and New York, became increasingly central. The emergence of newspapers—a clear sign of the regular work necessary for the craft's secure establishment—further demonstrates both the trade's success and the integral importance of the urban press.

Printing in the English colonies of North America began in 1638 at Cambridge, Massachusetts. The founders of the colony and its new Harvard College gladly accepted the offer of a British patron to bring a press, types, and equipment to the New World, primarily for the publication of religious works. By 1649 the office employed Samuel Green, the first colonist to have actually learned the trade on this continent; the first native-born American to learn the trade was, however, James the Printer (or James Printer), an Indian apprenticed in 1659 who ran off to join the uprising under Metacom in 1676. Throughout these years, the colonial General Court not only carefully confined printing to appropriate theological and civic tracts, but also ruled that "no Printing Presse be allowed in any Towne within this Jurisdiction, but in Cambridge."[2]

Over the years, the growing demand for printing forced the still cautious authorities to license other shops. By the 1670s, the General Court had authorized a Harvard graduate to open an office in Boston, and, upon his death in 1681, licensed a magistrate named Samuel Sewall to manage the press. In subsequent years, however, genuine printers trained to the craft won government licenses. By the second quarter of the eighteenth century, the most important shops—like that of James Franklin, Benjamin's brother—were yet closely regulated but clearly in the hands of working craftsmen rather than representatives of an elite. Moreover, despite its slow start, the colonial craft blossomed quickly; as early as 1700, the Boston book trade could claim to be a publishing center second only to London in the English-speaking world.[3]

Authorities elsewhere in the colonies shared this reluctance about relaxing their control of the press. Only two years after the chartering of Pennsylvania and the laying out of the city of Philadelphia, a recent Quaker immigrant, William Bradford, opened a printing office there. By 1692, however, he faced official charges of sedition for publishing material on the activities of the government.[4]

New York City benefited from the short-sighted policy of Pennsylvania's authorities. Self-exiled from Philadelphia, Bradford turned up in Manhatten and opened a successful office there in 1693. He and later colonial printers found regulations imposed in New York much less rigid than elsewhere. The famous 1735 sedition trial of John Peter Zenger demonstrated that local press had ceased simply to reflect the views of a homogeneous colonial administration.[5]

By that time, however, conditions had also changed in Philadelphia. Local authorities coaxed Renier Jansen to open an office in the city shortly after they had driven Bradford from the state. Mid-century saw Benjamin Franklin at the head of not only a successful printing business but also a political network.[6] The craft in Philadelphia, as in New York, had become an integral feature of colonial political life.

Furthermore, by mid-century the scope of the craft had expanded far beyond Boston, Philadelphia, and New York City. Not only had it appeared in each of the thirteen colonies, but some of the offices in smaller communities were among the best shops in the domains. John Peter Miller's little operation at Ephrata, Pennsylvania, serves as a unique example of the potential of such smaller offices for truly excellent work.[7]

With the steady increase in the white population, the number of items annually printed snowballed.[8] A single printing office produced a meager if steady output for forty years prior to 1670. New shops, particularly in the seaboard towns, began contributing over the subsequent twenty years. Coinciding with the prerevolutionary political crisis was a boom in printing, evident in an almost 75 percent increase for items in the 1770s over the total for the previous decade. In 1790 the American craft had a history of over a century and a half, but well over a quarter of the total number of published items had been printed in the previous ten years. Indeed, for each seventeenth-century publication, seventeen items had appeared since 1760.

This rapid spread of printing across British North America created unprecedented opportunities for the members of the craft. Generally, the ever-increasing urban demand for their product sustained and rewarded the efforts of Franklin and his peers to open and maintain new offices. If immigrant printers and men new to the trade found opportunity within it, those men born and bred to the craft particularly found their skills a source of genuine security. For example, the sons and grandsons of William Bradford—William Bradford II, William Bradford

TABLE 1. American Printed Matter before 1790:
Number of Items by Decade

Decade	Numbers of Items	Percentage of Increase over Previous Decade	Percentage of Total Items Prior To 1790
1620–1639	1	—	
1640–1649	29	—	
1650–1659	35	—	
1660–1669	95	—	
1670–1679	166	—	
1680–1689	284	—	
1690–1699	492	—	
Subtotal	1,102		3.69
1700–1710	687	39.62	2.21
1710–1719	972	41.48	3.31
1720–1729	1,388	42.48	4.63
1730–1739	1,677	20.82	5.6
1740–1749	2,389	42.46	7.98
1750–1759	2,821	18.12	9.42
1760–1769	4,038	43.14	13.48
1770–1779	7,046	74.44	23.62
1780–1789	7,834	11.18	26.15
Subtotal	28,852		
Total Items	29,954		

These statistics have several shortcomings. Up to a year's run of a
newspaper counts as only one item. Nor is any distinction made
between the title of a volume with hundreds of pages and one-page
broadside, nor between short and long press runs. Nevertheless, they
provide a general guide to the relative growth of the craft.

III, Andrew Bradford, and Thomas Bradford—attained a status ennabling them to make their own unique contribution to the art. Others, like Franklin, found that printing could lead to professional careers beyond the press.

At times, the typical colonial printing office became such a stable business, unfettered by either the whims of government or church contractors, that it had attained a life of its own capable even of surviving the inattention of its owner, who could then freely engage in other pursuits. Bradford's New York City shop provides an outstanding example of this new kind of secure publishing firm, but the most famous was perhaps that of Franklin. In partnership with the Scottish-born David Hall after 1748, Franklin worked almost twenty years before leaving the business. Hall simply took a new partner, William Sellers, and David Jr. and William Hall maintained the business well into the nineteenth century.[9]

Such stability required a steady flow of work that would free the shop from its immediate and precarious dependence on the uneven flow of small jobs like broadsides or announcements and book work that, in the short run, could not pay for itself. Regular contracts from political or church officials kept American presses busy from the first days of the Cambridge office, but, however important it was to the particular office, such patronage faded in importance relative to the development of a diversified and dynamic colonial commerce that required the printed word. Printers responded to the officials' need for regular work with the newspaper.

The newspaper regularized the work in many shops. While providing the reading public with material that had historically new and broader appeal than books or religious tracts, it also promoted the shop and demonstrated the quality of its work. Advertisements generated additional income. The emergence of newspapers, therefore, provides a useful gauge of the relative stability and security of the craft.

The innovative shops of the crowded seaboard ports led the way. Although Boston authorities suppressed the pioneering *Publick Occurrences* after its first number in 1690, the eighteenth century really saw local newspapers come into their own. The *News-Letter*, formed in 1704, lasted until American independence. There followed the *Gazette* of 1719 through 1749; James Franklin's *New-England Courant* of 1721 into 1726; the *New-England Weekly Journal*, which was started in 1727 and merged into the *Gazette* in 1741; and the *Weekly Rehearsal*, a forerunner of the *Evening Post*, which was established in 1731 and lasted until the Revolution. Several other publications also enjoyed a brief existence from the 1750s, notably a new *Gazette* that, under the editorship of Benjamin Edes and John Gill, became the leading voice of the incipient colonial resistance to Britain.

Despite a relatively late start, Philadelphia's newspaper trade rapidly eclipsed that of Boston. In 1719 Andrew Bradford launched the weekly *American Mercury*, which lasted thirty years. In 1729 one of its former employees, Benjamin Franklin, bought the year-old *Universal Instructor . . . and Pennsylvania Gazette*, building it into a major political force before selling it entirely in 1766 to his partner David Hall. Franklin also launched the first foreign-language newspaper, the short-lived *Zeitung* of 1732. Christopher Sauer issued another *Zeitung* in 1739 from nearby Germantown, and several other short-lived papers appeared. In addition, William Bradford III's office, in 1742, introduced the *Pennsylvania Journal* (later the *Patriot*).

At New York City in 1725, some years after his arrival, the elder William Bradford founded the *New-York Gazette*, which passed during 1743 into the hands of James Parker, who merged it with his own *Post-Boy*, a publication that lasted into 1773. In 1733 the *New York Weekly Journal* appeared under John Peter Zenger's editorship. The *New York Evening Post* lasted from 1744 into 1752. Hugh Gaine founded the *Weekly Mercury* in 1752. Another *New York Gazette* flourished from 1759 until 1768, when Gaine's *Mercury* absorbed it.

Outside of these three major cities, the appearance of newspapers did not bode as well for the security of the trade. After leaving Boston, James Franklin launched the *Rhode Island State Gazette* at Newport during 1732, but it disappeared a year later; a local philanthropist, Henry Collins, encouraged a 1758 effort by another Franklin with the *Newport Mercury*, which survived into our own century. New Haven's *Connecticut Gazette* of 1755 lasted into 1768, as did Daniel Fowle's Portsmouth *New Hampshire Gazette* of 1756. That same year, the *South Carolina Gazette* appeared at Charles Town and survived into 1802. The *Maryland Gazette* was begun in 1727, lasted into 1734, and was revived by Jonas Green from 1745 to 1839. Also, a succession of papers further south went under the name of the *Virginia Gazette*.

More generally, the years between 1743 and 1776 saw the Philadelphia and New York City offices surpass those of Boston.[10] The number of items printed in these three publishing centers grew from an average of 204 in the 1740s and 1750s to 367 for the 1760s and 1770s, an increase of 180 percent. Boston's presses accounted for annual averages of 73 and 80 items, lagging far behind those of Philadelphia, which more than doubled, from 45 to 94, and remained further behind New York City's, which rose from 30 to 71. Boston's proportion of the total colonial output shrank from 36 percent to 21.9 percent, while Philadelphia's rose from 22.1 percent to 27 percent and New York's from 14.4 percent to 19.2 percent.

With this general expansion of the craft at Philadelphia and New York, newspapers flowered during and immediately after the American Revolution. During these years, Boston printers issued only one of national importance, the *Massachusetts Centinel*, founded in 1784 and becoming the *Columbian Centinel* six years later. Those newspapers at New York City, however, included the *Packet*, which originated among the city's Revolutionary refugees at Fishkill during 1777 returned to the city in 1783, and lasted into 1792; the *Evening Post* (later the *Morning Post*), which was established in 1782 and lasted for a decade; the *Independent Journal* of 1783, which, like the *Daily Gazette*, lasted to 1795; and the *Daily Advertiser* of 1785–1806. The *Gazette of the United States* began at New York City in 1789, but moved to Philadelphia the following year. There, its competitors included the *Columbian Magazine*, established in 1786 and merging with the *Universal Asylum* four years later; the *American Museum*, published for five years beginning in

TABLE 2. Urban Printed Matter, 1743–1776		
Numbers of Items		
	1743–1760	**1761–1776**
Boston	1,321	1,278
Philadelphia	810*	1,580*
New York City	527*	1,129*
Total	3,666	5,862

Numbers of Items per Year (Rounded annual average)		
	1743–1760	**1761–1776**
Boston	73	80
Philadelphia	45*	94*
New York City	30*	71*
Total	204	367

*Includes foreign language publications: 1743–60—Philadelphia, 45, and New York City, 32; 1761–76—Philadelphia, 122, and New York City, 18.

1787; and the *General Advertiser*, established in 1790 and later becoming famous as the Jeffersonian *Aurora*.

The growing number of readers in eighteenth-century America relied on a rapidly expanding printing trade, increasingly centered in the two cities of the Mid-Atlantic seaboard. Boston had enjoyed an early and impressive start, but by mid-century Philadelphia emerged as the most important center for printing as well as the largest city in the colonies, and New York also surpassed Boston in both population and publishing. These years also saw Baltimore boom into a major city and, shortly thereafter, an important publishing center. The larger, more easily supplied and equipped urban shops set a standard of quality in the craft rarely matched elsewhere and a quantity never matched.

II

In these cities, the printers' workday began near sunup, as was customary in other crafts. Some of the more eager men started even earlier. Thurlow Weed, years later, recalled how he and James Harper "were both emulous to be first at the office in the morning." During the long summer days, they did "a half day's work before the other boys and men got their breakfasts." Meeting long before sunup, they "got the key of the office by tapping on the window" of their employer, who "would take it from under his pillow and hand it to one of us through an opening in the blind."[11]

Modern printing museums provide a glimpse into the world that such a key unlocked. Most American print shops of the 1780s tended to be smaller and to have less equipment than modern showcases for the old presses. Many began as virtually one-man operations, and often stayed that way. Almost half a century after the Revolution, old Hugh Gaine "with his almost solitary Gazette," sold "some three or four hundred papers, he himself being compositor, pressman, folder and distributor of his literary ware." At the same time William Hartshorne worked out of the basement of "an old Revolutionary building" on Brooklyn's Fulton Street with its "few hundred stands, etc., where he set type for a weekly newspaper (printed upstairs)," and "kept a small stationery store."[12] In the wake of the Revolution, such offices were less likely to arouse comment; they were simply the norm.

The technology of printing, like that of many other trades, had not outgrown the framework of domestic handicraft. Its practitioners could, and often did, ply their trade out of the first floor of their homes. For additional hands, they drew first upon family members. Wives might learn the trade well enough to provide competently skilled assistance in the craft work, in addition to managing its finances and the household. *Poor Richard* well knew that "industry, frugality, and prudent economy in a wife, are to a tradesman, in effects, a fortune. . . . "[13] Children, too, were such assets to the printers' work that they brought additional ones into their homes as apprentices.

The small scale of the operation and its reliance on family members and apprentices kept the hired adult craftsman a relatively marginal feature of the trade. In most shops, only a large project might require the temporary services of one or two hired men. Like apprentices, these men would generally find room and board with their master. Even later, when journeymen lived elsewhere, most preferred to stay very close to their workplace.

Aside from tasks common to all workplaces, like cleaning the shop at the end of the day or fetching firewood on winter mornings, the printer's craft required two sets of skills: composition and press work. Composing brought the printer before the type cases—the heavy drawers divided into compartments containing the particular lead characters. These were a good measure of a shop's prosperity. Greater amounts of type permitted a shop to do more than broadsides, pamphlets, and tracts. Book printing, for example, required a large investment of type in a project that would not yield returns for some time.

Keeping the press busy, particularly in a shop without a newspaper, depended directly on the piecemeal jobs, and what came to be called job printing was, indeed, the life's blood of most offices. The printer would begin with a manuscript left by a customer. If lucky, he had met the customer himself and discussed the job. If he had not, he may well have faced a difficult task of deciphering the handwriting and correcting the mistakes of grammar and spelling. Printers often complained of having to rewrite virtually an entire text in the process of setting copy from the hand of even the most refined gentlemen. In short, the early printer's job included proofreading and editing as part of the process of setting the type and composing the form.

Craftsmen usually made any necessary decisions about design. Choice of a typeface posed few problems. Imported from Britain, type was an expensive commodity passed from shop to shop until years of wear forced its reluctant replacement at great cost. If the shop was fortunate enough to have a set, the printer might well decide to use an elegant new set of modern types with thin, sharp, straight vertical strokes and serifs (the ears or feet of a letter) rather than the asymmetrical, more old style types.[14]

After choosing a face, the printer decided on the most effective way to fit the body copy onto the page. To do so, he might choose nonpareil characters—letters of six-point size. (Still used to measure type sizes, point refers to the smallest piece of lead that could be accurately measured and cast by the original type founders.) He stood or sat before the cases and pulled out the drawers with the appropriate size and typeface. Then he selected the type character by character, and placed each piece on a composing stick, with appropriate pieces of faceless type to provide spaces between words and as quadding to justify the type to a predetermined line length. Assuming that all the characters had been properly sorted after the previous jobs, a skilled compositor did not need to examine each piece but simply felt a niche to align it correctly with the others on the composing stick. He made the form by moving line after line onto a large, hard, flat surface, usually made of stone. He also had the option to set solid one line directly below the other or to put additional leading between the lines for more spacing and legibility.

Once the printer had completed the form, he turned to the actual printing of the sheet. As time went on, more and more shops had small proofing presses, but most eighteenth-century shops had only one large press. The big wooden machine in use at the time differed little from the modified wine or paper press adapted for printing in the fifteenth century.[15] Crosspieces at the top and bottom joined two large upright beams sometimes connected to the ceiling or walls for additional stability. A turned wooden screw or spindle penetrated the top crosspiece and gradually tapered down into a round point called the toe. A large nut collared the screw from which hung the hose, a box-like contrivance supporting a flat pressing board called the platen; the hose enabled the screw to turn independently while its toe rested in the stud, an indentation in the top of the platen. A bar fixed into the collar would be pulled to move the screw downward, sliding the platen down to dwell briefly upon the inked form.

The printer placed the form into a box called the coffin, which carried it back and forth from under the platen on a plank fitted with cramp-irons. Turning the handle of the rounce, a spit-like mechanism, moved the plank along the ribs of a frame called the carriage. The tympan, hinged to the coffin, was an inner and outer frame covered with linen or vellum that sandwiched cloth or similarly blanketing material, which would more evenly distribute the pressure of the platen and protect the type from unnecessary wear. The paper to be printed would be attached to the tympan at an exact register. A thin metal frame hinged, in turn, to the tympan covered the paper with the frisket, a protecting sheet of parchment or paper with windows cut into it to permit the type to print while protecting the paper from ink adhering to other parts of the form.

At the press, the printer—or a helper called a beater—used two inking balls to apply ink to the form resting in the coffin. Attaching the blank paper to the tympan, he closed the carefully cut hinged frisket over the tympan, and then the tympan over the inked form. Turning the rounce slid the coffin over the carriage under the platen and a short pull on the bar attached to the central screw lowered the platen, pressing the paper through the blanketing material of the tympan onto the inked form, which printed through the windows of the frisket onto the paper. Replacing the bar raised the platen, and a quick turn of the rounce pulled the coffin out from under the press. The printer then raised the tympan from the coffin and the frame with the frisket from the tympan. He would then replace the printed sheet with a blank one, making any adjustments to center the type or bring it into proper register.

When repeated for hours daily over years, this work press so changed a man that a trained eye could easily spot a craft brother. The repeated pulling of work at press, in particular, overdeveloped the muscles of the right shoulder and foot, causing printers to walk with a distinctively irregular gait.[16]

Not only did the process require well-trained automatic reflexes, but a necessary monitoring of the work required a great deal of visual and tactile expertise. At the end of a job, the types would have to be distributed again. Using a copy of the printed work, the printer could simply reverse the process used to set a line on the composing stick. If letter-perfect, the printer need not even check his characters, but simply spelled the characters back into their proper compartments in the case. If, however, individual characters needed for another job had been picked out of the form, the piece required close scrutiny; sorting such pied type was an unenviably tedious job.

Fortunately for the adults, such tasks were usually relegated to the printer's devil. As in other trades, some of these lads were virtually indentured by their parents or—in the case of orphans and other public wards—by the municipal or church authorities into the service of a master. Many of the boys, however, had also expressed a preference for printing. "There was to me in boyhood," recalled a later veteran of the industry, "a charm and an attraction about the type-case and press."[17] More than in other trades, apprentice printers wanted to learn their craft.

Shop custom generally assigned these boys the least interesting and enjoyable work. Some jobs made replacing pied type seem easy. One man left a vivid account of "treading the pelts," the process of cleaning the balls used for inking the type. The inking ball was "a dried sheepskin divested of the wool, immersed in the *slop pail* until well soaked, then taken out, rinsed [and wrung] by hand of surface water." Rolled in old paper, it would be placed on the floor for treading. Replacing the papers, the apprentice continued the process until the skin became dried and pliable. "Treading out a pair of skins was an epoch in a printers devil's life," he recalled, "which he will always remember until *odor* is lost in forgetfulness." Thurlow Weed, too, remembered the "green sheepskins, which had to undergo a sort of tanning process between your feet and the floor."[18]

Such labors created hazards for the workers that were unforeseen at the time. As was evident by the mid-nineteenth century, poisoning from the lead at the case and the chemicals at the press kept printers' lives relatively short, despite the continued denials of the craft's promoters. Although easily a dozen of the participants in the journeymen's societies of the early national period lived well into their eighties, many died very early in life. The *Columbian Centinel*, known for reprinting death notices from the nation's leading papers, noted the ages of nineteen others; of these, eight died in their forties, ten in their thirties, and one at twenty-four. Since it is probable the deaths of younger and less well-known men would be noted less often, the evidence indicates a high mortality among many working printers.[19] In 1850 one estimate gave the printers' life expectancy at only thirty-two and a half years, significantly below that of most crafts and less than half the life expectancy of a merchant. Indeed, later in the century, the new International Typographical Union thought the problem serious enough to form the first union-owned and -operated home for its retired and sickly members and its own sanitorium for the treatment of respiratory diseases. Yet, such dangers afflicted not only the journeymen but the master printer as well.

Moreover, competence at the case of press required time and patience. Employers had no real interest in pressuring the hired men for greater speed and productivity. Exceptionally hectic days notwithstanding, premechanized craftsmanship involved little intense labor. Even the ambitious and distractingly industrious Weed recalled nostalgically, "We took our time in those days. Nobody was in a hurry to get through the world. Nobody was 'fast'."[20]

In general most printers liked their work. Even in the middle of an alienated twentieth century, modern sociologists found an incredibly high rate of job satisfaction among New York City printers. Relatively few disliked or felt indifferent about their work, while almost three-quarters liked their jobs "very much," citing its lack of monotony and the imaginative, creative, and educational features of the required tasks.[21] Job satisfaction must have also been quite high before mechanization.

Printers spent most of the daylight hours from Monday through Saturday in or around the shop, but seasonal changes shortened the length of the work day for months at a time. Workers also took roughly half an hour to an hour each for meals, which included breakfast and supper as well as lunch. When work was slack, frequent work stoppages helped to stretch the jobs. When customers brought work to the shop, good business as well as courtesy required a break from the labors.

Their common labors at case or press predisposed printers to value their "art preservative" in a way distinctive to their trade. A sense of craft fraternity tended to be no less a part of their working lives than typecases and presses. This identification accompanied the printer when, at the close of the day, he turned the key in the shop door.

III

Studies of the mechanicks of the Revolutionary period indicate that, when the hired printers set aside the leather apron of their labors, they remained part of a characteristically artisan web of life shared with the coworkers within their craft, with their peers in other trades, and, to some extent, with the unskilled. The largest community that the craftsmen might have found outside the shop door in 1776 would have had fewer than thirty thousand residents. If a manual worker in these little cities faced greater chaos, filth, and disease than in the countryside, it should be remembered that rural life was hardly idyllic and pastoral and that centers of population offered men in pursuits other than farming the best opportunity to rise.

Hardly a citified people, these workingmen rarely felt compelled to wear the tailor-made clothes earlier worn almost exclusively by their social betters. As late as the 1830s, Horace Greeley and other newcomers to New York not only had obviously rural accents but also wore homespuns. A late nineteenth-century chronicler sketched the style of the early artisan: "a pair of yellow buckskin or leathern breeches, a checked skirt, a red flannel jacket, a rusty felt hat cocked up at the corners, shoes of neat's-skin set off with huge buckles of brass and a leathern apron, comprised his scanty wordrobe."[22] Significantly, differences in dress among mechanics reflected their distance from the rural life, not a distinction between the employer and the employed.

All craftsmen inhabited the same world. The American city of Revolutionary times had no tenements or massive boardinghouses to accommodate massive numbers of wage-earning renters, and the hired men often lived under the master's roof, earning room and board as well as a wage. Moreover, an independent proprietorship and full citizenship were well within reach of the hired craftsmen. Of twenty-six Philadelphia printers who went on strike in 1786, at least sixteen gained ownership of their own shops at some point in their lives, four of them issuing newspapers that lasted over a decade.[23]

American workers enjoyed a very favorable cost of living. An observer noted that provisioning in an early American city was "a full third cheaper than in similar places of Great Britain." The small size of these communities and the resulting proximity of their crowded public markets to the countryside kept food prices lower, and, at the right time of the year, city dwellers could easily take a Sunday excursion into the country to negotiate a good bargain for corn or potatoes. Fish, which may have tended to be a bit overripe at the time of purchase and had to be eaten quickly, formed a large part of the urban craftsman's diet. The homemade baked goods, meats, and fresh dairy products characteristic of the rural table remained hard to get for most in the city. Everywhere, certain types of produce like strawberries and grapes remained very rare, and Thurlow Weed doubted "whether, in 1815, a tomato was sold or eaten" in New York City.[24] European observers complained that Americans prepared their food in the easiest and quickest way, usually by frying it, and the hired hand, like his employer, tended to bolt his food in order to get on to other, more interesting and profitable pursuits.

Finally, the hired craftsmen shared with the employing mechanic the unpredictable risks of the economic fluctuations, the individual's budget, the nature of the craft, and any unexpected problems that still periodically disrupted work and income. Yellow fever epidemics, for example, brought commerce to a halt from time to time, leaving ships abandoned at the wharves and the workshops emptied. Large fires occasionally swept through sections of the city, financially wiping out those with homes or jobs in the area. A particularly harsh winter created crises among "the poorer laboring people" so severe as to require massive public aid in firewood and other necessities.

Changing government policies like the embargo against British trade in 1807 also did unexpected damage to the well-being of artisans of all sorts.[25]

The small-scale masters remained almost as vulnerable as their hired journeymen to the dangers of prolonged illness and loss of income. The Typographical Societies set their level of relief at three dollars weekly, or about half pay, to mitigate such potential disasters. Similarly, the death of the breadwinner was an expensive matter subsidized by the societies with between ten and twenty dollars, but the long-term loss of income to the surviving family generally proved devastating.[26]

Standards of living at home also differed from craft to craft. A chair-maker, for example, would logically have had better furniture. Tailors and cordwainers outfitted themselves and their families with better clothes and shoes. Butchers and bakers lived relatively well. Building tradesmen might, at some point, be better able to construct their own homes should they get the land. Similarly, printers had more books, old newspapers, and other products of their own craft than did their peers in other trades. Bartering and trading in kind enabled artisans to benefit from one another's skills.

Along with conscious business decisions and the exigencies of the local economy, age-old customs shaped the craftsmen's working lives. The American journeyman, like his British counterpart, could still claim Saint Monday as a holiday. With time, employers on this side of the Atlantic came to share the frustration of a particularly articulate London master who, when asked about the hours of labor, replied: "No man on earth can tell that; they begin in the morning when they like, but if any mortal thing happens, up they are from their stools and after it. . . . I never knew a dozen steady men among them in my life."[27] In earlier days, though, tradition generally defined efficiency.

On such a self-declared holiday, as in other leisure time, the employer had fewer options for recreation that were closed to his journeymen. John Binns, an immigrant British printer, noted the lack of attention "paid by working men of America" to leisure activities in general, and their preference to stay home.

Weed, too, recalled that "men lived at home" in early New York. Seldom, wrote Binns, did "these men and their wives and their children walk out together," as in the Old World, for, he reasoned, "no suitable places" existed "at convenient distances from the city for their recreation."[28]

Within the cities, however, the laboring people frequently lingered in the open areas, such as the old potters' fields of Philadelphia and New York City, which authorities closed to further burials in 1795 and 1797, respectively. Animals freely wandered there, women beat rugs, and garbage generally accumulated rapidly, but people had already begun to use such places as parks. Washington Irving sketched a typical summer scene at New York's Battery where "the gay apprentice sported his Sunday coat, and the laborious mechanic, relieved from the dirt and drudgery of the week, poured his weekly tale of love into the half-averted ear of the sentimental chambermaid." Not far away, Henry Wood, the young unionist brokenhearted after a tragic love affair, threw himself into the river.[29]

Of course, life in those small cities did not necessarily preclude fishing, swimming, sledding, ice-skating, and other outdoor activities. Philadelphians could pick blackberries beyond Sixth street between Chestnut and Walnut. Frequent picnic parties spent the day in Centre Square and tea parties gathered in Marhoes Woods above Ninth Street. Buncker Hill, beyond New York's City Hall, offered similar activities. "When of a Sunday afternoon we wanted fresh air," recalled Weed, "we would walk to the State Prison, then a prominent feature far away out of the city," directly on the Hudson adjacent to "the nucleus of what became the village of Greenwich." Another remembered "a crossing plank" over the ditch in "Lispenard's meadow" leading to "a well-beaten path leading from the city to the then village of Greenwich, passing over open and partially fenced lots and fields" not under cultivation. Similar walks led from Boston, Baltimore, and other cities to the adjacent open fields, farms, and villages not yet assimilated into the cities.[30]

Public houses and taverns offered nearer, if less reputable, entertainments and were a vital meeting place for workingmen as they began to form their own voluntary associations. Some occupations had their favorite taverns, usually located near enough to their work to provide a convenient refuge for breaks and after-hours recreation. Drovers and butchers, for example, gathered at a public house just beyond the city of Philadelphia. During major construction and renovation in the neighborhood of Independence Hall, the building tradesmen preferred a particular tavern. Although printing offices might be scattered across the city, individual workers moved from shop to shop enough to be familiar with those taverns near the larger workplaces which would have enjoyed a disproportionate number of typographical patrons.[31]

Even the most austerely industrious artisans of the period were not merely cogs in the mechanisms of production. Young Thurlow Weed, after his arduous day's labor, did more than work, eat, and sleep. Rather than return to his boardinghouse after work, he preferred to stop at "a porter-house in Fair (now Fulton street) to read the newspaper and drink a glass of Newark Cider."[32]

Early American printers lived in a world of artisans. Indeed, the survival and prosperity of his trade depended directly upon the often precarious services of other craftsmen. A printer depended upon cabinetmakers for his supply of specially made mallets, shooting-sticks, side-sticks and reglets; upon house carpenters for the type cases, turners for ballstocks, parchment makers for inking pelts (as well as for parchment); and upon whitesmiths for the chases. Before the widespread making of presses in the United States, printers employed men in such trades for assistance and for maintenance of their expensive and often irreplaceable equipment.[33]

IV

Nevertheless, the printing trades constituted a unique subculture in British North America. Not only were the physical processes of work distinctive, but printers as a group adhered to a common set of values and ideas. Even in his leisure time, the literate printer might be seen, like Weed at his porter-house, with a newspaper. Significantly, this craft fraternity made no rigid distinctions between masters and journeymen. Indeed, an often very thin line separated the proprietor from a hired worker. Theoretically a master could lose his office and still maintain a business for odd jobs, as might a freelance subcontractor, using somebody else's equipment. At the same time, a hired man could have an apprentice of his own, and, if anxious to earn some extra income, he might arrange with a master to become a partner in the printing of particular projects; after the owner of the press, paper, and type deducted fees, the "partners" then shared the profits of the enterprise.[34] The positions of artisan-businessman and artisan-laborer could not always be easily defined. Given the small-scale nature of production, the relatively favorable ratio of employed men and apprentices to actual proprietors, and the continued expansion of the craft, those craftsmen working for wages at any given point during these years could realistically expect the chance to follow the path of Benjamin Franklin.

On the job, ritualized activities unique to the craft involved printers of all ranks. Many of these were a residue of the seventeenth-century English *Mechanick Excercises* described by Joseph Moxton. Newcomers to the postrevolutionary craft generally still paid their customary entrance into the good graces of the chapel with drinks. Failure to do so invited a sanctioned ritual of censure and harassment that discouraged failures to care properly for the precious equipment and supplies. Printers also played games of chance, using type like dice. Other customs required the master to furnish refreshments from time to time, as when the shop put to press the signature "o." Weed recalled how at eleven in the morning "inevitably and too frequently afterwards," printers would "jeff" for alcoholic drinks. So endemic to the craft were such practices that they partially survived well into our own century, despite the steadily accelerating pace of work and periodically massive temperance campaigns.[35]

Masters, journeymen, and apprentices shared a bent for craft humor. Pun-loving typos drank toasts riddled with double-meaning references to their work, as to "Our Fraternity—May it never be disgraced by one whose *mackling* tongue would give *double impressions,* or cast a *slur* upon an absent member." Later developments gave a morbid turn to such humor, as when Philadelphia journeymen laughed over the document of an Alexandria Typographical Society mandating that members draw lots every four years, "the lots to fall on every third man,— and those on whom they so fall to be immediately hung till they are quite dead, and their bodies sold to the surgeons— money arising from which sale to go to the good of the society to which they belonged." (This paper also suggested hanging anyone in the trade serving less than seven years of an apprenticeship.)[36]

Individual printers shared the unique intellectual benefits of their craft, despite differing levels of formal education, ranging from charity and church schools to some time in universities. More than other artisans, they benefited from "the facility with which copies of literary works were multiplied," and "their consequent cheapness," which put knowledge "within the reach of every class of people." Hired printers particularly sought "eternal attributes" from the "effable progressions of infinity" in geometry, the "raptuous harmonies" of music, and history's "immortal shades of virtuous men." Largely reliant upon their own readings and discussions with their peers, they faced the problems of all those who strive for self-education and self-improvement. One complained that the constant work of his trade so restricted his intellectual development that he "knew but little of what was passing in the city outside of the printing offices." Another tried to compensate for the long working hours by spending late nights in bed, reading by candlelight, which he later called "an unprofitable and dangerous habit." In addition to the fire hazard, such studies lacked a system "as would have guided me to the right kind of books to read and dictated the arrangement or order in which I should read them." This "total want of system or arrangement" left him with "information and knowledge of various kinds" without an understanding of the dependence of one subject upon another, and he likened his mind to "a room full of books, into which thousands of volumes had been thrown hap-hazard without arrangement, one after another," leaving "a mob of information, not a disciplined army; organization was wanted."[37]

In a larger sense, though, the printers stood near the cutting edge of their civilization, and they knew the importance of their work as well as anyone. They regarded their craft as an integral partner of the Enlightenment. The printer called—and still calls—his workplace a chapel. Some commentators held that the term originated from the location of one of the earliest English print shops in what was formerly a church. Nevertheless, the tenacity of the term reflects printers' belief that theirs was the "art preservative of all others," an essential force in the shift of western civilization from a world centered on the church to a secular world grounded in science and reason embodied in the printed word.

Indeed, individuals later active in the organization of the hired craftsmen printed religious titles, almanacs, scientific works, statistical reports, and political tracts. They proofread completely, set character by character, stacked line by line, printed page by page, and bound volume by volume American editions of works by John Locke, Jean Jacques Rousseau, and other Old World theorists of liberty. Indeed, little of the wisdom or folly of their day has survived to our own without first passing through the calloused, ink-stained hands of the printer. As one observer later warned, "think not the printer is altogether a machine—think not he is indifferent to the gem of which he is but the setter. . . . "[38]

In this craft, journeymen as well as masters had close contact with the statesmen and men of letters of their day. The promising young poet Philip Freneau wrote verses for Francis Wrigley, a Philadelphia journeyman later active in the organization of hired men. David Bruce "had frequent opportunities of seeing Mr. [Thomas] Paine at the printing office in which he was engaged" at Philadelphia. It was Paine's "usual custom" to invite Bruce and the other workers "to partake of a supper and refreshments which he had ordered at a hotel in the vicinity." Another printer later recalled his meeting men like Paine, Franklin, and Dr. Benjamin Rush, who took walks past his door. Another remembered his experiences as a journeyman and spoke frequently to young Walt Whitman of "the personal appearance and demeanor of Washington, Jefferson, and other of the great historical names of our early national days." Yet another had "frequently seen General Washington, and loved to speak of the noble appearance of that man."[39]

Understandably, printers as a group felt a particular affinity for Franklin, especially those in Philadelphia. In the small circles of the trade, many had at least a nodding acquaintance with the great figure. One had served as an apprentice with Franklin's grandson Benjamin Franklin Bache and worked as a messenger for Franklin himself during the sessions of Congress in Philadelphia. Wrigley and Samuel Lecount had emigrated from Britain during Franklin's term there as the colonial agent; their craft, their settlement in Philadelphia, and the former's employment with Franklin's old firm indicate that they carried with them letters of recommendation from Franklin, who remained eager to recruit new printing talent to his city.[40] Throughout the century, local printers' festivals marked Franklin's birthday across the country, providing, in some communities, an early indication of organization in the craft.

Printers generally tended to find inspiration in Franklin's scientific and political contributions. A Boston journeyman, for example, later praised him for having "combined the virtues and talents of the patriot, the sage, the universal friend of man." Franklin's "inquiries were spread over the whole face of nature." With truth as "the sole object of his researches, he was of course no sectary; and as reason was his guide, he embraced no system which that did not authorize." If the image of Franklin towered above the man, it was nonetheless a compellingly effective ideal. "If there be talents, we can never hope to equal,—if there be a series of good fortune, we can never expect to enjoy" those of Franklin, his journeyman admirer suggested. Yet, the craft might still "become acquainted with habits which it may be prudent to adopt,—and discover virtues which we cannot fail to applaud."[41]

Printers like Ebenezer Mack, a New York journeyman, also drew inspiration from the tremendous odds that had faced Franklin's generation in its struggle for national independence.

"Is it not, then, at the power of arms alone that tyranny has to tremble?" he asked. "No! It is the enlightened mind, which knows and feels the dignity of human nature—which scorns to bow beneath the yoke of oppression." Another discussed the importance of a free flow of ideas in any attempt to understand such natural law and wondered whether advocates of restrictions on the press would also desire "that the sun be extinguished from the firmament, because the serpent basks as freely in its beams as the swallow?—because it warms alike to vegetation the noxious weed as the nutritious plant?"[42]

Mack and his peers discussed their faith in reason and implicit centrality of that faith to their own work. He explained that "SCIENCE is the sister of LIBERTY; and PRINTING, though of later birth, is the guardian of both . . . LIBERTY must preside o'er the PRESS, and the PRESS be the watch-tower of LIBERTY. By SCIENCE must the PRESS be illuminated, and the PRESS shall disseminate the rays of SCIENCE." While the press might sometimes falsify the truth, he argued, it should never be restrained, for "with the antidote before us, why should we fear the poison? A free privilege of inquiry, and unbiased judgement—where the mind is thus enlightened, TRUTH will ever, in the end prevail."[43]

Because of this relationship, declared George Churchill, an officer of the Albany union, printers "should be men of integrity and wisdom—men who will keep constantly in view the permanent interests of mankind, and will never be diverted from the path of rectitude by a mercenary love of gain, by a servile fear of power, or by the capricious and fluctuating tide of public opinion!" He suggested: "let us strive to encourage virtue, to depress vice, to wrest from tyranny the iron rod of oppression, to enlighten the public mind, and to promote genuine philanthropy."[44] Shoemakers, carpenters, tailors, and other craftsmen felt a similar impulse to make a product of quality, but the very nature of the printing trades imbued its practitioners with a uniquely ideological sense of public service.

V

The context of craft production in the printing trades of 1790 had changed in quantity but not quality in its three hundred year history. A century in the New World had rooted printing into the infrastructure of commerce, religion, and politics, particularly characteristic of the cities of the eastern seaboard. Communities that prided themselves on the unbounded possibilities for individual growth and prosperity provided the framework within which working artisans shaped their lives and tried to understand their world, their country, and the changes they saw around them. Building upon a tradition of craft fraternalism, printers nurtured a unique social conscience and sensitivity. Already, however, great forces prepared to transform the craft with unimaginable consequences for all concerned.

If, indeed, Franklin was an appropriate patron of the art, it should be remembered that his was an ambiguous legacy. His virtues were neither those of a modern entrepreneur nor those of an old-fashioned master. He cherished the paternal ideals of craftsmanship and the fraternal harmony of the employing and employed mechanic while counseling amition, industry, temperance, and self-improvement.[45] Franklin did not introduce to this country the work ethic and competitiveness associated with the Protestant Reformation. Nor did those values melt the more leisurely pace of handicraft labor and the ethics of fraternalism in his day. Yet, after 1780, forces emerged to redefine the values of craftsmen in Franklin's own trade. In the process, Franklin's legacy encouraged the transformation of the craft into an industry.

On the other hand, those craftsmen who made their living by selling what they had—their skills and labor—judged their successes and prospects by Franklin's standards, and when pressed would also assert the role of conscious, human choices in the shaping of individuals' lives and of a new society. They, as well as their employers, claimed the artisan legacy of Franklin.

One

Birds of Passage

The Emergence of the
Wage-Earning Printer

Wanted—A Printer ... a mechanical
curiosity with a brain and fingers—a
thing that will set so many type a day—a
machine that will think and act, but still a
machine—a being who undertakes the most
systematic and monotonous drugery, yet one
the ingenuity of man has never supplanted—
that's a printer. ... He must not think of the
future, not recall the past—must not think of
home, nor kindred, of a wife or babe—his
work is before him, and thought is chained to
his copy.
—*New York Exchange*

In the early national period of American history, few
could have more realistically aspired to follow in the footsteps
of Franklin than Henry Collins Southwick, a Newport printer
named for the local philanthropist who had assisted both his
father and Franklin himself. Bred to his craft, he enjoyed the
benefits of ties and influences which, in colonial days, might

have secured a bright future. Before the age of nineteen, he launched his own newspaper, the *Rhode Island Museum*, which collapsed in the same year, 1794. The ambitious young man then sought work elsewhere, turning up later among New York City journeymen as an officer of their Typographical Association. Moving on, he established another office that printed the *Albany Chronicle*. Apparently losing that business in 1798, he tried elsewhere with the *Poughkeepsie Journal* but in 1800 again found himself serving as an officer in the hired men's society at New York. Southwick then joined Richard Crooker in printing the *American Citizen, and General Advertiser* in 1802, but seems to have been unable to secure ownership of a shop until 1806, when he did so with a member of the Hardcastle family, prominent in the local trade. However, 1812 found Southwick assuming control of his brother's newspaper, the *Albany Register*, from which office he also issued the *Christian Visitant*. Four years later, from Auburn, he began publishing the *Advocate of the People* and produced a rather famous *Southwick's Almanack*. A fellow printer later recalled how Southwick, then "in hope of retrieving his fortunes" after the Panic of 1819, "embarked in a wild real estate speculation, which utterly ruined him. He bore up, and struggled on with indomitable industry and courage for more than twenty years" in his quest for economic security and social mobility. His death in 1821 ended his frantic, if ultimately unsuccessful, efforts.[1]

Southwick's experience illustrates the drastic nature of the changes that had swept the postrevolutionary craft. Political and economic independence for the American states encouraged an unprecedented increase in the volume of printing, which required major changes in the workplace. As the need for printing grew, the number of men involved in the trade increased dramatically. Most importantly, however, it radically reshaped the craft, disproportionately increasing the number of hired printers. This trend redefined the roles of master-proprietor and journeyman-laborer and locked men like Southwick out of their own shops.

I

With national independence, printing quickly grew from a colonial handicraft into an infant industry. Despite an impressive, though short-lived, boom at the start of the Revolution, the annual product of the trade just before and immediately after the beginning of the conflict generally fluctuated between 550 and 700 items.[2] By the close of this period, it regularly reached totals in excess of 3,000 items—a roughly five-fold growth.

A growing number of those items represented those regular, periodical sources of work, newspapers, the development of which particularly demonstrates the dynamic nature of the Philadelphia craft. In addition to the *Pennsylvania Gazette*, the *American Museum*, which failed in 1792, the *Pennsylvania Journal*, which collapsed the following year, and the *National Gazette* of Philip Freneau, which went under in 1793, local printers issued the *General Advertiser*. Renamed the *Aurora*, it took its place as one of the most important national organs of what became the Democratic-Republican opposition. The *American Daily Advertiser*, begun in 1793, became *Poulson's American Daily Advertiser* at the turn of the century.

The New York trade also produced many notable papers. The older *Packet* survived until 1792. The *Independent Journal* became the *Daily Gazette* in 1795. The *Daily Advertiser* lasted until 1896. The *General Advertiser and New York Evening Post* also secured a regular readership, as did the *Columbia Magazine*, which became the *Universal Asylum* in 1790; the *American Minerva* appeared in 1793 and was renamed the *Commercial Advertiser* four years later. The *Argus*, established in 1795, became the *American Citizen* in 1800.

Other cities, too, experienced an expansion of the newspaper press. Boston's *Massachusetts Mercury* appeared in 1793 and came to be known as the *New England Palladium* after 1813, and the politically Republican *Independent Chronicle* joined the *Columbian Centinel* as a major local newspaper. Baltimore, the boom town of its day, had its *Federal Gazette* from 1796 and, three years later, the *American*. The new national capital on the Potomac had the *Federalist* from 1800 until 1809 when it was superseded by the *National Intelligencer*. During this period, newspaper publishing penetrated each of the United States and most of the territories.

The dramatic increase in the demand for printing reflected

TABLE 3. Annual Increases in Printing Output:
Number of Items Produced by Year,
1776 through 1815

Year	Items	Year	Items
1776	874	1796	2,186
1777	739	1797	1,939
1778	686	1798	2,343
1779	687	1799	1,964
1780	587	1800	2,661
1781	579	1801	1,778
1782	591	1802	1,969
1783	767	1803	2,101
1784	753	1804	2,266
1785	695	1805	2,312
1786	958	1806	2,251
1787	976	1807	2,401
1788	967	1808	2,615
1789	1,062	1809	2,579
1790	1,264	1810	2,913
1791	1,254	1811	2,487
1792	1,441	1812	3,239
1793	1,801	1813	3,052
1794	2,094	1814	3,258
1795	2,265	1815	2,996

These figures have shortcomings similar to those of Table 1. They
especially understate the growth during the later years, when propor-
tionally more items represented large volumes and tended to have
larger press runs. Most significantly, perhaps, the figures minimize the
importance of newspapers, which grew in number and circulation in
the early national period.

the changing character of society. White settlement had expanded rapidly after the Revolution with new villages and towns sprouting along the advancing lines of Euro-American cultivation and commerce. The establishment of new printing offices followed the white frontier's westward movement. At the same time, this expansion transformed villages into towns and towns into small cities, including those in the hinterlands of the great urban centers. Designated political centers like Albany or the planned Federal City of Washington particularly nurtured the expanding printing trades.

In the four great ports—Philadelphia, New York, Boston, and Baltimore—printing grew, in great part, to keep pace with a massive population growth. Revolutionary Philadelphia had less than 30,000 residents, but, by the turn of the century, 69,000 people lived in the city or its environs, and in 1820 the city and the adjacent communities (the Northern Liberties, Southwark, Kensington, Penn Township, Spring Garden, Passyunk, and Moyamensing) counted over 137,000 inhabitants. New York City had 22,000 on the eve of its wartime occupation by the British, but reached over 60,000 by 1800 and, twenty years later, the future boroughs had over 150,000 people. In those same years, Boston grew from 16,000 to 25,000 to over 63,000. Baltimore, which had less than 7,000 at the time of the War for Independence, expanded to almost 63,000 by 1820.[3] In half a century, then, the four largest American cities of the early national period together grew to over five times their Revolutionary populations.

Not only did the people increase in number over a broader area, but they also enjoyed a greater literacy, allowing them to indulge the curiosity that kept pace with the complexities of their world. Moreover, as roads improved and distances became less formidable, the markets for printing reached beyond the city into a national network of urban and rural readers. Such changes fueled the growth of the craft.

Such growth required the introduction of technological innovations. By 1789 American craftsmen had built printing presses at New Haven, Hartford, Philadelphia, Charleston, S.C., and Fayetteville, N.C., and, in the process, began slowly to incorporate improvements, like the use of rollers to ease the movement of the carriage and screws to steady the platen. The use of newer hairline typefaces required greater impressing power, attained by thickening the central screw, which reduced the rate of declination and increased the pressure that could be applied. By the American appearance of the first new Stanhope press during 1811, pressmakers in the country had already begun to develop an indigenous iron press, the Columbia, although its cost remained virtually prohibitive for small offices.[4]

Other innovations also emerged from the postrevolutionary boom in the demand for printing. To avoid the continued importation of paper, Americans experimented in using more easily accessible materials like currier's shavings and corn husks. Stereotyping, the English technique of making casts of the form, eliminated the need to repeatedly typeset copy for frequently printed works like the Bible. A change particularly welcome for apprentices came around 1814 when inking balls of more easily cleaned dressed deerskin replaced the green sheeps' pelts stuffed with wool.[5]

Nevertheless, such technological changes in the craft pale before those that were to come. For example, before the advent of the linotype machine in the late nineteenth century, type continued to be set in the same way it had for centuries. So, too, the presses of 1815—or even the later Washington press with its toggle-joint mechanism—more closely resembled the press of three centuries before than the powered presses of 1830.

Employers met with the increasing new demand for printing less with technology than with a thorough reorganization and expansion of their premechanized workshop. At the turn of the century, for example, one Boston office had five presses in continual operation, requiring the attention of ten journeymen working at press and a number of other hired men and apprentices setting the type. Soon after, some urban shops had as many as nine or ten presses in operation.[6] The sizes of the shops and the greater numbers of workers permitted a division of labor between compositors and pressmen, for example, with each workman gravitating toward the most efficient use of his labors. Such chapels came increasingly to resemble factories awaiting mechanization, and human relationships grew differently in this environment than in the small-scale shop of Franklin's—or even Southwick's—youth.

Masters of such shops had new concerns that reshaped the ideals and values of the old-fashioned paternalistic masters. They revived a guild tradition to meet common needs and solve acutely felt problems, but the needs and problems of master artisans in the new environment often shaped what were, primarily, employers' associations like the Philadelphia Company of Booksellers formed in 1792 or the Company of Philadelphia Printers formed two years later. Boston masters made a better effort in 1805 by forming the Faustus Association, which branched into a Conservative Fire Society in 1811.[7] Masters elsewhere engaged in concerted activity without building a formal association.

With or without organizations, however, large-scale masters pursued goals analogous to those of similar formations of proprietors in other crafts and the broad societies of mechanics in general. Artisan-businessmen in the printing trades readily helped distribute one another's respective publications, pooled their resources to meet the expenses for joint publishing projects beyond the reach of one shop, and held elaborate literary fairs to place their wares before the public.[8] For the master printers such activities blended personal advertising with craft promotion.

The concerted efforts by masters to promote the craft also involved two related campaigns to secure government protection of their trade from foreign competition and internal trade regulation. They petitioned the political authorities to raise higher tariffs on the importation of printed matter in English and to minimize the import duties on hard-to-get supplies like types and ink. In their protectionist memorials to Congress, too, masters demonstrated the unity of both their patriotic and self-interested motives.[9]

Shopkeeper-printers also sought to regulate the prices charged by the local trade to prevent being undersold by their peers. Eleven leading New York firms reached such an agreement in 1795, while their Philadelphia peers sought the same goal. Boston masters agreed upon a schedule of prices in 1805 but failed to maintain it for more than a few years. Part and parcel of this effort was what Philadelphia's Company of Printers called the power "to determine the terms for employing journeymen."[10]

In short, the radical growth of the craft and its reorganization polarized printers into the employers and the employed. The promotion of business had particular importance for the more securely well-off masters whose larger shops enjoyed a disproportionate power within the marketplace and whose concerns took priority in shaping the craft's norms.

II

Integral to the transformation of the workshop was the disproportionate growth of its hired work force in the craft. "Of all the articles of domestic manufacture, and general consumption, none perhaps offers more facility for its triumphant establishment" than printing, wrote one promoter of the craft in 1802. Soon, he predicted, it "would employ many thousand hands" and become a mainstay of the economy.[11]

The city directories of Philadelphia and New York City reveal much about the growth of the craft. The numbers of New York printers annually listed jumped from 15 to 68 in the decade following 1786, and from 77 in 1805 to 146 in 1815. In Philadelphia, the decade after 1785 recorded a growth from 37 to 81, by 1806 to 131, by 1815 to 175.[12] These figures indicate that the trade in its two largest American centers grew between four- and ten-fold in a mere thirty years.

Significantly, such records drastically understate the real increase in the numbers of wage earners—precisely the most rapidly growing group within the craft. The sixty-five journeymen printers who signed the Philadelphia wage schedule of February 22, 1802, provide a measure of this inaccuracy. Composed of men actively working at the craft during the winter of 1801–02, the signatories represented much of the relatively stable core of the trade, which had seasonally shrunk from the larger work force of the warmer, busier months. Nevertheless, of the sixty-five only fifteen could be identified with certainty in either the 1802 or 1803 directories. Conversely, at least fifty-four journeymen—and no doubt others had not signed the memorial—worked in the city's trade without appearing among the 138 printers listed in the 1802 volume; the real size of the craft at that time probably exceeded two hundred. Such dubious sources have shaped wildly inaccurate scholarly estimates that wage earners comprised only as little as a half of the craft.[13]

Similarly, the early national period also saw the development of particular skills related to the printing trades. Engravers, bookbinders, pressmakers, type founders, ink makers, paper makers, and other specialized crafts began to labor in increasing numbers to meet the needs of the printing industry.

Finally, the very nature of this growth blurred the facile distinctions between who was and was not a printer. Ideally, of course, a craftsman had clearly discernible skills setting him apart from half-way or two-thirds journeymen, those green hands who had not served a regular apprenticeship. However, the need for more workers eroded some of the distinctiveness of skilled labor. Masters tended to accept apprentices into the workplace as much to get cheap labor as to give them an introduction to the craft. As men these apprentices entered the work force with a fraction of a full journeyman's skills, and, like the few women and free blacks in the trade, they earned less than the duly trained journeyman with more rounded skills.[14]

Like late twentieth-century trends in the graphic arts, the early national experience in the printing trades simply dissolved preexisting standards. In 1810, for example, the New York Typographical Society labelled one applicant for membership a "half-way man," although his name had appeared in seven of the annual city directories as a printer. Another member accepted as fully qualified by the Philadelphia journeymen's society later faced suspension for incompetence by the New York union, which had accepted him as a full member. European apprenticeships, of course, provided yet another perplexing obstacle to easily distinguishing the genuine craftsman.[15]

This explosive expansion of the local crafts also permits several generalizations. Significantly, the numbers alone made

TABLE 4. The Growth of the Work Force in Printing:
Philadelphia & New York City, 1785–1815

	Philadelphia			New York City		
Year	Allied Trades	Printing & Bookbinding	Total	Allied Trades	Printing & Bookbinding	Total
1785	48	46	94	—	—	—
1786	—	—	—	13	16	29
1787	—	—	—	14	18	32
1788	—	—	—	12	20	32
1789	—	—	—	17	29	46
1790	—	—	—	21	31	52
1791	46	68	114	25	32	57
1792	49	53	102	28	32	60
1793	55	76	131	32	39	71
1794	73	93	166	49	54	103
1795	76	103	179	56	81	137
1796	84	117	201	73	81	154
1797	83	125	208	66	71	137
1798	85	120	205	66	75	141
1799	82	102	184	64	73	137
1800	92	111	203	53	70	123
1801	85	122	207	59	74	133
1802	89	175	264	63	85	148
1803	92	178	270	62	101	163
1804	91	168	259	66	109	175
1805	100	163	263	71	107	178
1806	94	171	265	73	108	181
1807	102	193	295	70	109	179
1808	100	192	292	79	115	194
1809	106	216	322	76	131	207
1810	124	217	341	76	135	211
1811	151	261	412	78	167	245
1812	139	204	343	79	167	246
1813	151	261	412	82	175	267
1814	160	269	429	90	193	283
1815	147	228	475	90	201	291
1816	159	270	429	90	217	307

it impossible to sustain the old system of workingmen earning an income with room and board found under the employer's roof. This not only physically separated the hired men from the employer but also left the well-being of the former exclusively dependent upon a monetary wage.

Only a minority of these newly enlarged numbers of hired craftsmen could have been following the pursuits of their fathers. Membership rosters reconstructed from the extant records of the typographical societies of journeymen confirm such suspicions, with a few notable exceptions. The more outstanding of these, in addition to Southwick, included Neal Green of the Philadelphia Typographical Society, a man descended from the printing family that had established the pioneering seventeenth-century shop at Cambridge. Another was Robert Skeotch Aitken, the grandson of the colonial publisher who had hired Thomas Paine upon his arrival in 1774; the young Aitken had seen his father reduced to alcoholism and his aunt, Jane Aitken, forced to assume the responsibilities for his grandfather's press. Despite frequent losses to creditors, she maintained the family business consistently enough to give some means of employment to her brother and nephew.[16]

Moreover, although Aitken worked at the trade in the city of his birth, few of the new workers involved in an early labor organization could have been native to the area. Most, no doubt, had originally entered the urban craft as part of a seasonal stream of rural and small town mechanics into the cities. Many came from backgrounds like that of Arthur Merwyn, the protagonist of a 1799 novel, *Arthur Merwyn*. An ignorant youth from rural Chester country, anxious to find "other manual occupations besides that of the plough," Merwyn sought his fortune in Philadelphia. His creator, Charles Brockden Brown, like later authors, shaped his character from the experiences of those around him. The continued improvement of roads and communications drew such men into an ever-widening, increasingly national network of exchange in which workmen as well as their products circulated freely. The New York Typographical Society complained in 1811 that its members, "the professors of the noblest art with which this world is blessed, have become *birds of passage*, seeking a livelihood from Georgia to Maine."[17]

Most workmen in Philadelphia shops clearly came from offices outside of the city. Of the eighty-seven men proposed for membership in the Philadelphia Typographical Society from July 5, 1806, through October 25, 1810, forty-one mentioned their most recent work experience. Of these, five had held positions in Wilmington, Delaware; four each in Lancaster and New York City; two each from Easton (Maryland), Alexandria (Virginia), London (England), and Harrisburg and Carlisle; and one each came from Gettysburg, Williamsport, Northumberland, Washington, and Pittsburgh in Pennsylvania, Trenton and Elizabethtown in New Jersey, Baltimore, Washington, Utica, Hartford, Springfield, Providence, and Raleigh. A few simply claimed to have worked in North Carolina, Virginia, Ireland, and Europe. As in later years, immigrants played an important role in the American craft. Philadelphia and New York City offices employed not only British, Irish, and Scottish journeymen, but also natives of Germany, Switzerland, Sweden, and the West Indies.[18]

This diversity made the urban chapels scenes of a new kind of cultural interaction. Workmen themselves often noted "a marked difference between the journeymen who came from Boston, Hartford, and other New England towns" to New York, where they showed themselves to be "temperate and frugal," and "those who came from Baltimore, Philadelphia, etc., etc.," who tended to be "thriftless or dissipated." Others also "thoroughly enjoyed the thrifty and intellectual example of the Yankee" in the print shops of the city.[19]

George Churchill's career illustrates the nature of membership in early labor organizations. Although he played a major role in the organization of his fellow journeymen at Albany, he soon set off in pursuit of fame and fortune. After five months in New York City he had enough savings to leave for Philadelphia, where he turned again to the press to rebuild his funds. When he had enough, he moved on to a Pittsburgh shop. Repeating the process, he arranged to travel down the Ohio River with some Cincinnati merchants on a flatboat. From that city he went on to Louisville. Finally, after taking a keel-boat to Shawneetown, Illinois, he proceeded on June 11, 1817, to walk toward Kaskaskia. By the end of the month he was working at the press in St. Louis, setting aside money to buy a farm in Madison County, Illinois.[20]

The establishment by other union printers of short-lived newspapers as well as their obituary notices indicate that they crossed and recrossed the country from Michigan to Louisiana, to the west beyond St. Louis, back to the Old World, and south into Latin America.[21] In part, of course, such men simply followed a long tradition of tramping British and European workingmen who sought to improve their skills, but the possibility of more immediate success also provided a particular lure to American craftsmen.

Less dramatically, but perhaps more significantly, some urban printers moved out into, as well as from, the small towns of the cities' hinterlands. One historian of printing in upstate New York mentioned the early trade societies as having "little influence upon the country printers," but no less than thirty of the country printers he studied held membership in a journeymen's organization at some point in their working lives, and many more must have been associated with the Albany Typographical Society, for which little membership information has survived. Weed, as a tramping New York journeyman, encountered many former union brothers from New York City who later "established themselves in neighboring cities and villages, and became influential and prosperous publishers or editors."[22] Many less successful journeymen also roamed the country.

This individual movement from place to place also reflected the relatively young ages of the known participants in journeymen's societies. Francis Wrigley may have been about sixty when he participated in the wage dispute at Philadelphia during 1802, but few of his co-workers were half that age. As journeymen's societies secured the closed shop, workers joined upon completing their apprenticeships at ages eighteen through twenty-one, keeping still lower the average age of their first involvement with concerted workers' action.[23]

Insofar as the new hired workers took pride in their craft as a worthwhile and vital contribution to the well-being of their civilization, they may well have expected an income sufficient to secure a comfortable life for themselves and their families with some hope of setting up their own, independent offices. Their aspirations may have differed little from those of the old colonial tradesmen, but the world they confronted had changed radically.

III

The experience of the journeymen varied widely, but their employers' use of less skilled labor and the disproportionate growth of the wage-earning portion of the craft justifies two related generalizations: the decline of real wages, and the slow closing of the channels by which journeymen became proprietors.

A journeyman's pay for his sunup-to-sunset workday varied greatly depending on the city in which he worked, the state of the trade at any given time, and the difficulty of the particular job in which he was engaged. Nevertheless, available figures indicate the general norms. An observer in 1789 described the wages of colonial printers as very great compared with those in Britain. Workers in New England, he wrote, got three to eight dollars weekly. Those in the Mid-Atlantic received five to ten dollars. In the South, where skilled labor was rare, eight to twenty dollars or even twenty-five could be made.[24]

Between 1760 and 1830, the wages of urban printers in the Mid-Atlantic states remained well within this range. Philadelphia journeymen sought a minimum of six dollars, roughly a dollar per day in 1786. The Franklin Typographical Association in New York City secured that minimum scale in many of the local shops at the turn of the century, and the Philadelphians sought, apparently without success, to establish a weekly rate of eight dollars in 1802. Thirteen years later, Weed and Thomas Kennedy "seldom lost a working hour" to earn as much as twelve dollars weekly and more, making them the most highly paid printers in the city, and probably in the country as well. The frequent complaints of the Typographical Society about members earning less than the established scale of eight dollars weekly on the evening and nine dollars on the morning papers hint at more representative wages. A reasonable estimate of the average wages for those working at the established scale probably ranged from $5.75 to $6 in the late eighteenth century, increasing gradually to $7.50 to $9 by 1815.[25] Printers made more than shoemakers, tailors, and hatters, but somewhat less than the seasonally employed workers in the building trades.

Clearly, the hired craftsmen battled to sustain their standards of living in a very different context than had the Revolutionary artisan. Vast urban growth had introduced a new element in American life. For the hired man, the changing city of the early national period offered some of the worst elements of the developing system of rationalized production without any major departure from the decaying preindustrial standards of sanitation and housing. As "CLEON" noted in the *Aurora*, the new urbanite could not "raise his food and manufacture his clothes" as could his fellow citizens living in the surrounding countryside. At the same time, the city offered not a refuge from, but a concentration of the stench and squalor of preindustrial life. Cowherds, for example, daily gathered the numerous livestock still raised in Philadelphia and New York City to drive them to the fields. As late as 1817, some twenty thousand hogs rooted about New York City, competing with goats, dogs, and the unwashed children of the poor, yet too young to work.[26]

City growth strained older levels of municipal planning that measured its achievements primarily by its ability to keep the surveyed streets passable and to minimize the further construction of clapboard houses, which were fire hazards. Stagnant water, sewage, garbage, and dead animals collected freely in the yards, open lots, cellars, and streets; the privies, cleaned perhaps once in ten or twelve years, failed to contain the corporation pudding, as New Yorkers called it, that seeped into their wells and drinking water. Workplaces of soap boilers, tallow chandlers, butchers, and other craftsmen, also contributed to the atmosphere of the early city. Even an enthusiast for contemporary urban life admitted that postrevolutionary New York had become "a vastly disagreeable place of residence."[27]

The congestion of the cities resulted partly from workers'

desire to live close to their jobs. However, in what was still a walking city, they probably resided in all parts of the community. Urban historians argue that city growth had been too great and too rapid to permit the development of distinct neighborhoods of the rich and of the poor, who were generally seen simply as the unskilled. Nevertheless, despite the possible presence of the odd large house belonging to a well-off family that had yet to move away, working poor certainly predominated in some quarters.

Working class residents lived virtually alone on many streets of the port area. Philadelphia's Water Street, which ran "but a little above the surface of the tide," and its lack of any proper space between the buildings left it "much confined, ill aired" and "more nauseous." In 1820, when the yellow fever reappeared along the wharves below Market Street, the outbreak centered on Water Street, "the narrowest, yet one of the most populous in the city."[28]

In New York City, too, "near the margin of the two rivers" clustered "the poor, uncleanly and destitute classes of the community." Over decades, the city had filled parts of the East River, pushing back its original banks along Pearl Street to add Front, Water, and eventually South streets, a district characterized by maritime and waterfront labor and called Top-sail or Canvas Town. Along "several dismal lanes, courteously denominated streets," the poor disproportionately resided. By 1815 sections of the west side, along the North or Hudson River, contended for the reputation as "the worst quarter of the city."[29]

Badly engineered landfills helped channel the expansion of these poorer neighborhoods. New York authorities had long been engaged in filling the old Collect Pond on the east side above the new City Hall, leaving only a stagnant, filthy pool that inspired nearby residents to call it the "Collick." When buildings on the yet-unsettled fill began to sink and tilt, rents dropped and it became yet another site of congestion, poverty, and disease. In Philadelphia, Dock Creek became an open sewer, a "large and offensive canal" running through the most populous part of the city before being bridged, partly covered, filled, and renamed Dock Street.[30]

Builders tried, with marginal success, to accomodate new urban growth. The early national period saw the rise of the row house; buildings often covered the entire front of the lots for an entire block. Baltimore's rapid expansion gave that city a particular flexibility in its spread over newly surveyed blocks. Elsewhere, builders often fit their works into the spaces between older houses. Contemporaries often and correctly noted that these practices, on such a scale, would effectively preclude adequate ventilation for the interior of the buildings.[31]

More typically, multiple buildings haphazardly crowded onto single lots to shelter the growing numbers of city dwellers. Franklin Court, a row of three houses built across the fronts of several adjoining lots in central Philadelphia, inspired wide emulation. The practice soon degenerated into packing the poor into shabbily built backyard houses, shanties, and sheds. Such additional construction often assumed the addresses of the narrow alleyways like Philadelphia's Elbow Lane and Strawberry Alley, which, as early as the 1790s, provided space for 137 additional buildings in the interior of the block bounded by Second and Third, High (or Market), and Chestnut streets. On nearby Apple Tree Alley, where forty people died in the 1793 epidemic of yellow fever, only ten of the twenty-four heads of households may have been day laborers, with artisans, no doubt, accounting for most of the rest; still, few contemporaries would have failed to recognize such places as abodes of the working poor.[32]

In this environment, the hired men, unable to find board with their employers, scrambled for what accomodations they could afford. Few had the means of setting up their own household, for men known to have been working in the craft during a given year generally do not appear in the city directory. Those with families in the city simply stayed with parents and relatives as long as was possible and tolerable. Edward and John Whitely, for example, remained unlisted in the city directories or the Federal census as heads of households during the years of their active involvement with the Typographical Society, and almost certainly lived in the only household in the area with their surname, that of Elizabeth Whitely, a widow who kept a boardinghouse and was probably their mother, aunt, or other relative.[33]

More established workingmen doubled up to share rent. Often crowded "into very small confined apartments," some moved their entire family in one room. If one had a garret or an extra room, its rent would provide a welcome addition to a family's income.[34]

Such boardinghouses as Mrs. Whitely's provided homes for the locally least-known workers, including the newcomers. About thirty or forty lived in a typical place "not far from Peck's slip" in New York City. Some such places were better than others, but officials generally viewed them as "the abode of dissolute characters and scene of frequent disorders." The authorities tried to insist that they "be neat and clean, and no more lodgers shall be admitted than the City Inspector shall think" proper, under penalty of fine.[35]

Journeymen's wages generally protected them only from the worst places in which to live. For example, many families, "particularly among the Irish emigrants," resorted to "the necessity of living, or rather existing, in damp cellars." In "these numerable miserable" places, "the greatest number of the poor," especially the immigrant poor, resided. Not only did "one of these half-under-ground huts" serve "as bedroom, kitchen and shop, to a whole family," but "the offals cast from every part of the house" fell outside the windows, if there were any. Some "subterranean apartments" got light only through an open hatch door, which, when shut, left the inhabitants "buried alive."[36]

New kinds of poverty fostered the development of crime. Certainly, the wise traveler avoided certain areas of the early cities, including those smaller cities, for the victims were not limited to the well-off. When Ichabod Hoyt of the New York Typographical Society went to New Orleans, for example, he was "robbed and thrown into the Mississippi, where his body was found the next day."[37]

The yet-compact size of even the largest American cities meant that workers enjoyed some access to the cheaper, undeveloped land adjacent to the city, but such lots were only inexpensive relative to those already within the rapidly expanding line of construction, and even the more well-paid artisan had to move quickly. Weed recalled a walk taken in 1815 or 1816 with George Mather, a friend and fellow member of the Typographical Society. After years of saving, Mather had purchased "a vacant lot situated near the now corner of Spring and Mercer" outside the city where he hoped to "erect an ink manufactory" of his own. He and Weed strolled into the countryside beyond the present site of Canal Street only to find a flurry of new construction where Mather had expected "that the adjoining property would not be occupied for many years, and that he should never be distracted by neighbors!"[38]

The interior of the journeyman's home would have generally been quite bare. The very poor often "had not even a stool to sit on, nor a bed to lie upon," although the hired mechanic who had been in the city for a while had a few sticks of furniture. Everyone, however, required warmth in the winter, and newcomers found firewood very dear in the larger cities, making a constant, extraordinary drain on a worker's budget.[39]

In summary, a year's labor on a scale of $8 placed an annual income of near $400 at the journeyman's disposal. In 1809 the hired carpenters met in New York to compose a sample budget demonstrating the difficulties of maintaining a family of five locally on that income. According to their estimates, house rent took $55, firewood $30, and food $162.50; the worker's clothes, tools, and contingent expenses another $60, $10, and $20, leaving a mere $62.50 for the family members' clothes, education, recreation, medicine, and emergency needs.[40] Significantly, their employers' responses challenged none of these figures.

Other considerations demonstrate that even these rather grim approximations of printers' incomes and standards of living tend to be optimistic. As we have seen, a significant part of the hired work force in the printing trades earned less than scale. A hired man, in the early years, generally made his pay based on the numbers of sheets printed or ems of type set; the struggle of the typographical societies to establish a guaranteed minimum weekly rate reflected the hazards of an income based exclusively on the piecework system. That system made workers bear the burden of the ebb and flow of orders, mechanical difficulties with the press, and the variable need for manuscript corrections as to grammar, spelling, and punctuation.[41]

Even if a printer did work for the scale, he rarely worked constantly. The end of a particular job order often meant the end of regular work for the hired man. Wage-earning printers, as one observer later noted, "lived well or ill, according as they have or have not permanent situations." The lot of the man forced "to run from office to office, obtaining a week's work here and a few days employment there, is not one to be coveted."[42]

Nor did journeymen necessarily collect this wage in easily negotiated currency. English pounds and shillings and Spanish dollars circulated freely in the early national period, as did paper certificates redeemable only in the immediate locality or even at a particular shop with which the employer had some arrangement. As late as 1815, Weed received his extraordinarily high wage in twenty-five and fifty-cent shinplasters issued by a local bank.[43]

Finally, the long-term trend in wages must be considered. It is a sobering fact that the desire to secure a scale first attained in 1800 inspired the organization, half a century later, of the current New York Typographical Union, and that a leading local newspaper in 1864 remarked "that nineteen-twentieths" of the local trade "did not average $6 per week."[44] The oft-quoted references to the higher incomes of American craftsmen need an increasingly critical eye as one discusses conditions in later years. Wage earners began to feel the efforts of this long-term degeneration in their standard of living in the early national period. During these years, hired printers began to claim that the salaries proposed by their employers would place them at or even below a mere subsistence; their complaints, particularly by men with families, were demonstrably well-justified.

More significantly, the structural shifts in the craft restricted a worker's ability to rise to the ownership of his own shop. Even a modest printing office in a small town with cheaper rents required an initial outlay of several hundred dollars, with additional money needed to relocate and support the printer and his family, to repay loans, to purchase paper and inks, and to maintain the equipment. The total capital that was required roughly equalled more than a full year's wage. Even then, those who did prosper, as one scholar noted, became "entrepreneurs rather than craftsmen."[45]

In the city, the ambitious printer took fewer chances. Higher rent and greater competition for business plagued the urban shop, but equipment and supplies cost less, and the ultimate price could be minimized, for, when business went badly, one could always find work in another shop. Moreover, skilled hired men might also be able to strike a bargain with a master for the use of his equipment.

The real test of mobility within the craft might begin, at least, with the proportion of journeymen able to establish their own printing offices, but the sources permit no easy answer concerning these "birds of passage." For example, one of these very mobile workmen active in the New York City trade during 1810 may well have earlier had his own shop in rural Massachusetts and may have later opened another in New Jersey without either experience having made an imprint whatsoever on the New York City sources.

However, membership rolls from early typographical societies provide a valuable opportunity to roughly gauge mobility during these years. The extant minutes of the Philadelphia Typographical Society and the New York Typographical Society permit a more or less complete reconstruction of the rolls. In addition, men who had their own presses for any length of time tended to print newspapers, at least for a while, and Clarence S. Brigham's *History and Bibliography of American Newspapers* includes national listings for all extant American newspapers published prior to 1821.

A comparison of the 598 known participants in the typographical societies with those printers of early newspapers yields some useful figures. At least 160 of the early unionists, somewhat over a quarter of the total, did operate their own papers; of this total, 58 did so before their involvement in a labor organization and 115 afterwards, with a handful who had shops both before and after their involvement with a journeymen's society.[46] A liberal margin for others who had shops without having issued a known newspaper might swell the estimated proportion of unionists who became proprietors at some point in their lives to as high as one-third of the total membership.

Nevertheless, several considerations dampen any optimistic view of mobility among early national printers. First, the nature of such a success seems dubious in most cases. "Every journeyman expects to become a master—it is the regular line of preferment," noted one observer, "but few masters expect again to be journeymen."[47] Information on the printers indicates that they should have. The vast majority of the 160 printers of newspapers who also, at some time, had membership in a labor organization could not maintain newspaper publication for more than a few years, and only twenty-three retained their proprietorship for longer than a decade. Genuine and permanent mobility, as opposed to an apparent mobility, seems to have been quite rare.

Second, the truly significant successes attained by some of these printers involved men whose associations with the journeymen's societies tended to be very brief. John Binns, for example, established a powerful press with strong political ties before coming to Philadelphia, where he apparently held membership in the Typographical Society during a few weeks of work as a journeyman before launching the *Republican Argus*, the predecessor of his very successful *Democratic Press*. Joseph Gales, Jr., the son of a prominent North Carolina printer and political figure, spent no more than a short time in the Philadelphia society before going on to Washington, securing government printing contracts and launching his career as a journalist and editor. Similarly successful printer-publishers had relatively marginal ties to journeymen's organizations.[48]

Finally, the long-term dynamics of craft development tended to erode any high rate of success. As the demand for printing increased, shops grew larger, and technology evolved, the disproportionate growth of the wage-earning section of the trade became ever more acute. Furthermore, the mobility figures for just the twenty-six Philadelphia strikers of 1786 provide a useful point of comparison. Over 61.5 percent of their number gained shops of their own, with 50 percent issuing newspapers, and roughly 15.5 percent keeping their own businesses for over ten years.

The lack of exactness in the statistics is less instructive than their reflection of an obvious restructuring of the craft, which strangled upward mobility among journeymen. The case of John Hewes provides a rare and notable exception proving the rule. A man with substantial unionist credentials, having served as the president of the Baltimore Typographical Society, he entered into a small printing partnership in 1804. After two years, he expanded the business, taking control of another press formerly run by Daniel Lawrence (who had himself participated in the Philadelphia strike of 1786) and assuming ownership of the *Federal Gazette*. His ability to make further necessary investments near the point at which other small operations tended to fold was unusual but less mysterious than it seems. During March 1805, he, along with a cabinet maker, had won ten thousand dollars in the Roman Catholic Cathedral lottery.[49] Blind luck often courted economic independence and security more surely than did hard work and individual initiative.

Individuals formulated several strategies to circumvent the obstacles to mobility within the craft. The sort of horizontal mobility—individual movement from place to place—discussed above in part reflected their personal searches for markets capable of sustaining their own shops. Indeed, the data on their establishment of newspapers indicates a great deal of moving about the country. Some sought a place in the specialized niches of the developing industry. Two prominent members of the Franklin Typographical Association, David and George Bruce, formed a printing partnership in 1805 that gained success by branching into a type foundry and stereotyping. Wrigley, the Philadelphia journeyman, showed a similar ingenuity in 1806 by opening his own business as a manufacturer of printing ink, as did George Mather later in New York.[50]

Journeymen's lives beyond the workplace also inspired efforts to escape the strangulation of mobility within the shop. A number of men involved in the typographical societies tried to open and maintain public houses wherein they might combine a profitable business with pleasure. Such a course seems to have been quite common among early American craftsmen.[51]

A few men involved in the typographical societies also left the craft entirely to enter professional life as doctors or clergymen. Some sat among the many "unprofessional friends" of John W. Francis, New York City's printer-turned-physician who, unlike most of the city's medical profession, "repudiated all absolute and unworthy concomitant of the big-wig, gold-headed cane, and solemn dignity of the doctors who practised before the schoolmaster was abroad in the world." Journeymen printers participated with small masters in the Franklin Society, formed in 1788 around a constitution that directed its last two members to divide the remaining funds in a prescribed way, contributing the remainder to the American Philosophical Society for scientific research. One early unionist, Stephen Sewall, became so interested in herbal medicine that he tried his hand at its practice. Another, writing as "an advocate of universal improvement," issued his own text on the treatment of consumption.[52]

Some journeymen also dabbled in historical and literary pursuits. Respected men of letters well knew their printers, and the most famous American poet of the day, Philip M. Freneau, wrote holiday verses for future unionist Francis Wrigley. As a journeyman and union member, Thurlow Weed passed "most of my leisure hours" reading or at the theater, and Binns's love of the Philadelphia stage rivalled Weed's "passion for the drama" in New York, where the fifty-cent tickets "left but little of my earnings." More interestingly, they soon tried their own hand. Wrigley's friend, Jacob Berriman, went on stage himself, and the two collaborated on an early children's history of America. John W. Scott wrote a history of his Presbyterian parish and published his own poetry. Theophilus Eaton's doggerel *Rambles through the City* must have been one of the first such celebrations of the urban experience. Other poets among the organized printers included David Bruce and, most famously, Samuel Woodworth, whose "Old Oaken Bucket" idealized the pastoral virtues of his rural New England.[53]

Several besides Southwick also tried to follow Franklin's path of journeyman printer to publisher to political leader. After all, a printer with a knack for political journalism, the connections to bolster his fragile business with government contracts, and the possibility of establishing a statewide network of political allies could find both fame and fortune. Members of journeymen's societies like Binns, Weed, Gales, Peter Force, Ebenezer Mack, and Sheppard Church Leakin later gained considerable influence in local, state, and even national politics, a few even winning high public office. Stephen B. Leonard, a former leader of the Albany journeymen, went to the Federal Congress, and John Norvell, formerly an officer of the Baltimore Typographical Society, later won election to the U.S. Senate by the Michigan legislature.[54]

Again, although such men may have had the most marginal ties to later organizations, printers seized on any evidence of such opportunity for years to come. By the outbreak of the Civil War, the appointment of a St. Louis printer to be a postmaster at St. Joseph inspired a trade paper to advise the "little fellows who are mounted on boxes in obscure corners of printing offices picking up type" to "be of good cheer! your turn will come by and by. Aim high be faithful and persevering, and you will reach the goal."[55] To aim high by mid-century had clearly meant something less than in the days of Franklin.

More efforts, apparently farfetched, to change their occupations hint at colorful and charming personalities. Jacob M. Berriman, who had worked in the Philadelphia printing trades as early as 1785 and had, with Wrigley, printed various pieces for the local stage, regularly showed his own flair for the dramatic. In 1799 a Connecticut broadside reprinted a selection from his journal kept "during his tour to the westward of Fort Recovery" in the wilderness of what became the Ohio-Indiana border. Referring the skeptical to a skin in William Peck's collection, it described his encounter with and the killing of a monstrous snake over thirty-six feet long and a yard in diameter. Shortly after his participation with Wrigley and fifty-eight others in the wage struggle of February 1802, Berriman left the craft entirely for the stage.[56]

Leaving the trade, however, did not guarantee success. The name of William Cornely, one of Berriman's and Wrigley's comrades in the wage struggle of 1802, alternately appeared in local directories as a city constable, a pump maker, a shingle-dresser, and an accountant. Success could be elusive outside as well as inside the craft.[57]

In summary, a peculiar kind of upward mobility remained possible for journeymen printers of the early national period. While many rose to the independent status of a small-scale entrepreneur, almost all lost their own shops within a few years and returned to the workbenches of others. As a result, prospects often seemed brighter outside of the craft. Short-lived efforts at both sorts of success created a layer within the hired work force of men who were neither permanent wage laborers nor employers in the modern sense of the term, but who nonetheless spent most of their lives working for others.

IV

Structural changes within the craft, rather than the lack of personal industry, account for both the disproportionate expansion of the wage earners within the trade and their declining wages, standards of living, and mobility. In their changing world of work, jouneymen, with ideals, values, and aspirations shaped by earlier conditions, engaged in prolonged personal struggles against long odds. In these efforts, hired printers forged strong, if rarely documented, friendships and personal bonds with each other.[58] In addition to politics, religion, and cultural matters, hired workers discussed the questions affecting their craft and became increasingly aware of the structural changes in the trade. Their response was not the simple, almost instinctive reaction to economic compulsion so often depicted but a carefully calculated course of action, informed by a common understanding of their plight and historic appreciation of their prospects.

Journeymen printers also had before them many examples of self-organization. Wrigley and other workmen who went on strike in 1786 participated not only in later printers' clubs like the Franklin Society, but also in other kinds of voluntary associations. Wrigley's coworker, John W. Scott, for example, became active in his church and in a church-based mutual aid club, the Provident Society, and New Yorkers like Isaac Collect and Ebenezer Mack became prominent freemasons.[59] Still others held membership in volunteer fire companies, political societies, and social clubs. Like many Americans of their day, when confronted with grievances, the wage-earning printers turned to committees, petitions, and resolutions. In short, they began to organize.

Two

All As One

The Organization of the
Typographical Societies

E very labourer in the vineyard of literature
is richly worthy of his hire. . . .
—New York Typographical
Society, 1816

However different our education has been;
however dissimilar our situation in life;
however opposite in opinion, with regard to
politics, religion, or any branch of art, science,
or literature,—yet, when associated, as we
now are,—*we are* ALL *as* ONE;— we know of
no *distinction*, but that *brother*, or of *friend!*
—William Burdick, 1802

In September 1810 journeymen printers in New York City held general meetings of their craft to discuss and publicize a stand out or turn out. Their resolution that they highly approved of the action was no less militant and combative because the strike had been called by their peers in the Philadelphia trade. Baltimore unionists held similar meetings in support of their striking brothers.[1] In a few short years, these hired printers had not only organized themselves to challenge the exclusive control of their trade by the employers, but also coordinated their activities in different communities.

The surviving record of printers' activities in the early national period indicates the scope of their achievements not only at New York City, Philadelphia, and Baltimore, but at Boston, Washington, Albany, and New Orleans. At New York and Philadelphia, their oganizations emerged alongside associations of hired men in other unregulated, "free" trades like the cabinet- and chairmakers, house carpenters, tailors, and shoemakers. Baltimore had associations among the carpenters, the tailors organized in Boston, and the shoemakers acted in concert as well at Pittsburgh, Lexington, and a few smaller communities. Scattered Philadelphia sources also refer to organizations among painters, ship carpenters, masons, saddlers, blacksmiths, brick-layers, stonecutters, hatters, goldsmiths, and curriers (leather workers). The historical record on the early printers' unions, however, most clearly represented the qualitative dimensions of the journeyman's achievement, their reevaluation of the artisan experience, and their articulation of ideas and values distinctive to labor. Finally, the nearly complete records of the Typographical Societies in Philadelphia and New York permit us to see some of these hired men not merely as the faceless, dehumanized creatures of economic circumstances, but as individual workers with diverse backgrounds, ideological commitments, and personal aspirations that shaped some of the characteristics of their early unionism.

I

In the shadow of the American Revolution, the hired printers made their earliest efforts to participate in decisions that shaped their lives and prospects within the craft. Late in 1778, printers in British-occupied New York City held a series of informal meetings, issuing a statement to their employers on November 9. "As the necessaries of life are raised to such an enormous price," they argued, "it cannot be expected that we should continue to work at the wages now given." They denied any desire "to distress the Master Printers at this time, on account of the scarcity of hands" or to "take an ungenerous advantage of the times—we only wish barely to exist; which is impossible to do with our present stipend." The Tory editor James Rivington used their statement and his agreement to a wage hike to justify his increasing charge for advertising.[2]

Seven years later, more serious trouble flared at Philadelphia. In the spring of 1786, as master printers planned to slash wages, twenty-six local journeymen organized the first known turn out in the American trade. They left work and refused to return until employers agreed to restore the old scale. The apparent ease with which the wage earners defeated their masters may well have reflected the tacit support of the strikers' goals by Franklin, the aged but mentally alert and open-minded patron of the craft.[3] More broadly, the ideals of the Revolution itself, as well as the economic changes it had engendered, played a role in stirring the journeymen to action.

In the wake of this sharp clash in the local trade, an important early society formed under the patronage of Franklin himself. Near the close of his long life, he sponsored a meeting on March 8, 1788, to establish a permanent society of the Philadelphia craft. It included not only men who owned their own shops, but also journeymen; at least five of its members—Thomas Lang, Francis Wrigley, John Doyle, Richard Folwell, and John Bushell—had been active in the strike movement two years before. After the death of their esteemed founder, the members changed the name of their organization to the Franklin Society. It collapsed in the wake of the yellow fever epidemic of 1793 and seems to have been unable to recover, although 1796 saw some sort of printers' association, thanked in a formal resolution by the Federal Society of Journeymen Cabinet-Makers for its support during their strike that spring.[4]

In the spring of 1794, over fifteen years after New York City journeymen had gained a wage increase through their short-lived group, the hired printers of that city formed the New York Typographical Association (also called the New York Typographical Society). They ratified a constitution, elected officers, such as Southwick, to exercise interim powers between its quarterly meetings, secured a minimum scale of one dollar per day, similar to the Philadelphia rate, and survived into 1797.[5]

Shortly after the failure of their organization, the New York journeymen made another effort that seemed to have directly inspired the development of organizations elsewhere. In November 1798 veterans of the defunct association such as Southwick and Thomas Ringwood became involved in holding formal meetings that established a new society. The Franklin Typographical Association (or Franklin Typographical Society) constituted itself in 1799 and met monthly rather than quarterly, rapidly gaining fifty members and waging a successful strike that autumn to secure a new wage scale. The yellow fever epidemic that hit New York in the summer of 1803 seems to have severely damaged this effort, which lasted only into the spring of the following year.[6]

A wave of activism swept the craft after the New York victory. A protest against pay cuts at the Philadelphia *Aurora* may have inspired the 1799 formation of the Asylum Company of Journeymen Printers. Many members must have been among the sixty-five journeymen who signed a new wage schedule in February 1802. Their effort to gain a minimum weekly wage of eight dollars was possibly aimed at achieving the scale recently won in New York City.[7]

That same year, journeymen printers organized in two other cities. A Boston Franklin Society petitioned the U.S. Congress concerning protective tariffs and, in the following year, a Boston Typographical Society functioned, indicating a reorganization of the older group. Five months after his participation in the Philadelphia wage struggle of February 1802, Alexander Boland helped to start a Baltimore Typographical Society.[8]

In Philadelphia itself, participants in that 1802 wage dispute and members of the earlier Asylum Company formed one of the most influential of these early labor organizations. The Philadelphia Typographical Society organized in November of 1802. Although it formally withdrew from trade-regulating activities in the summer of 1810, the society yet survived as a mutual aid club well into the present century.

Elsewhere, journeymen had to periodically rebuild their fragile organizations. The Baltimore union failed in 1807, but reor-
ganizing efforts began as early as February of 1808; by June, the
new association had elected George Tomlin, another veteran of
the Philadelphia struggle of 1802, as its first president. The
Baltimore society lasted at least into late 1810. Some journeymen
at the new national capital, Washington City, issued a call for
organization on November 2, 1807, but without immediate
results. After the failure of Boston's Franklin Society, journeymen there began a new organization in August 1809. By June
1810 a New Orleans Typographical Society had formed.[9]

In New York City, where the older societies had collapsed,
a new Typographical Society appeared in the summer of 1809.
Based upon at least fifteen years of efforts to establish an
organization, the journeymen of the city built a militant trade-
regulating body. Although it renounced the unionist regulation
of the craft in the winter of 1817–18, the society, like its
Philadelphia counterpart, survived as a mutual aid association
well into the twentieth century.

In the lesser centers of the trade, efforts also continued. A
Baltimore Typographical Association, formed early in 1812,
lasted until 1815. The Albany Typographical Society, formed in
March of 1813, later described itself in a letter to the New York
City group as "a branch of your Society"; the upstate journeymen immediately established a new pay scale and secured an
even better agreement with their employers late in 1815. On
November 25, 1815, Boston printers reorganized their association
yet another time, but nothing is known of its fate.[10]

These efforts culminated in the participation of veteran
unionists in a historic ferment among the printers of the
District of Columbia, where the seasonal demands of government printing regularly drew large numbers of journeymen from
across the country. The British sacking of Washington during
the summer of 1814 seriously disrupted the lives of the residents.
Journeymen, impatient with the conditions imposed upon the
generally transient work force, started the Columbia Typographical Society the following winter. Later called the Columbia
Typographical Union, the body has survived into the present

as probably the oldest trade union in the Western Hemisphere, Local 101 of the former International Typographical Union, now part of the Communications Workers of America.[11]

II

Each one of these unionist efforts built upon the achievements of its predecessors, through four stages of development. Sporadic outbursts of journeyman activity between 1778 and 1793 sought first to influence trade regulations. From 1794 to 1801, short-lived societies emerged in New York City and Philadelphia. Between 1802 and 1809, the idea of organizing, if not its realization, became deeply rooted in those two cities and the initial short-lived associations at Boston and Baltimore. Finally, the years 1810 through 1815 saw the spread of ongoing efforts to maintain societies at Boston and Baltimore, as well as at New York and Philadelphia, coupled with the appearance of rudimentary societies elsewhere.

Each new local body drew strength from the presence of similar organizations in other communities. Again, very real, if rarely documented, personal ties between these transient pioneers of American trade unionism provided a sense of continuity to those efforts. Even the incomplete records of most of these associations indicate that some members and leaders had participated in earlier efforts. Peter Konkle, a former leader of the Philadelphia Typographical Society, moved and joined that of New York, and still later joined the Columbia Typographical Society at Washington. Former co-workers frequently kept track of each other, often through third parties in the craft, creating an important informal network of uncertain dimensions hidden behind available sources.

Such ties enabled new societies in some degree to learn from the experiences of their predecessors. The course of organization in Baltimore, for example, benefited greatly from the presence of unionists trained in the Philadelphia struggles. Several New York City journeymen assisted in one of the many reorganizations of the Boston society. At least thirteen former members of the Philadelphia Typographical Society, along with some former members from Baltimore and New York City, helped to shape Washington's Columbia Typographical Society.

The similarity of the names journeymen chose for their organizations intimates these rudimentary national ties. The name of the Franklin Society, Philadelphia's old fraternal order of 1788 through 1794, remained a favorite with new organizations of wage-earning printers for several years. When Baltimore printers chose simply to call their union a Typographical Society in July 1802, groups of their peers followed the example in Philadelphia that same year, New York in 1809, New Orleans in 1810, Albany in 1813, and the District of Columbia in 1815. That a similar process operated in other crafts is evident in the 1804 organization at New York of the United Society of Journeymen Taylors, echoing the choice of their Baltimore counterparts, whose United Journeymen Taylors Society began in 1795.

An older sense of craft fraternalism also predisposed printers to cooperate with their brothers in other cities. When New Yorkers faced an outbreak of the yellow fever in 1803, the new Philadelphia Typographical Society and the still younger Baltimore Typographical Society—along with, perhaps, the Boston Franklin Society—mustered their own feeble resources to assist the stricken journeymen of the Franklin Typographical Society. When the Philadelphia group assigned a committee "to forward the above amount [$83.60] to suitable persons in New York," it inspired Jacob Franks, the president of the New York union, to assure them that needy local printers "shall not fail of tasting the sweet cup of their friendship, so amply filled by their brethren," nor of remembering the "honourable token of their friendship and benevolence" as "an act which should be recorded in Golden Letters."[12]

Employer tactics also drove hired workers relentlessly toward this broader vision. Masters often responded to a strike, or the organization of a new society capable of waging a strike, by placing advertisements in out-of-town newspapers announcing large numbers of jobs for journeymen in their city. The unionists might then face a work force disproportionately composed of trained but desperately unemployed newcomers, an effective, if perhaps personally reluctant, counterweight to strikers or potential strikers. To counter such tactics, journeymen often published official, public replies and developed an elementary national network of communications. When Philadelphia masters placed such advertisements, the new Typographical Society published notices of their own, to warn the members of other associations, specifically the Franklin Society in Boston, the Franklin Typographical Association in New York City, and the Baltimore Typographical Society.[13]

A similar logic moved them toward a common national perspective in their efforts to regulate the craft. As the month-old New York Typographical Society moved toward a strike in 1809 to secure a new wage scale, its board assigned secretary David H. Reins to "open a correspondence with the different Typographical Societies in the United States" to propose an exchange of information concerning former members of journeymen's groups who had, by breaking a strike or similarly violating the organizations' rules, betrayed their fraternal pledge; the presence of such "rats" could be a major consideration in union strategy. John Childs responded that news of the organization of a typographical society at New York had inspired "inexpressible pleasure to the members of the board and of the Society in general" at Philadelphia. They hoped that the New York City craft had "broken their manacles with a determination that they shall never be riveted again" and advised them that "no great end was ever yet attained without danger and difficulty." He then described the request to exchange lists of rats as involving "a principle not readily acceded to" by some of the officers of the group (himself included) but with which they would comply.[14]

Ultimately, only the removal of temptation would assure the societies that workers would not be easily coaxed into an area of higher wages which, in the process, might reduce those wages. In November 1815 the New York Typographical Society sought the support of the other associations, particularly "those of Philadelphia and Albany," for a national campaign "to raise their prices to the same standards as ours," establishing a uniform wage scale along the upper eastern seaboard.[15] Integral to the earliest stages of local unionization was the beginning of a long struggle toward national organization.

Clearly, these short-lived groups and societies of hired men constituted genuine trade unions, although the term itself did not become common until the mid-nineteenth century; as such, they represented something new in American life, the self-organization of hired men to exercise power together on questions of wages and working conditions, control of which had previously been left to the exclusive determinations of the masters. "The profession required such an institution," explained a committee of the New York Typographical Society, whose members had earlier been "scattered and exposed to undue influences of the currupt in power. A great spirit gave it birth."[16] Describing these typographical societies as unions does not, of course, preclude certain peculiarities unique to the working-class condition of the period, such as the fraternal concerns about mutual aid or a sense of identity that continued to include small-scale master printers.

During these years, journeymen—indeed former unionists—became employers and began to reappraise their stance. Upon gaining their own shops, once-leading unionists could become the officers in employers' associations. Two of the most successful ex-unionists among the Pennsylvania shoemakers, for example, later led the masters' organizations at Philadelphia and Pittsburgh that initiated legal proceedings against their former brothers in blatant attempts to break the unions they had earlier helped to organize. So, too, the same journeyman who brazenly defied union protests to work below the established scale might join the same union shortly thereafter or even help to organize one in another city.[17]

Prominent members of the journeymen's organizations also articulated some of the best expressions of that persistent legacy of craft fraternalism. New York's *Independent Mechanic*, for example, was operated by Joseph Harmer and George Ashbridge, two former members of the journeymen's Typographical Society. Years before, in 1801, the union gave nine hearty cheers and drank a toast to the employers' Printers and Booksellers Association of New York for the latter's efforts to promote the craft's prosperity. John Clough, the journeymen's speaker, declared that "while the *employers* are using every endeavor towards the advancement of the Typographical Art, the *employed* are not less anxious for its promotion," and "while we endeavor to prove by assiduous attention to business, that we are actuated by motives of *mutual* benefit," he assured his peers and their masters, "we shall ever receive the commendation of discerning men."[18] After all, printers of every status still had a great deal in common and sought to promote the welfare and prosperity of the craft as a whole.

The earliest workingmen's associations also did their best to maintain their old tradition of craft self-education. They ordered Isaiah Thomas's *History of Printing,* sent their formal congratulations to the inventor of the new Columbian Press, and endorsed the quality of various printing inks. In the temperate spirit of Franklin, they sought to find a meeting place "other than in a Public House."[19]

So, too, the New York Typographical Society began its regular monthly meetings with a lecture by one of the members and even sponsored a literary club for those wishing to master "the theoretical parts of that Science." Conversely, that the society never forgave those who degraded such studies became clear in 1810 when it assigned its annual oration to Joseph Gleason, who had earlier addressed Boston's Young Democratic-Republicans. After a respectable performance for the New York society, Gleason declined persistent requests for a publishable copy, explaining that, "not being overambitious to appear before the public as a literary champion," he had not the time to polish the manuscript, which he had sent to his brother in Massachusetts anyway. Nevertheless, in late July, other members found it "in the most *complete* order for publication," a previously printed commencement address from Harvard University plagiarized by the unfortunate Gleason, who soon left town in disgrace.[20] Early typographical societies, as a body, placed a high value on original literary and rhetorical achievement.

Unionist expressions of these traditional craft concerns meant that, as a body, the societies never passively accepted their permanent status as wage earners. Rather, the emerging organizations resisted the grouping of the small master with the successful manufacturer. Philadelphia journeymen appealed to the former with their hope that "the time is not far distant, when the *employer* and the *employed* will vie with each other, the one in *allowing* a competent salary, the other in *deserving* it." "Let us become rivals to each other in the performance of our respective duty," suggested Clough. "Let us be emulous to obtain the respect of those by whom we are encouraged—Let the general tenor of our conduct evidence the purity of our intentions, and our Society will be respected." A "professional tenet of our constitution" required "justice to our employers, as well as to ourselves," argued Ringwood. This needed the great care of members to maintain, for "our association will thereby support that credit which it has been gradually attaining since its establishment." He urged the "numerous society" to "endeavor to conciliate the esteem of our employers," "be united as we have heretofore been," and "soar above the *malevolent attacks* of any who may, from *principle* or *prejudice*, profess themselves our enemies."[21] Clearly, journeymen's affinity for the ideal of the small-scale master craftsman remained strong.

Threats to the trade by foreign competitors concerned all printers. Indeed, one of the few known acts of the Asylum Company of Journeymen Printers in Philadelphia or the Boston Franklin Society involved their memorials to Congress on this subject. New York's Franklin Typographical Society, upon hearing of the formation of the Philadelphia Typographical Society, invited it to work jointly "for the purpose of draughting a petition to Congress for laying an additional duty on imported European works." The project so impressed the Philadelphia directors that they assigned three of their leading members to compose one of their own and a fourth to send word to the New Yorkers of "the results of the letter received from them."[22]

Early unions also shared an anachronistically non-unionist concern with establishing reliable assistance for injured or sick members and the families of recently deceased members. Perhaps this preoccupation reflected the tendency of their organizers and leaders to be the most residentially stable men in the local crafts, with a greater number of dependents. Efforts to regularize such aid provided a fruitful source of internal conflict in all of the early unions. Even the very militant Federal Society of Journeymen Cordwainers in Philadelphia had a history of actually participating with their employers in "another society for assisting the distressed and disabled men of the craft," and New York cabinet- and chairmakers abandoned their union for the much needed security of such an association.[23]

Issues of mutual aid also sparked some of the sharpest conflicts within the early printers' organizations. All of the associations for which any information has survived had strong benefit features. The New York Typographical Society even subscribed to the City Dispensary to ensure medical treatment to its members, and the Philadelphia society had a similar plan. Clough desperately assured the New York City masters that "the sole purpose" of the journeymen's organizing their own society was not the desire for "a greater emolument for our labor" but involved the "very different motives" of relieving the needy among them and their families.[24] His words, though, may have swayed few of his listeners, most of whom, no doubt, retained vivid memories of the society's bitter strike of a year before to establish a minimum union wage scale.

In practice, the great issue that polarized the printers' societies was the tension between their function as trade unions and as benevolent associations that often led to efforts to secure legal incorporation by the state legislatures. While banning efforts by the society thereafter to regulate trade matters, incorporation ensured the group's funds. After eight years of existence as a trade-regulating body, the Philadelphia Typographical Society, in 1810, decided to pursue that course. The following year, George Asbridge suggested that the year-old New York Typographical Society also obtain "the sanction and protection of the state" for its treasury, but it did not do so until 1818. Later, only one vote defeated the advocates of incorporation in the Columbia Typographical Society.[25] Another generation passed before organized journeymen in the trade came to view the perspective of "alimoners," those interested exclusively in mutual aid, as incompatible, in the same organization, with the approach of the "industrialists" who advocated trade regulation. In any case, the typographical societies included members who had not consciously rejected the sufficiency of older, fraternal forms of association as inadequate.

This early conflict presaged a tension central to the history of American labor unionism. A combination of official repression and sanctioned arbitration gradually pruned the labor movement in the United States in the direction of its current status as legally entitled to engage in trade regulation but only under the ultimate authority and supervision of governmental bodies like the National Labor Relations Board. Even the first generation of trade unionists felt such pressures. Their high turnover of membership, the lack of continuity in leadership, and personality conflicts complicated debates over employer membership in the society, and the extent of appropriate regulatory activity. Extant records of typographical societies illustrate the wide spectrum of solutions unionists posed to these issues.

III

The Philadelphia and New York Typographical Societies sought to build stable organizations on shifting foundations. The traditional technique of holding protest meetings over specific grievances seemed sufficient to many of the often transient hired craftsmen in both cities. Too, new groups had to supercede older mutual aid clubs as the Philadelphia journeymen bypassed the Asylum Company in early 1802. Even after its organization, the union there coexisted with non-associated journeymen who met periodically to protest developments in the craft. Through the winter of 1802–03, the union sought simultaneously to counter the efforts of five masters to glut the local job market and to discourage "any further overtures . . . in support of the business" by nonmembers "as the Philadelphia Typographical Society is no doubt competent at all times to support its interests and its rights." In 1809, despite years of organizing efforts, the New York City journeymen still faced pockets of independent action at the edges of their city. The strike that year, for example, rallied a group of Flatbush printers to the society. After months of unsuccessful attempts to get information on the trade, wages, and conditions there, it simply disclaimed any desire to regulate such matters beyond Manhattan on which only those members working on the island would vote.[26]

A membership drawn from such a work force posed an immediate challenge to the survival of any journeymen's society. For example, fully a third of the participants in the wage dispute of February 1802 did not participate in the November founding of the Typographical Society. A committee of the New York group found that, two years after its formation, it had lost "more than two-thirds" of its original members. In September 1811 the secretary sadly noted the absence of a quorum at its board meeting. Of the sixteen subsequent board meetings, six had only one item of business, one adjourned due to "no business," and two lacked quorums, as did the October general membership meeting. In 1812 the outbreak of war and fear of invasion created a "peculiar state of public affairs, which necessarily affects the pecuniary concerns of almost every class of citizens"; that year, membership meetings were rescheduled in July, cancelled in August, and mustered no quorum in October. After the war's end, only nineteen members still paid dues, of whom "only half" seemed concerned with sustaining the union.[27]

Wage disputes inspired journeymen to organize in both cities. However, the Philadelphia society emerged in the wake of the conflict, while in New York the process of organization preceded a conflict "to establish equitable prices for our labor." In the latter case, a society existed to compile a unique record of early strike preparation. Certainly, wages remained a central concern, even in the initial informal meetings during the spring and early summer of 1809 at the home of David H. Reins, a twenty-six-year-old Newburgh native who had spent some years at sea before entering the trade in New York.[28]

That year, the journeymen found themselves in position to take the initiative. They avoided such provocations as the firing of two of the society's founders by the *American Citizen* and chose their own battleground, a demand for a guaranteed minimum of eight to nine dollars weekly. Masters who failed to agree soon found their shops vacated by members and their sympathizers. A group of employers attempted to formulate a common response of their own. Although the society's leaders charged that it "savoured much of despotism," they held a special membership meeting that debated the employers' proposal in "a spirit worth the cause in which we are engaged, and an eloquence that would have graced a senate house." They concluded that "neither the justice of our claims nor the honour of our body will permit us to deviate" on the essential demands. With the uncommitted falling by the wayside, the society still did not hesitate to expel members like the man who engaged in "unworthy and ungrateful conduct" (probably strikebreaking) or the individual who had reported in Philadelphia that the strike had collapsed. Its firm resolve, in turn, drew new recruits like those nonmembers who walked off the *Mercantile Advertiser* to join the strike. By November the society had won in all but a few offices.[29] Similar tribulations challenged all early unions.

Both societies faced a perennial crisis of leadership. Their constitutions had vested most of what authority these unions had in the hands of twelve-member boards and executive offices—president, vice-president, treasurer, and one or two secretaries—but the high turnover in membership meant even greater practical power. So much so that, in Philadelphia, members referred to their board of directors informally as "the directory." Extant minutes reveal that, there, ninety-two of the known participants—over two-thirds—held office at one time or another and that more than half of these won election to more than four months in office, the equivalent of an executive post, or more than one term as a director. Moreover, the actual number of officeholders must have been even higher, given the gap in that society's minutes between January 1804 and June 1806. So, too, in New York between 1809 and 1818, at least ninety-four members held office, of which sixty-seven served for over four months.[30] In short, almost any member willing to assume the thankless responsibility of such offices could do so.

However, only a small group of activists seemed regularly inclined to seek the responsibilities of an official position. Only six men held office in Philadelphia for more than half of the period of time covered by the minutes, with only eight serving for as much as a year and a half. Of the thirty-six who held office by 1804, twenty-three had signed the original wage scale, and these founding members accounted for fourteen of the seventeen elected to serve more than four months. New York had even less continuity in office, with only its unusually reliable treasurer Henry McKee holding a post for more than three of the nine years recorded.

Such leadership proved insufficient to avert periodic crises. In mid-1803 the Philadelphia directory decided to purchase shares in a new bank, entrusting the allocation to George White, the society's president and the former president of the ad hoc coalition of 1802. Thereafter, he missed meetings for several weeks and, that fall, announced his resignation. The startled board voted that "the room be cleared, on account of private business," "came to order & adjourned," decided "that the Adjournment be reconsidered," and appointed a subcommittee to recover the funds. This subcommittee included both secretary William Little and treasurer Bartholomew Graves, who had since 1802 opened his own shop on North Fourth Street. The subsequent delays seemed not to irritate White's successor, former vice-president John Childs, apparently a member of the Childs family that was prominent in the east coast trade as the "printers of the laws of the United States." After many weeks, Childs finally agreed, over Graves's objections, to summon White to a hearing where he answered questions only "through the medium of the President."[31]

The society did not easily extricate itself from this crisis. The board finally expelled White, who left town a few years later, published several papers in New York, and apparently became vice-president of the Albany Typographical Society. However, Graves's balking, together with his ownership of a shop, created such resentment that he left the society and seems to have become quite a vocal opponent of unionism. So, too, Little's reluctance to act against White ended in his resignation from office and the board's polite acknowledgment of his services; he left the city for New York.[32]

A similar crisis revolving around the presidency erupted in the New York Typographical Society shortly after its formation. Its first president, apparently one of the Sherman family of printers at Trenton, also resigned. When he did so, John H. Sherman also presented a bill for various services rendered, such as publishing expenses for the society's 1811 Fourth of July oration. However, when he found that the board had deducted his debt to the society from his reimbursement, his temper flared. Cursing and threatening, he walked out, later refusing to apologize for his conduct. Sherman, like White, rather quickly started his own printing office.[33]

Such a presidential crisis amounted to little more than a sideshow in the New York society, but sparked an ongoing factional conflict in Philadelphia. The White-Graves-Little leadership left a beseiged Childs presiding in their wake. Directors like Samuel Sewall, who badgered Childs for action against White, gained important allies in November and December 1803 when the membership elected to the board two other veterans of the original 1802 wage dispute, John McIlvaine and William W. Wands. Among the printers of "high reputation in their day," Wands had published his own paper in upstate New York before coming to Philadelphia in 1797, going to work at the *American Daily Advertiser* office, and becoming an active unionist for the rest of his life.[34]

Once the Sewall-Wands-McIlvaine bloc gained the support of Childs, they proposed a series of reforms that superceded the controversy over White. They increased fines for financial misconduct, reasserted the prohibition against working with untrained men, and instructed Childs to write to the Boston, Baltimore, and New York societies about the masters' job advertisements placed in those cities. The board decided to permit members "to attend a meeting of printers" called by nonmembers, reflecting a growing concern for the trade, and even wrote a new "List of Prices." Finally, their experience with Graves, the member-turned-master, inspired a motion that "none but journeymen Printers be members" of the society.[35]

An unexplained gap in the society's minutes from early 1804 into mid-1806 obscured the organization's retreat from such positions. The 1805 and 1806 prosecutions of strike leaders among the local shoemakers for criminal conspiracy may explain this, for other unions destroyed or mutilated their own records to evade court action.[36] Perhaps a similar threat entrenched the Childs leadership, which had firm control of the society by 1806.

Still, an opposition eager to regulate the trade confronted Childs. Its most vocal advocate on the board was Peter C. Konkle, who later turned up in the New York union and, still later, became a cofounder of the Columbia Typographical Society. When Childs reported a member's working below scale, Konkle moved for expulsion. For three meetings, he blocked the president's recommendation to admit a man who had served only a year's apprecticeship. He and Wands protested vigorously when Childs lost his bid for reelection in November 1806 but secured a revote through adept parliamentary maneuvers. Thereafter, Konkle blocked Childs's motion to relieve master printer John Alexander, whose membership remained in doubt. Childs responded by attending only one of the next five directory meetings, and that to forestall threats of censure at the general meeting of January 1807.[37]

Matters grew worse for Childs in February when the membership elected to the board Lewis C. P. Franks, the iconoclastic democrat who later chose as the motto of his own short-lived *Independent Balance*, "I claim a charter as large as the wind, to blow on whom I please." Charging that members had "tamely submitted" and "in some instances connived" to undermine regulations, Franks proposed a new report largely by himself and Konkle on condition in the craft and moved to exclude permanently those who procured jobs for nonmembers in preference to members, excepting "strangers in distress, or immigrants from Europe." Counptercharges followed by Childs and the newly elected director Joseph Gales, Jr., son of the prominent Sheffield printer active at Raleigh and Washington. When Childs vacated the chair to address the meeting—as was his frequent parliamentary practice—Konkle rose as well, "declaring them not in order," and when the president threatened Franks with expulsion, Konkle resumed his place to discuss the impeachment of Childs, who fined him twelve and a half cents for having left his seat. Later meetings stifled the report of the committee on conditions and refused to reconsider fining Konkle, who wryly moved that each member should "pull off his hat, when-ever he shall have occasion to ask information from the board or address the chair." In May the board finally heard Franks's report that the "great body of journeymen" suffered under "the gang of pettifogging master printers" who had monopolized the craft's reputed prosperity. He proposed concessions to "the few respectable masters" in return for a closed shop, the permanent expulsion of members working below scale, and a settlement of Alexander's status. Under Childs, the board voted down all but the last, reducing a broad spectrum of grievances and pro-posals to the question of an individual master's integrity.[38]

The Childs leadership weathered the Konkle-Franks opposi-tion of 1806–07 as it had the Sewall-Wands-McIlvaine group of 1803–04. By June 1807 Konkle had already begun to vote with Childs against Franks on some issues and even accused his former ally of working below scale himself. A week later, a supporter of Childs pressed new charges based on the testimony of a new member that Franks attended meetings "for the pur-pose of irritating the president" and hoped to "form a new society." After the board—with Konkle's vote—suspended Franks for a year due to his disloyalty, Konkle finally paid his twelve and one half cent fine. However, the board expelled the witness against Franks for getting another member fired that fall. In the summer of 1808, Franks rejoined the troubled society, which again placed him on the board, where he resumed his campaign for regulation that, he argued, might yet save the union. His new committee reported in December, but the min-utes record nothing of its content, debate, or vote beyond Franks's being fined twenty-five cents for disorderly conduct.[39]

The New York union never experienced such internal con-flicts, partly because of a concensus among its leaders on the necessity for trade regulation. It followed its initial conflict of 1809 with a survey of the local craft in 1810 that uncovered not only a large proportion of half-way journeymen but also boys who weekly earned as little as $4.50, $4, or even less. Sidney W. Andrews, its former vice-president, proposed various inno-vations to secure the society's hold. Leaders there refused to accept Daniel Fanshaw's effort to gain membership for James

Fanshaw, a minor. Nor did they hesitate in the fall of 1813 to defeat one master who refused to give the scale, discharged members, and advertised for journeymen elsewhere. In May 1815 the society voted to revise the wage scale, an effort that collapsed when employers argued that city pay had to retain a rough equilibrium with that elsewhere on the seaboard. Deeming job action inexpedient, the New York society nevertheless adopted a new rule concerning apprentices and established a new scale of nine dollars and ten dollars weekly for evening and morning newspaper work.[40] In short, what would be regularly debated and defeated in Philadelphia became the standard in New York.

The New York union of 1809 had had a crucial seven years more experience than had the Philadelphia society when it began. Although perhaps exaggerated by the more complete nature of the New York records, the difference may have been decisive. Of the participants in the 1802 dispute at Philadelphia, the only known veteran militant had been Francis Wrigley, probably a member of the defunct Asylum Company and its predecessor of 1796, and certainly a survivor of the old Franklin Society of 1788–93 and the strike of 1786.

The New York Typographical Society, in contrast, included a number of identifiably experienced men. Its secretary, Thomas Ringwood, had participated in both local efforts during the 1790s; when he later fell ill, the usually tight-fisted society acknowledged his organizing role as well as "his pecuniary circumstances and distress" by not only sending the standard three-dollar weekly allotment but extending relief and even raising more money in a general membership meeting. The society also aided Hance Gird, once proprietor of his own paper at Alexandria, a member of the old Franklin Typographical Society, and an active member of the new union until his death in 1812, whereupon Fanshaw coordinated an independent subscription for Gird's family that raised $92.82. Walter Heyer, another veteran of earlier local associations, lent his experience to the effort to reorganize the trade. Union leadership at New York also benefited from the participation of former officers of the Philadelphia society like Konkle, Thomas Kennedy, and William Neil.[41]

In the end, both societies sought incorporation by the state. This alternative secured their treasuries and conferred a certain respectability, but it was hardly an easy one. Postrevolutionary lawmakers had largely abandoned their old mercantilist traditions of government regulation, and the crafts, too, had outgrown self-regulation. Legislators' fears of such organizations' exercise of undue political or economic forces had long blocked the persistent efforts of New York City's General Society of Mechanics, but it succeeded in 1793, in gaining incorporation by the state. Thereafter, societies of mechanics, manufacturers, and tradesmen, as well as guild-like associations of masters within the crafts, reorganized and petitioned their legislators.[42]

The Philadelphia Typographical Society plunged toward incorporation, partly as a viable alternative to the militancy of Franks, for state law would prohibit involvement in trade regulation. A committee of directors spent the spring of 1809 exploring the possibilities and, whether deliberately or not, mistakenly reported that the legal ban on "keeping up prices may easily be obviated by inserting an article in the act reserving to the society the power of making bye laws." Although even Childs balked at first, he and Thomas Kennedy became warm advocates of making "alterations in the constitution as would enable the Society to get an incorporation." Ignoring the protests of Franks and others, the union began making revisions that took a full year. By midsummer 1810, the society reconstituted itself and elected new officers, including the most persistent officeholders prior to reorganization: Childs, Kennedy, John Scott, and John Cooper—all leaders through at least part of 1802–03. Two others elected in 1810—Horatio Boate and George Barnhill—had also held office during the old society's first year.[43]

Even as Philadelphia reorganized, incorporation first came up in New York. However, its adoption largely reflected the work of one man, Adoniram Chandler, who moved to petition the legislature in the fall of 1815 and won election to the society's presidency. Unlike Childs, Chandler was neither a founder nor

an early activist in the society, joining in 1810 after the initial
strike. Even as Chandler gained a certain influence in the New
York society, a man by the same uncommon name published
the *Maryland Republican* at Annapolis through 1811. Apparently
the astute, if opportunistic, organizer may have managed his
own business elsewhere while he reoriented the union of hired
printers. Indeed, in the late 1820s and early 1830s, Chandler spoke
in the name of the workingmen to denounce the infidelity of
Robert Dale Owen, the son of the British socialist Robert Owen
whose New Harmony community in Indiana had drawn
national attention. The younger Owen had subsequently moved
to New York where he became involved in an independent
political movement of Workingmen. Shortly thereafter, Chandler campaigned as a Whig in opposition to the local Workingmen's party; he subsequently became a leader of the long
conservatized General Society of Mechanics and Tradesmen.
Ambitious and far-sighted, he seemed to have easily dominated
the New York society, decimated by inaction and wartime
conditions. In 1816 the state assembly complied with its petition
and the society finally reorganized in the spring of 1818.[44]

Regardless of the different means and motives, the results
left the craft in a shambles. The 1810 Philadelphia strike that
so inspired printers across the seaboard represented not the
work of a revitalized society but that of the local journeymen
who persisted in holding sporadic protest meetings. Conditions
there degenerated until, in 1816, local pressmen complained that
they had been "less rewarded for their services than is awarded
in any of the other cities in the Union."[45] That very year, the
New York assembly incorporated the Typographical Society on
Manhattan, where the depressed economy after 1819 accelerated
the decline of the printer's organization.

Nevertheless, a genuine trade unionism had taken root in
the craft. The institutionalized regulatory practices reflected
the hopes of working craftsmen to gain redress of their grievances. As the most prosperous of contemporary American labor
unions have discovered, even the healthiest treasuries and most
organizationally stable institutions may be helpless in the
absence of a unionist sentiment deeply rooted in the work

force, for where the sentiment exists, solutions will follow. Even the complete absence of organization can—and will—be overcome.

IV

The articulate journeymen in the printing trades provide an important, if largely neglected, key to the more general process that shaped an early American labor history. They shared in a preindustrial tradition of fraternalism and even self-regulation which, in British North America, embraced the personal drive to rise in the world. These framed the self-perception of a distinctive class of hired men that emerged in the postrevolutionary craft. Their efforts to build unions heralded a new consciousness among that growing proportion of the craft that made a living as wage earners. Unionism, like all new ideas, represented largely a later application of older values amidst new realities, an innovative defense of an older craft fraternalism.

There were two immediate obstacles to their success. First, the nature of the trade kept journeymen on the move: This, in turn, permitted unionism to rapidly assume a national scope, while keeping it weak locally. Leadership in these circumstances tended to rest with the most residentially stable and relatively secure men. Secondly, the policies of such weakened societies reflected the tensions between their assimilation of an artisan republicanism and their unique ideological interpretation of those values. Understandably, they desperately sought refuge in the embrace of the government.

Unionism long outlived the societies that first expressed it. Workers continued to articulate certain key ideas irreconcilable with those of their employers and to build upon early printers' confrontation with the virtually exclusive power of their masters over the crucial decisions that affected them. From the beginning, however, their nascent labor ideology bequeathed a legacy that involved both a militant working-class activism and an acceptance of political and legal measures to regulate and ultimately reinterpret such militancy. In one form or another, millions of American working people came to share the reasoning of those long-forgotten craftsmen and its ambiguities.

DAVID BRUCE, *a leader of New York's Franklin Typographical Association during the late 1790s, later went into partnership with his brother George in an effort to establish and secure their own shop. Their business became one of the few successes achieved by former journeymen who sought economic security within their changing trade. Their success rested initially upon their introduction of new stereotyping techniques into the American trade and later upon their typefounding. From* New York Typographical Union No. 6 *by George Stevens, courtesy New York Department of Labor.*

GEORGE BRUCE, *another former officer of New York's Franklin Typographical Association, long outlived his brother and retained some pro-labor sympathies, running for office on the Workingmen's tickets of the early 1830s. Later, in the midst of economic hard times, he loaned type to the young Horace Greeley to help launch the New York* Tribune. *From* New York Typographical Union No. 6 *by George Stevens, courtesy New York Department of Labor.*

SAMUEL WOODWORTH, *the Yankee editor and poet, became a prominent leader and intellectual influence among organized printers at New York. The author of many poems on patriotism and printing, he attained much of his lasting popularity for "The Old Oaken Bucket," extolling the pastoral virtues of his New England childhood. From* New York Typographical Union No. 6 *by George Stevens, courtesy New York Department of Labor.*

November 26, 1848

PETER FORCE *was an officer of the New York Typographical Society from 1812 until he left the city. Later the editor of Washington's* National Journal, *the voice of the Adams administration, he received contracts for Federal printing, compiled his own edition of historical documents as* American Archives, *and served as mayor of Washington in 1836–40. Unlike other craftsmen, printers had a possible if not easy route to respectability through writing, editing, or the political power which accompanied these. Such cases, often cited as proof of a Franklin-like upward mobility among craftsmen, actually demonstrate the closing of opportunities within the trade itself and the necessity for ambitious printers to move to the fringes of the old craft and beyond. From* New York Typographical Union No. 6 *by George Stevens, courtesy New York Department of Labor.*

THURLOW WEED, *arguably the most famous member of the early printers' unions, had been an active and influential, if short-lived, member of the New York Typographical Society before moving to Albany. There, his management of the* Evening Journal *and government printing contracts, combined with astute business and political maneuvering, made him the master of a powerful statewide machine. He is shown here in later life, as a leading force behind the scenes of Whig and later Republican politics in the state. From* New York Typographical Union No. 6 *by George Stevens, courtesy New York Department of Labor.*

ELLIS LEWIS, *a small town youth in the New York Typographical Society, soon returned to Pennsylvania, where he studied law and gained admission to the bar. His position as Chief Justice of the state supreme court crowned a prominent career in politics and legal scholarship. From* New York Typographical Union No. 6 *by George Stevens, courtesy New York Department of Labor.*

THE "ALLEGORY" OF THE PHILADELPHIA TYPOGRAPHICAL
SOCIETY *later decorated its certificates of membership.
Liberty, wrapped in the American banner and accompanied
by an eagle, holds a scroll bearing the Society's motto while
revealing the press as a source of enlightenment to the
world; the four female figures represent Europe, Asia, Africa,
and America. Above the press—demonstrating both its light
and its power—the figure of Intelligence overthrows
Ignorance, depicted in chains. To the front, alongside the
books and periodicals, are the fragmented instruments of
war and destruction. In the distance, the Temple of Fame
sits atop an almost inaccessible hill. At its foot cowers a
king with his crown rolling in the dust and his former
subject, erect with fetters broken.*
    *The engraver, John Sartain, had been a student of William
Blake before emigrating to Philadelphia, where he embraced
the socialism of Charles Fourier. This work and its adoption
by the Typographical Society demonstrates their shared
assumptions and outlook, rooted in an older tradition of
artisan republicanism and a certain persistent plebeian faith
in the Enlightenment. From* The History of the Typographical
Union *by George A. Tracy, courtesy Communications
Workers of America.*

Three

More Humble Followers

*The Deferential Citizenship of
Union Printers*

I s it not reasonable to believe that a man
will feel a much warmer interest for his
country's welfare, when he has a knowledge
of the laws, and is made acquainted with the
policy that governs it? And does he not
imbibe a reverence and a love for that country
which entrusts him with these important
secrets? He has a natural right of inquiry to
the conduct and measures of men, with
whom, as a sanctuary, he has deposited his
liberty and life, for the enjoyment of both in a
state of refinement, and the benefit of social
society.
　　　　　　—George Asbridge, 1811

Journeymen printers regularly gathered to celebrate
American Independence on the Fourth of July, a day which, by
"a glorious coincidence" and "a happy omen," also saw the
founding of both the Franklin Typographical Association and
its successor, the New York Typographical Society. One member

of the latter organization praised the Founding Fathers and asked rhetorically, "Shall we forget their more humble followers, who shared in their toils; who assisted them in all their plans of wisdom and bravery?" Moved to verse, he proclaimed,

> Though high in honor, yet of humble birth,
> Their names may perish with them from the earth
> But Time's rude progress Memory shall defy—
> Their glorious deeds shall never—never die![1]

In his audience sat men like Samuel Woodworth, the son of a Continental soldier. Indeed, some participants in the initial efforts to unionize the craft had themselves stood among those humble followers in the movement for American independence.

Significantly, Asbridge's assertion of workers' "natural right of inquiry" did not entail an insistence that workingmen had a right to equal participation with their social betters in the political life of the country. Notwithstanding scholars' enthusiasms for artisan republicanism, these heirs to the regulatory legacy of the old crafts and to the mechanics' role in the revolution already had a history of civic deference. Periodic flashes of autonomous artisan activism should not obscure the overall conservative nature of the colonial revolt. For the most part, followers remained just that, and what Bernard Bailyn called "the contagion of liberty" flared only sporadically in those years. With some exceptions, notably in Pennsylvania, the elite leadership of the colonial resistance retained control not only over "their more humble followers" but also over the imaginations of those who, as unionists, commemorated the victory of that leadership.[2] Distinctively artisan values did not shape workers' civic sense and political self-perception in the early national period.

Among union printers, this civic deference had several sources beyond the regulatory legacy of the crafts. The fundamentally deferential nature of artisan participation in the colonial resistance and the American Revolution eased their acceptance of elitist institutions as the embodiment of an institutionalized and mystified republican tradition. As laborers in a craft central to the promotion of ideas, it is hardly surprising that their language and perspectives echoed those of men sanctioned to generate and promote ideas. Such considerations shaped the peculiar republicanism of the postrevolutionary United States that kept "followers" in their place. By 1815 that legacy of political deference had withstood important pressures.

I

At union banquets, journeymen orators praised liberty as institutionalized in American government and society. Insofar as the early unions published these addresses in their own names, the tracts provide a crude reflection of sentiments not atypical of those of the group as a whole. These speeches, by men who had a particularly strong exposure to the rhetoric of the political elite, articulated few ideas that did not faintly echo what they had spent their working lives hearing, reading, and printing.

The first trade unionists served their ideological apprenticeship as mechanics. Hired men had historically identified with a craft rather than a class or, more broadly, with handicraft workmen as a social group. In late eighteenth-century Anglo-America, Craftsmen and their dependents accounted for only about a tenth of the population in the more sparsely populated districts, but, along with their less skilled counterparts, they easily constituted the bulk of the town dwellers.[3] In the course of the colonial conflicts and revolutionary activity of the day, these artisans often acted as a coherent political and social force.

Recent scholarly interest in the mechanics has focused on Philadelphia, New York City, and Boston, where craftsmen lived and labored in numbers large and concentrated enough to cohere into what one historian termed a community.[4] Many common values, beliefs, experiences, and concerns united those city dwellers fortunate enough to have a trade. Clearly, too, their efforts to shape history grew from the economic, social, and political interests of the tradesman-proprietor: the self-sufficient, working shopkeeper eager for personal advancement and practical self-improvement that involved concerted action with, and mutual assistance among, one's peers.

The coherence of the artisans in the eighteenth-century American seaboard cities often defies modern approaches to historical analysis. Scholars have frequently and inappropriately turned to Marxist analytical tools honed for an appreciation of social contradictions and conflicts in a mechanized, industrialized world. Some, citing the manual nature of craftsmanship and surmising that most artisans must have been hired workmen, have imbued the early crafts with a proletarian character, while others emphasize the allegedly middle-class concerns of tradesmen and, while acknowledging that mechanics constituted the base of the early American cities, argue that "the bottom was a bourgeoisie."[5] So, too, the modernization model carried the assumptions of western social scientists about non-industrialized societies in the twentieth century to those societies that first became "modern"; it also implies the universal applicability of a reality constructed from the statistical techniques developed to describe the quantifiable data of contemporary mass societies. Both approaches might have a certain value as standards of comparison, but anachronistic models are less informative or accurate in defining social reality than the analytical tools forged by that society for understanding itself.

The social categories of the day provide us with concepts that seem blunted and unwieldy. Contemporaries used terms like "the middling classes," "mechanicks," "the industrious poor," or "the lower orders." Scholars have erroneously concluded from this that social classes did not exist, that class barriers remained permeable to the truly ambitious, and that the terminology existed simply to obscure social reality. In fact, the scientific precision demanded by modern scholars is neither possible, desirable, nor accurate when discussing the yet-unspecialized categories of work and class, particularly at the base of a rapidly changing society. Preindustrial reality is best read from the inside out.

Those contemporaries addressed artisans as a discrete social group. When Andrew Adgate, Philadelphia's popular religious writer, issued a tract aimed at craftsmen, his lengthy eighteenth-century title revealed much of its contents and appeal:

The Mechanics Lecture: Showing the Usefulness of Mechanic Arts; and who was the First Mechanic; and giving a Short history of Taylors, Masons, Carpenters, Ship Carpenters, Joiners, Cabinet-Makers, Blacksmiths, White Smiths, Bakers, Barbers, Weavers, Fullers, Hatters, Tanners, Shoemakers, Cobblers, Dyers, Carvers, Coach-Makers, Saddlers, Sail-Makers, and Printers. Reverently Dedicated to those respectable supporters of Liberty and Property, the Mechanics of Philadelphia, by their faithful Servant, and Fellow-Laborer, Absalom Aimswell, Esquire. By these we support our Families and Enrich our Country. To which is affixed, The Mechanics Song, composed and set to music by a Native of the United States[6]

In such a statement, the religious propagandist followed in the footsteps of political leaders who, by 1790, had dealt with the city mechanics as a distinct social group for a quarter of a century.

As a group, these mechanics first came into political awareness and activity under the tutelage and influence of the elite advocates of resistance in the colonial seaports. Pursuing a radical strategy of actually blocking the enforcement of imperial measures like the Stamp Act of 1765, the Sons of Liberty reached out to gain the active support and cooperation of the craftsmen who had played, at best, a very minor role in colonial political life. Several more well-off and influential artisans even sat in the inner circles of Boston's Loyal Nine, the secret steering body of the popular opposition to the Stamp Act. Printers like Benjamin Edes and his partner, Thomas Gill, the editors of the *Gazette*, played particularly important roles in these local circles of propagandists.

Boston politics reveal the often contradictory nature of artisan involvement. On the one hand, the most famous of the early artisan rebels, Paul Revere, the Boston silversmith on the patriots' intelligence committee, won a certain immortality for his famous ride of 1775. While the colonial gentry resisted accepting a craftsman of any sort into their midst, Revere was no mere manual laborer but a prominent manufacturer, owning a prospering business that employed other artisans and offered prospects of an even brighter and more prosperous future.[7]

On the other hand, such individuals alone could not organize the successful resistance to British law in the ports. The need for massive and carefully controlled mobilizations left the elite "Sons of Liberty" reliant on what was, to them, the least respectable and rowdiest of the urban commoners, whose political participation on any level had rarely been welcomed. In Boston, the Loyal Nine turned to the shoemaker Ebenezer Macintosh as their voice in the streets. Aside from one outstanding incident early in his career when he led the Boston "mob" on a general rampage against the symbols and property of the authorities, Macintosh proved to be a reliable, plebeian agent of the radical wing of the rebellious local elite. Despite the victory of a revolution for which both had worked, the two mechanics had very different destinies. While Revere ended his days as a wealthy and respected Boston manufacturer, Macintosh died forgotten in a Vermont poorhouse.[8]

After the 1766 repeal of the Stamp Act, the British authorities began imposing a series of duties on goods imported into the colonies, inspiring the radical leadership to resort to nonimportation. This new strategy had a particular appeal to the mechanics as domestic manufacturers of goods. They tended to accept and promote much more readily a boycott of British imports, while some colonial merchants with often close and vital links to the transoceanic network of trade, politics, and culture frequently remained unenthusiastic. As the campaign continued, some of the latter tended to drift from the ranks.

As a result, artisans played an increasingly prominent and independent role in the development of the resistance strategy mapped by their betters. Craftsmen clashed with the authorities in such incidents as New York's Battle of Golden Hill and the Boston Massacre. Also artisans combined to confront and to thwart efforts to break the unity of the colonial front in the strategically vital ports. Here and there, more or less distinct committees of mechanics began to appear under the general auspices of radical political leaders like Samuel Adams in Boston, Christopher Gadsden in Charleston, Isaac Sears and

Alexander MacDougall in New York City, and James Cannon, Timothy Matlack, Thomas Paine, and others in Philadelphia.

This legacy bore directly on the course of those later journeymen who formed unions. Some had close personal ties to the development of the mechanic wing of the colonial resistance. John Bushell, later a participant in the 1786 printers' strike at Philadelphia, served his apprenticeship with a Portsmouth, New Hampshire, master who had left Boston in 1756 after printing a tract politically offensive to the royal authorities; as his apprentice, Bushell would have participated in his master's efforts to organize and expand the Portsmouth Sons of Liberty in those crucial early years of the struggle against the crown.[9]

Others had family ties to those early pioneers of colonial resistance. Benjamin Edes, an officer of the Baltimore Typographical Society, was the grandson of the printer Benjamin Edes, ally of Revere and Samuel Adams, of Boston's Loyal Nine. Nathaniel Willis, father of the Boston unionist of the same name, actively promoted the goals of the local resistance and participated in the defiant "tea party" of December 1773. Similarly, Henry C. Southwick's father operated the *Newport Mercury*, the press of the Rhode Island opposition. The grandfather of Robert S. Aitken, the Philadelphia unionist, had given Thomas Paine his first job in the colonies.[10]

Such connections strengthened the attitudes of the later union printers to those early political battles. Thomas Ringwood of New York's Franklin Typographical Association explained to his audience that "the industrious of all classes" in the colonies had worked only "to enhance the riches of haughty Britain." Little wonder that, as resistance hardened into revolution, a "GLORIOUS enthusiasm nerved every arm; the old, the young, the right, the poor, alike flew to and rallied around the standard of freedom."[11]

The American Revolution itself was an inescapable personal fact in the lives of such men as sat in Ringwood's audience. A handful of the older men had even participated in this process. "Ardent in his devotion to the cause of liberty," William Price Young, a participant in the printers' strike of 1786, had "spent the flower of his youth in the service of his country" during

the Revolutionary War. His fellow striker, Samuel Lecount, shoul-
dered a musket in the Pennsylvania Line of the Continental
Army. Other participants in that early strike who had done
tours of duty with the local militia during the Revolution
included John Bushell, John Albright, Leonard Yundt, John
Switzer, and Francis Wrigley, who had also worked as a printer
of Continental money at Hall & Sellers.[12]

The Revolution also directly touched the lives of younger
men. Southwick, for example, had been inadvertently left
behind when his family fled the British occupation of Newport
in 1776. The authorities, anxious to close his father's radical
printing office, had raided their home, capturing the family's
nurse and the future union leader, then scarcely one year of
age.[13]

The ranks of early printers' unions also included numerous
sons of Revolutionary veterans. Samuel Woodworth, for example, was the proud son of "a soldier of the Revolution [who]
had consequently no legacy to leave his children, except the
testimonial of Washington, under his own signature, of having
faithfully discharged his duty." Other sons of Continental soldiers included David H. Reins, prominent in the organization
of the New York City union in 1809, and Judah Delano of the
Columbia Typographical Society at Washington.[14]

Significantly, though unionists cherished the memory of a
Revolutionary experience, they, like their artisan predecessors,
generally remained humble followers of the Founding Fathers
who moved the newly independent states toward a Federal
Union. During these years, urban mechanics, like their betters,
had a direct economic stake as well as patriotic motives in
supporting the formation of a central government strong enough
to bar cheaper British goods from the American markets. When
self-proclaimed Federalists within the country's political leadership proposed the replacement of the Articles of Confedera-
tion with a new constitution, artisan spokesmen vociferously
brushed aside objections and objectors in their own communities. In Philadelphia, for example, although a handful of old
radicals like George Bryan and David Rittenhouse, once popular
among local mechanics, opposed the new document in 1787,

they could muster only a few hundred votes as opposed to over 1,200 for a Federalist slate that even included such former antagonists of the craftsmen as James Wilson. Two years later, a New York City election resulted in a Federalist sweep of 2,342 to 373 votes. The Federalism of the majority of New York City craftsmen even overwhelmed their old revolutionary leader John Lamb, whose home was mobbed—by the same local artisans who had once followed him into the streets against stampmasters and imperial tax collecters—when he tried to organize local opponents of the Constitution. Such evidence led one historian to discern a virtual "absence of any division of opinion in the towns" over the issue. Not only residents of the larger ports— Boston, New York, and Philadelphia—but also the citizens of Portsmouth, Newport, Providence, Albany, Norfolk, Savannah, and Charleston had been almost unanimous. Of the cities, only recently urbanized Baltimore remained relatively well-divided, and there only three of ten voters opposed the Constitution.[15] This mechanic Federalism, along with their role in the Revolution, shaped the perception of an ideologically coherent social force that had its own unique blend of social self-interest and broader patriotic and republican considerations.

Given such a history, when hired craftsmen thought about ideas like natural law, they invariably turned to the short history of their new nation. "Does not our western world furnish sufficient subjects of this nature to excite our admiration," queried John W. Scott, the Philadelphia printer, speaking before a local mutual aid society. "Yes, America, highly favored land!" he exclaimed. "The bright star of liberty irradiates they hemisphere," and "the breezes of every clime" salute its flag. Peace, prosperity, and learning "filled her fragrance on thy inhabitants," "the useful and fine arts flourish in they congenial soil," and benevolence "dispenses joy to every heart." The well-deserved loyalty of its people "environs thy coast with amunition invulnerable by Tyranny," and a new age for humanity was to dawn in the young republic. The colonists, he explained, had fled the oppressions of the Old World, preferring to brave the dangers of nature in order to enjoy the blessings of liberty and the full fruits of their labors. In America, their labors had cultivated a wilderness, developed a viable commercial life, and expended the nation's potential for economic and social development.[16]

The perception of such achievements had not required artisans to depart from their role as humble followers, and the earliest unionists readily embraced the course of their betters as their own. Although craftsmen had played an important role in different phases of the Revolution's development, hired men like Asbridge did not speak of mechanics when he recalled the "zealous intercession of the glorious heroes of our revolution" through which "the high executive of heaven has granted us the charter of Liberty and Independence." Universally, of course, the hired men in printing remembered their craft brother, Franklin, but their addresses also recalled a host of other Revolutionary heroes, reserving the highest of their praise for George Washington, the personification of the American Revolutionary tradition.[17] Only one of the speakers whose published oration survives coupled to praise of the Founding Fathers an acknowledgement of "their more humble followers."

Journeymen's addresses published by their craft societies veritably glow with rhetorical flourishes about their country's "days of danger, the hours of trial." "The progress of time," argued Mack, "steals not a tittle from its importance." The spirit of that Revolution lingered still. "We do not take a pleasure-excursion to Harlem, not to admire the green fields of Long Island," he said, "but we behold the sacred spots where heroes' bones have mouldered—the verdant soil, once stained with patriots' gore! Even perhaps, the spot of earth over which we are now assembled, has been drenched with the blood of our fathers!"[18] Rightly or wrongly, early unionists placed themselves not only on the grounds of traditional craft fraternalism and self-regulation, but also on a battlefield of patriotic devotion.

II

While the rhetoric of republicanism clearly meant different things to different people, unionists left no sources to indicate that they viewed their values in the civic realm differently from that of their social betters. Early unionists as such did not articulate an idea of liberty that directly challenged the civic premises of the American state. As a group, they did not challenge the implicit national boundaries of liberty, the racial and ethnic exclusivity of society in the New World, nor even the very limited nature of their own access to political power.

Insofar as these men of the "lower orders" experienced nothing to contradict the standards of the society around them, they tended to assimilate the prevailing values. The Vermont-born Albany union leader George Churchill, who was a vocal critic of black slavery all his life, nevertheless echoed praises of the British colonial ventures on the Asian subcontinent as an effort by English-speaking Christians to rescue India from its "pagan darkness."[19]

Individually, some early journeymen, like Jacob Berriman of Philadelphia and William Hartshorne of New York, went far enough into the west to encounter American Indians within their own culture. The latter's manuscript account of his stay of 1793 among the Indians of what later became Michigan is noted for its portrayal of Indian life. More philosophical and theological considerations motivated one Philadelphia printer to ponder, "May we not anticipate such a dispersion or error, such an irradiation of truth, as that not only 'the lion shall lie down with the lamb, but that the Indian and the negro shall be equally free with the white?'"[20]

Other union printers had experience with the institution of black slavery. After moving to the Missouri Territory, Churchill boldly used the St. Louis press to denounce its admission into the Federal Union as another slave state. Later, although preferring his new life as a gentlemen-farmer in Madison County, Illinois, he campaigned in the 1820s for a seat in the legislature, where he helped to thwart an effort to reintroduce slavery into that state. His pioneering work in support of the antislavery press in Illinois also contributed to his reputation as a "thorough-paced abolitionist all his life."[21]

Such antislavery concerns were not unique among Churchill's peers. The poetry of Theophilis Eaton bitterly chided not only New Yorkers' complacency about slavery but also their smug sense of radical superiority. Daniel Lawrence and Leonard Yundt, two participants in the 1786 Philadelphia strike, later gained their own press, from which they issued a series of tracts denouncing the "peculiar institution." Upon retirement, the latter sold the press to John Hewes, the former president of the Baltimore Typographical Society and "an intimate of Yundt's" who continued to befriend antislavery and reform causes.[22]

Such ideas contrast sharply with the limited thinking of their age, race, culture, and class. Indicative of the more general attitudes of skilled white workingmen might have been the course of the crowd activities that greeted the War of 1812 in Baltimore. Led by several former members of the local shoe-makers' union, local mobs followed the course of all too many other nineteenth-century manifestations of the urban plebeian crowd in the United States when it redirected its violent and hysterical Anglophobia toward a more accessible scapegoat, the blacks.[23]

The ethnic diversity of the American craft did not add any cosmopolitan dimension to their language of liberty or modify its chauvinistic adulation of the government of the new republic. A steady stream of printers from Great Britain, including some ideologically committed republican activists, fed the growth of the printing trades in the United States without substantially modifying the narrow nationalism of its rhetoric. John Binns, a native of Dublin and a leader of the London Corresponding Society, had chaired a mass meeting estimated at about 150,000 and spent a year in prison before seeking a new life in the Pennsylvania trade. About the same time, Joseph Gales, Jr., the son of a prominent Sheffield printer, fled with his family when the authorities moved against his father's shop for selling Paine's *Rights of Man*. George Bruce, prior to his emigration, had been involved in "a radical political club in Edinburgh, called the 'Friends of the People.'"[24]

Veterans of Irish republicanism also worked in the American craft and its early labor organizations. The New York Typographical Society included some men like Daniel Fanshaw and Henry W. Clayton, later printers of the *Shamrock*, which both reflected and articulated the ethnic spirit of the growing numbers of Irish on the American seaboard. At least one veteran of the uprising of 1798 became a prominent American labor activist. In the years prior to the revolt, Timothy Byrne had been old enough to assist the underground work of his father, Patrick Byrne, who had become the first Roman Catholic admitted to the Dublin booksellers' guild after the repeal of its denominational ban. The elder Byrne clashed repeatedly with the authorities over his political publications, which included the writings of Wolfe Tone, and his shop served locally as "the literary rendevous of the United Irishmen," the center of the city's underground republican organization. Only its infiltration enabled officials to dissolve the Dublin movement on the eve of the rebellion. Upon its defeat, the family resettled in Philadelphia, where Patrick became an eminent bookseller, and Timothy went to work as a journeyman printer.[25] As such he not only joined the Philadelphia Typographical Society but also participated in the Flatbush association that merged into the New York Typographical Society in 1810, and, some years later, became a member of the Columbia Typographical Society at the capital.

Some journeymen also took a lively interest in the possibilities of the French Revolution. At least a few working printers sought out Citizen Genet, Gouveneur Morris, Thomas Paine, and others who had been there. By 1813 the Albany printers' union as an organization responded to Churchill's praise of the people of Paris for the storming of the Bastille by voting to publish it. Significantly, however, his purpose in discussing the course of the French Revolution centered on its relation to the American experiment. Citing a widespread literacy and a popular understanding of the issues involved, he portrayed not only the anger of the French people raging against their aristocratic oppressors but its destiny as "buried in the ruins" of the republic by a new imperial authority. Along with some unflattering comparisons between Napoleon and Washington, another journeyman proclaimed, "It is still tyranny—whether reigning in adverse darkness, or amidst delusive and guilty splendor. We would wish them—not a change of oppressors; but a thorough emancipation from every kind of oppression."[26]

Nor did a broad idea of liberty completely explain some of the curious ventures south of the border with which some of these men became involved. Such activities certainly blended the desire to promote liberty with the promise of travel and adventure, and perhaps, interests foreshadowing those of later filibusters so central to nineteenth-century U.S. expansionism. In late 1811 or early 1812, Samuel B. Johnson, William H. Burbridge, and Simon Garrison arrived in Santiago, Chile, to place the skills of New York City craftsmen at the service of the nation, which had broken with Spain in September 1810. Their *Aurora de Chile* was the first newspaper of the country. Although the authorities there expelled Burbridge and Garrison for "misconduct" in June, 1812, Johnson remained at the press in Santiago until 1814.[27]

Some years earlier, two Trenton journeymen joined the expedition of General Francisco de Miranda, the Venezuelan inspired by the American and French revolutions to plan the independence of South America from Spain. When the tiny group fell into the hands of the Spanish, both John H. Sherman and John M. Elliot witnessed the execution of their comrades and, later, escaped from imprisonment to return to New York City. In spite of these adventures (or, perhaps, partially because of the notoriety that resulted from them), Sherman won election to the presidency of the recently organized Typographical Society. Shortly thereafter, during 1810, Elliot reappeared in the city, went back to his trade, and, of course, joined the union.[28]

Indeed, the Latin world of monarchy and state religion remained alien to the secularist concerns of Anglo-American printers. On the Iberian peninsula, they told themselves, an unproductive and decadent elite sapped the labors of "the poor misguided peasantry" whose superstitiousness and illiteracy left them "passive slaves of despotic power and ecclesiastical duplicity."[29]

In summary, American journeymen found little elsewhere to foster an expansive and cosmopolitan view of republican liberty. "Although the old world has beheld the dawnings of many revolutions," declared Ebeneezer Mack, "tyranny still maintains its ascendancy." Elsewhere, Asbridge reminded his peers, the lack of liberty abroad created a general "apathy and indifference" in the citizen who remained "in total ignorance with respect to national concerns, and the strength of that political arm which should shield him from oppression."[30]

Anglo-American chauvinism found justification in some very material considerations that, the journeymen argued, made the United States a more secure homeland than the Old World. "O, Europe!" cried Mack, "Humanity weeps for thy crimes, thy follies and thy sufferings, but turns with disgust from the scenes of thy degradation." Historically, Ringwood noted, "many of the oppressed of Europe sought a sanctuary" in the United States in order "to enjoy the glorious privileges of conscience—of political and religious freedom." In 1801 union printers at New York offered a toast to "Peace—May the calamities of war which we witness at a distance with horror, teach us the value of this lovely fugitive, who flies to America for her last refuge." The United States, they felt, had "no privileged orders—no constitutional division line between the rich and the poor—no plebians [sic]—no patricians" by virtue of its republicanism. Breaking from the heritage of the Old World, the new nation had "not built upon their systems—and so long as she maintains her original purity of government can have no fear of their fate."[31] Although artisans almost immediately began to protest the loss of that original purity, their dissatisfaction did not lead to a general questioning of a mechanic patriotism echoing that of the American elite.

Formidable obstacles prevented journeymen from participating in the political life of the American republic they so highly praised. The Constitution of the United States and those of the various states had governmental structures shaped by the concerns of their writers, none of whom had been working craftsmen. The various American states also imposed property qualifications for voting and office holding that, while differing from state to state, more or less precluded the development of any coherent or distinctive political tendency among either the mechanics in general or the hired mechanics in particular. The elaborate system of checks and balances institutionalized at all levels in the new governments provided an essential safeguard both against possible electoral victories by political outsiders and against the effective use of the government by non-elite groups in the unlikely event of their electoral victory.

Beyond the constitutional and legal obstacles to the acquisition and exercise of power by the working citizens, a party system had already begun to emerge. So, too, interpretations of the partisan differences that divided Federalists and Democratic-Republicans as having any direct relevance for the non-slaveholding, propertyless, hired workingmen represent little more than the partisan preferences of the interpreters. Conflicts within the political elite of the new nation—which did not include craftsmen of any sort—shaped the emergence and organization of the early political parties.

Finally, the demands of the everyday working world restricted the possible civic lives of hired men. Even Weed, the future politician, had time to go only "occasionally to political meetings" and to visit the state legislature only "on two or three occasions toward the close of its session, more to see the prominent members of whom I had heard rather than to listen to the debates."[32]

These considerations make it remarkable that the early union printers left any record at all of their allegiances in the great partisan political battles of the 1790s. The decade that saw the breakdown of the apparent political unanimity among city artisans left some mechanics loyal to the old Federal promise of political stability and economic growth, while many of their social peers came to sympathize with the Jeffersonian critique of that Federalism. Local factors moved the craftsmen of different cities at a different pace. Baltimore craftsmen, for example, seem to have broken with Federalism more quickly than their peers in New York City, and the old order retained a longer hold on Philadelphia artisans and enjoyed an even more persistant and loyal following in Boston.

Clearly, though, a few unionists were among the most ardent Federalists. Richard Folwell, a striker in 1786, became one of the most notorious apologists for the party of Washington and Adams. John H. Williams, an officer of the New York Typographical Association in 1796, shortly thereafter gained his own newspaper, from which he excluded items that reflected unfavorably on the Federalist government, labeling the curious talk of journalistic objectivity to be irresponsible and comparable to the confused testimony of a witness at a trial unable to decide what he had seen. A leader of the Boston Franklin Society, William Burdick printed and probably wrote a parody of the rationalist, republican, and anticlerical works of Thomas Paine.[33]

Another future unionist had been so intensely pro-Federalist that it nearly led to bloodshed. William W. Wands maintained a couple of short-lived newspapers during 1794 and 1795 amid a rising tide of anti-administration sentiment in upstate New York. Among those printers who enjoyed "a high reputation in their day," according to a contemporary, he so rigorously defended the policies of the Washington and Adams administrations that a local Jeffersonian challenged him to a duel, publicly taking "the liberty of declaring Mr. W. W. Wands a Rascal and a Poltroon."[34] A duel was barely averted.

Other pioneering unionists also favored Federalism. Both Harris Sage and Samual Huestis, for example, retained their memberships in the Federalist Washington Benevolent Society as late as 1810. Typographical associations also included former and future printers of Federalist newspapers like Ira Jones, John Bernard, John W. Allen, Elliot Hopkins, Henry Gird, Ephraim Conrad, John W. Scott, and Henry Nichols. Still other unionists, like John H. Sherman and John Pasteur, shared the surnames of and were probably related to some prominent Federalist printers.[35]

Many unionists certainly followed the general shift in artisan political allegiances to the Democratic-Republicans at the turn of the century, a course reflected in Southwick's career. His first newspaper, established in 1794, clearly favored the Washington administration, insofar as it dealt with politics. His second, lasting only for a short while during 1797 and 1798, took decidedly Federalist positions, while a third, surviving from 1798 into 1800, remained independent but increasingly tended toward the Jeffersonians. By 1812 he owned and operated a militantly partisan Republican press.[36]

Republican printers from abroad accounted for several of the key Jeffersonian newspapers. Binns's association with the Jeffersonians dated from his refusal of an editorial post on the *Aurora* six years prior to his immigration; his political journalism in the United States nearly involved him, like Wands, in a duel, and his *Democratic Press* eventually gained national influence. Similarly, Gales, through his *National Intelligencer* at Washington, D.C., became an unofficial spokesman for several Republican administrations.[37]

Other Philadelphia printers took Jeffersonian positions as well. One early historian referred to Bartholomew Graves as "a famous Democrat," and, after leaving the Typographical Society, Graves operated the Lemon Tree tavern, known also as the Wigwam due to its connections with the local Tammany Society. Lewis C. P. Franks later established a paper which, like himself, remained "devoted to the support of the Democracy of the Old school." Another participant in the internal battles that plagued the Philadelphia Typographical Society during 1803–04, George White also printed a Jeffersonian paper. Further, a few other participants in early labor organizations also had a place in the ranks of the Democratic-Republican political clubs of the period, like the Tammany Society.[38]

Such findings provide no basis, however, for the claim often implicit in some scholarly writings that some affinity existed between early trade unionism and Jeffersonian Republicanism. Although the relatively egalitarian rhetoric of the Jeffersonian Republicans may have appealed to some unionists, its Southern and agricultural preoccupations did not, and, if Federalism's emphasis on economic regulation and protective tariffs had a certain appeal to mechanics, the reputedly overt and predominant elitism of its leadership had little attraction.

If the rhetoric of journeyman printers accepted a notion of liberty that neglected non-whites and slighted the importance of republicanism elsewhere in the world, it also locked the journeymen themselves into a passive citizenship. Heirs of the "more humble followers" of the Revolutionary years, the early union printers, in their civic lives, remained deferential to their elite contemporaries. Historically, the extent of their acquiescence would face ever more severe tests with the future development of the nation.

III

Some early workingmen clearly hoped that the new American republic would rapidly outgrow the hierarchical institutions and practices of the Old World. Elliot Hopkins, a leader of the Franklin Typographical Society, for example, issued a tract declaring *War Inconsistent with the Doctrine of and Example of Jesus Christ*, and Daniel Lawrence, an old striker of 1786, reissued it a few years after Hopkins' edition. George Churchill, along with his criticisms of duelling, condemned "the still more barbarous and impious wars in which the whole Christian world is engaged," and "the honors bestowed by a *religious* and *refined* people upon those who have displayed the most skill in the art of destruction." Although history had "justly and universally exploded" barbarous religions which "alone could justify" war, he sadly found his contemporary fellow Christians "proud to imitate the *conduct* of those, whose *principles* they hold in utter contempt." Men "whose lives are marked by bloodshed and devastation—whose only glory consists in enlarging the sum of human misery, have, in all ages, received from mankind those plaudits which are due along to their *real* benefactors." Even as they met, he told his Albany audience in 1813, men still followed "their ambitious and tyrannical rulers to the field of slaughter and bloodshed."[39]

Yet the potential of the American republic remained fragile and faced a seemingly hostile world. Asbridge wondered, "How long will your peaceful citizens be permitted to cultivate their soil in quiet, unmanured by the blood of brothers—uncontaminated by the sacrilegious tread of despotism? How long shall they be indulged in the unmolested prosecution of their useful labours, of perfecting the arts, of improving the sciences?" Reviewing examples from the past, he asked whether "a few presumptuous bigots" would one day "impiously dare assume the judgement seat, and arraign their fellow man, for differing in his speculative reasonings from their doctrines of these absurd theorists, and the creeds they have established—pronounced judgement on the culprit, and, snatching the rod of authority from the sovereign hand, arrogantly declare him the object of divine vengeance?" Burdick explicitly declared the threat to be "malignant and depredatory foreign birds of prey hovering over our glorious situation and prospects." Should American liberty face such threats, he predicted that "all parties would reciprocally unite in defense of our liberties."[40] In 1812 American trade unionists had their first experience in such a defense.

If early American laboring men made no unique and coherent contribution in terms of voting and civic activism, they did contribute to the survival of the nation and its "original purity," if through distinctively traditionalist and plebeian channels. Some of them had, at some point in their lives, served tours of duty in the regular military and naval forces of the United States. For example, Silas B. Hand, a native of Sussex County, New Jersey, probably held membership for a time in the New York Typographical Association before or after operating his own short-lived printing office there in 1796. After working his way to Philadelphia, he enlisted in the Marines for three years on August 3, 1798, and served subsequently with John Barry's Atlantic and West Indian squadrons during the naval war with France and Tripoli. Later, he joined in the Philadelphia movement for higher wages in February 1802 and, shortly after, returned to the Marine Corps.[41]

Militia musters provided many more unionists with personal civic lessons in martial glory. One English journeyman found such inspiration from "the awkward squads of the Pennsylvania militia, armed with muskets and rifles, clubs, sticks and cornstalks, while the banner of freedom waved over them" that he took his first oath of allegiance to the United States, and later became very active himself in the militia. Eager and patriotic American workingmen could, at times, enter into particularly elite militia outfits. Thomas Dean of the Boston Franklin Society and William W. Wands gained places, respectively, in the Ancient and Honorable Artillery Company of Massachusetts and the Philadelphia Light Horse, known as an elite and aristocratic unit from its colonial origins.[42]

Merging the journeyman's identity as a citizen, as a craftsman, and as a unionist, the societies often participated in the periodic work on the coastal defenses. As a group, printers' unions joined in the construction of fortifications to protect their cities during the troubled years of the Napoleonic Wars. Various associations of the different crafts, including the journeymen's societies, took the responsibility for organizing different phases of the project at their assigned times. Particularly in New York City, which had experienced enemy occupation during the Revolution, each trade took its day to "handle the mattock and shovel" in the various efforts between 1798 and 1812 to fortify the harbor.[43]

With the outbreak of war in June 1812, printers played a vital role in the propaganda to mobilize the nation's sentiments. Samuel Woodworth, David H. Reins, and George P. Morris of the New York Typographical Society published *The War*, which, like *The Massachusetts Manual* of William Burdick, reported on the events of the day. The former even wrote what became the second most famous song of the War of 1812. Inspired by the work of the trades on the fortifications of New York City, his "Patriotic Diggers" warned the enemy:

> *Better not invade; don't forget the spirit*
> *Which our dads displayed and their sons inherit.*
> *If you still advance, friendly caution slighting,*
> *You may get a chance a bellyfull of fighting!*
>
> *Plumbers, founders, dyers, tinmen, turners, shavers,*
> *Sweepers, clerks and criers, jewelers and engravers,*
> *Clothiers, drapers, players, cartmen, hatters, tailors,*
> *Gaugers, sealers, weighers, carpenters and sailors!*
>
> *Pick-axe, shovel, spade, crowbar, hoe, and barrow,*
> *Better not invade; Yankees have the marrow.*[44]

Although the United States had commenced the formal hostilities by declaring war on Great Britain, the fact was lost in the realization that a conflict with the great naval power meant that the fighting would take place in large part on this continent.

The appearance of British invaders on American shores eclipsed the issue of the justice or injustice of that declaration of war, transforming it into a "Second War for Independence." Thus, the New York Typographical Society listened with approval to Mack's description of the issues at stake in America's conflict "with the very power from whose claims she has been emancipated. Is this contest right—is it just on our part?" he asked rhetorically. "Is it not a contest to MAINTAIN those rights, that liberty, which our forefathers ACQUIRED?" Denying any desire "to pursue the inquiry," "prolong the subject," or "enter into an examination of its merits" before a politically neutral labor organization, Mack nevertheless made clear his own opinion, and the union membership, by publishing his speech, indicated that, in the main, it tended to share his views. Regardless of the causes of the war, he felt, the threat of British invasion sufficiently endangered the republic to drive every patriotic workingman to its defense.[45]

Invasion and the problems of national defense, however, had a dual edge early in American history. For example, John Lambert Hoppock of the Philadelphia Typographical Society was killed in action on April 27, 1813, during the capture by U.S. troops of York, the present city of Toronto.[46] Probably the first American trade unionist known to have died in one of his country's wars ominously did so not in an embattled defense of his homeland, but on foreign soil in the uniform of the invader.

Prominent leaders of the New York and Philadelphia typographical societies appear on the rosters of local military units. "Most of the printers volunteered" in New York, many serving in a company raised by David Reins, with George Bruce serving as paymaster. Even in Boston, the heart of New England opposition to Mr. Madison's War, most of the few known members of the local printers' union were in the militia. Moreover, these records of local service tell only part of the story, for some of those former and future members, like Weed, only arrived in the city after having served elsewhere.[47]

The most dramatic mobilization of early unionists in the course of war came in response to the invasion of Maryland.

When British regulars landed at North Point near Baltimore on September 12, 1814, many members and former members of that city's primitive labor movement hurried to join in the efforts to harry the enemy's advance, particularly with the third militia brigade. Moreover, official service records severely underestimate their contribution. William Pechin, a former officer of the local printers' society, simply closed his office and took its entire staff to join in the desperate battle. When Baltimore itself came under seige and Fort McHenry was bombarded, Judge Joseph Nicholson and his brother-in-law, Francis Scott Key, desperately hurried from shop to shop, anxious to put into print the latter's poem, "The Star-Spangled Banner." To their dismay, as they later explained, they found that every adult printer they sought, whether summoned into militia service or not, had gone to defend the city.[48]

Workingmen paid a heavy price for their role in the war. Early unions lost men like Hoppock in military ventures such as the invasion of Canada, and others fell to casualties more common for the warfare of that age; Walter A. Corry, an officer in Hoppock's union, had marched off with a company of the State Guard mobilized with the First Regiment of Pennsylvania Volunteers, but contracted a disease and died at nearby Wilmington on November 6, 1814.[49]

More generally, war required unionists, along with other citizens, to face continued sacrifices in their day-to-day lives. The outbreak of hostilities closed the young republic to foreign commerce even more completely than had the earlier embargo policies, forcing a reliance upon and the development of domestic manufactures, but it destroyed the prosperity of those crafts directly dependent on the transoceanic trade. Speculative sales and investments in the necessities of life made prices soar, and urban residents—including the working mechanics themselves—came to regard a new pair of shoes, a stick of furniture, carpentry work, books, newspapers, and other artisan goods and servides as unaffordable luxuries during the wartime economic crises.[50]

Such conditions impoverished the sentiment for unionism. Where journeymen's societies existed, they found themselves unable to regulate the conditions of employment in the increasingly unstable and transient wartime work force. Some early unions simply suspended such functions entirely or threw themselves into the war effort and the relief of the families of members that were away in the service.[51]

Self-interest had little to do with their participation in the war effort. Certainly, the conflict enabled a handful of former unionists who had become masters or foremen to legitimize their new personal status by serving as officers. Scarcely a decade after his arrival in this country from Britain, Colonel Binns plunged into the war effort, freely using his own money to build a unit of troops. "I presumed I could afford it," he wrote later, "which presumption, I subsequently ascertained was not so well founded as I had supposed." Other unionists and former unionists with commissions included Hoppock of Philadelphia, Reins and Daniel Dodge of New York, Joseph Gales at Washington, Thomas J. Leakin, James Holmes, and James Massey of Baltimore.[52]

The participation of journeymen in the War of 1812 had deep cultural and psychological roots as well. Men like Woodworth and Delano, whose fathers had fought the British in the Revolution, eagerly went to war in 1812. The opportunity for such service validated their claims to be their fathers' sons. For journeymen without such immediate ties to the nation's Revolutionary past, the war provided an opportunity to participate in that legacy of the armed American populace, aroused by invasion to a defense of its republican government, jealous of its rights, and even vigilant in defense of their liberty.[53] In short, it revealed that many journeymen had remained as much humble followers of the political leadership of 1812 as were their artisan predecessors to the rebels of 1776.

IV

Despite the massive political mobilization of urban craftsmen from 1765 through the Revolution, their efforts had, for the most part, remained within the general guidelines encouraged and approved by one or another competing faction of their "betters." Later craftsmen, including hired printers, placed themselves within a similar framework. Their oratorical praise of liberty lauded its embodiment in the social and political institutions of the new nation.

Yet, American civic culture inspires such loyalty, in part, through a flexibility that enables ordinary citizens to reshape, in their own minds, the institutions and figures that dominate that culture. Most Americans, for example, have come to view the Constitution as the cornerstone of democracy in the United States, although it had been formulated, promoted and accepted as a stable, institutional bulwark against democracy. Similarly, union orators paid homage to Franklin not only as an individual political leader but as "the poor's universal friend," a "truly philanthropic son of nature," and "a useful companion to all, who had the advantage of his acquaintance." Washington, too, in their eyes, became a friend of the working poor and "the needy ever found a cheerful welcome in his bounty."[54] Insofar as unionist tributes to a status quo established by their betters expressed a different perception of that status quo, it hinted at attitudes more complex than a traditionalist deference.

So, too, the rationalistic and mechanistic philosophy at the heart of enlightened republicanism soon proved itself to be quite flawed when applied to human society. People—even "humble followers"—constitute an unreliable and unpredictable fulcrum for change of any sort, because they themselves learn and evolve in the process of being so used. In the late eighteenth and early nineteenth century, some of those Americans who mobilized to attain the limited goals of national independence began to flush periodically with a fevered "contagion of liberty." Already, here and there, a Hartshorne might find the American Indian a fit subject for something other than removal, a Daniel Lawrence issue his antislavery tracts, or a George Churchill denounce the waging of war. Some of these actors began to translate the rhetoric of natural rights into realities unimagined by those who had first directed them onto the stage of history. The organization of hired printers, by hired printers, and for hired printers created a dynamic that promised an original, plebeian interpretation of the American liberty for which they had contended and were contending.

Four

Let None Be Deterred

*The Plebeian Crowd, Labor
Ideology, and Solidarity*

There is nothing more common than to
confound the terms of the American
Revolution with those of the late American
War. The American War is over, but this is far
from being the case with the American
Revolution. On the contrary, nothing but the
first act of the great drama is closed.
  —Dr. Benjamin Rush

In Revolutionary days mechanics, seeking a symbol of
their movement and societies, adopted the image of a workman's
arm with its hand grasping a hammer. Later it adorned the
pages of artisan newspapers like the *Independent Mechanic* and
the *Mechanic's Gazette* and was emblazoned on the streets of
New York at the close of the War of 1812 with the slogan: "Peace,
the Mechanic's Friend." By the late 1820s, the burgeoning labor
press adopted it as its own, using it extensively in papers like
the *Mechanic's Free Press* and *Workingman's Advocate*. By the
last quarter of the century, the arm-and-hammer insignia
became exclusively identified with the socialists.[1]

An ideology distinctive to labor evolved slowly from a long history in the United States. Like the image of the arm and hammer, an autonomous, non-deferential idea of liberty unique to hired workers began to emerge in the early national period upon precedents that included the sporadic "crowd" outbursts of the Revolutionary years. Unionists intellectually justified their efforts in the language they had learned as followers, redefining terms like "social contract" and "natural rights" to articulate a fundamentally new and unique interpretation of human freedom as the foundation of labor ideology. That hired men in various crafts shared this experience is evident in their common fraternal efforts to unite workers regardless of craft distinctions.

I

The victory of the rebellious colonial elite required the broadest possible popular support, particularly in the port cities. The mobilization and management needed to pursue strategies of resistance, nonimportation, and revolution required mass education in a Whig ideology further bolstered by the political debate over the contours of the new governments. Despite the general political hegemony of the Revolutionary leadership, some discontented farmers and artisans did act on their own from time to time to bend the course of events to their own purposes. These efforts ranged from small sporadic outbursts of the crowd to regulate flour prices in the cities to massive, if localized, rebellions like that which swept western Massachusetts in 1786 and 1787. The episodic autonomy of these urban mass activities expressed particular relevant artisan concerns.

There, colonial politicians had rarely called for action by the petty shopkeepers, craftsmen, laborers, and waterfront workers of the city, deeming it better by far to leave them to the apathy, passivity, and deference that characterized traditional plebeian behavior. Resistance to British policy in the summer of 1765 required popular mobilizations that violated this gentlemen's agreement, inspiring great forebodings, particularly among the more articulate and imaginative Loyalists. They predicted dire consequences, should propertyless and near-propertyless colonists begin to reshape public policy. When the royal governor of Massachusetts surveyed Boston while it was in the hands of the Stamp Act rioters, he warned: "Terrible will be the Anarchy and Confusion which will ensue; Necessity will soon oblige and justify an Insurrection of the Poor against the Rich, those that want the neccessaries of Life against those that have them." Another later wrote that, with the turmoil of the Revolution, "the laboring classes, instead of regarding the rich as their guardians, patrons, and benefactors, now look upon them as so many overgrown colosuses, who it is no demerit to wrong."[2]

Rebel leaders in Boston and Newport quickly learned that, once aroused, the mob could express opinions of its own. In the initial battles of August 1765, the chosen agent in the streets, Ebenezer Macintosh, led thousands of his peers on a rampage that cleared the city of the British authorities and utterly demolished several buildings belonging to detested figures in the local gentry. When fearful Sons of Liberty faced a similar outburst at Newport, they collaborated with the royal authorities to arrest their street leader, an obscure seaman named John Webber, and they soon found themselves and their homes, as well as thoses of stampmasters and crown agents, threatened by the mob.

Frustration and desperation alone cannot explain the sporadic outbursts of political autonomy by traditionally passive craftsmen, laborers, and seamen. A pattern of grievances and protest emerged most clearly in the peculiar course of the Revolution in Philadelphia, where the crowd appeared regularly to influence political life for several years. There the presence of British troops and the hegemony of radical nonimportation had kept artisans for the most part politically loyal to the limited perspective of the older resistance leadership, but the resort to arms in 1775 and the political battle for independence brought to the fore a secondary radical leadership composed of Thomas Paine, Dr. Thomas Young, and other virtually unknown men. They won the local artisan-based militia to their side and, in effect, toppled the existing government of Pennsylvania. Their Committee of Privates took the initial steps toward establishing a new government that rejected the standard Anglo-American practice of balanced government with its institutionalized checks and balances on popular will. Their government based on a single assembly elected by an expanded suffrage provided a more straighforward republican model advocated by the more democratically minded revolutionists elsewhere.[4]

In the process, what one scholar called "the mob element" among the radicals continued to influence the local course of the Revolution. As flour shortages inspired one writer to a local newspaper to warn of popular insurrection against forestallers, ordinary citizens of Philadelphia began petitioning their new Revolutionary government, which responded in the fall of 1778 by appointing a commission of inquiry. The events of the following year clearly show the dynamics of this process. In January 1779, about 150 seamen demanding higher wages to keep up with spiraling prices began unrigging outbound ships; the local authorities, backed by the military force of General Benedict Arnold, arrested at least thirty of the strike leaders. That spring, when a local merchant took a large quantity of scarce flour from the city to sell it for a higher, unregulated price in Maryland, the artillery unit of the city's militia issued a formal protest against speculation, and the radicals summoned a public meeting on May 25, described by critics as "a Mob . . . assembled to regulate prices." On October 4 the militia seized prisoners and surrounded the home of James Wilson, a long-time critic of "the Mobility" in politics, and a heated exchange of words erupted into shooting that ended only with the arrival of the president of Pennsylvania at the head of other troops.[5]

Although events after the Fort Wilson affair clearly discouraged agitation of the internal divisions within the Revolution, the subsequent experience of Samuel Lecount reveals the ongoing implications of such popular autonomy for the mechanic citizen-soldier. The son of a London fan-stick maker, he had grown up in the St. Martins Le Grande neighborhood of the city, been apprenticed to a printer in 1765, and indentured himself to reach Philadelphia in 1775. The outbreak of armed hostilities opened possibilities for him as well as for his betters. Although printers as a rule had a skill more needed on the home front, the paper shortage severely curtailed employment in the trade, and military service would have dissolved the obligations of his bondsmanship. Lecount had probably drilled as one of the Associators, the mechanic-based city militia which played a prominent role in both the emergence of a new radical leadership and the agitation against profiteers. Enlisting as a private in Company E of the Second Regiment, he served in a unit of the Pennsylvania Line that fought at Princeton, Bound Brook, Amboy, Brandywine, Paoli Tavern, Germantown, Whitemarsh, Monmouth, Paramus, and Connecticut Farms, and wintered at Valley Forge in 1777–78, Middlebrook in 1778–79, and Morristown in 1776–77, 1779–80, and 1780–81. Not surprisingly, perhaps, these soldiers often showed a capacity to act on their own. For example, in the fighting of July 21, 1780, at Bergen Heights, New Jersey, they became frustrated with the failure of light artillery to reduce a British position and staged what Washington called an "act of intemperate valor" by organizing a heroic but unsuccessful assault of their own, directly ignoring the orders of their officers.[6]

Lecount's unit also participated in the most famous such incident of the war in winter quarters at Morristown. On the night of January 1, 1781, after some obviously prearranged disturbances and diversions, small groups of soldiers, repeating rumors of an imminent enemy attack, assembled with arms and knapsacks on the parade. Unable to dissuade or intimidate them, the officers quietly withdrew, after suffering several casualties and confronting a Board of Sergeants that had taken control of the encampment and, professing their continued loyalty to the Revolution, declared its intention to seek a redress of their grievances. After gathering equipment and provisions, the Line then marched on Philadelphia to take up the matter with the Continental Congress. Nervous Pennsylvania officials convinced the Board to stop the Line at Princeton, where on January 5 the soldiers presented their case, demanding a general amnesty, adequate provisioning, the settlement of back pay (often as much as six months in arrears), and the discharge of all who had served their three years with the option of reenlisting and collecting bounties. Reluctantly, the government ceded victory to what one historian correctly termed "a well-managed strike."[7]

Many discharged veterans of this successful "mutiny," including Lecount, felt their grievances settled by the spring of 1781 and returned to join two provisional battalions assembling at York. A lingering resentment, coupled with the government's failure to meet its January promises, revived discontent. For further acts of mutiny that spring, the officers punished at least six enlisted men (three of them tried and shot, and a fourth apparently executed without a trial). After marching south, where they fought at Green Springs and Yorktown, the soldiers of the reconstituted Line spent 1782 campaigning in the Carolinas, where some carried placards asking: "Can soldiers do their duty if clad in rags and fed on rice?" Officers reacted by killing another sergeant. In June 1783, Pennsylvania officials themselves sparked final rebellion by trying to disperse the soldiers without paying months' back wages or properly provisioning them for their trips home. Lecount, in returning to Philadelphia, probably participated in the march of three or four hundred of the enraged veterans who threatened the newly formed Bank of North America and forced the Continental Congress and other officials to barricade themselves inside their "public" buildings.[8]

Lecount's career spanned the poorly documented crowd outbursts of the Revolutionary period and the early days of trade unionism among hired artisans. Aside from brief service during 1785 in the city militia, he never went back to the military. Rather, he returned to the printing trades.[9] As a Continental soldier, he had apparently participated in three collective refusals by enlisted men to follow direct orders and two instances in which the threat of their doing so had been serious enough to compel officers to execute their own men. Such experiences informed Lecount's participation in a new kind of mutiny as a hired printer involved in the Philadelphia strike of 1786.

Strikers like Lecount and their successors shared much of the mistrust of unregulated economic activity that characterized the sentiments of Revolutionary crowds in and out of uniform. Mechanic citizens in eighteenth-century America generally supported a good deal of municipal and state efforts to set legal levels for prices and wages. The mercantilist legacy of an ordered economic life faded slowly in the postrevolutionary American city. Although tradesmen in the municipally licensed and regulated crafts—such as butchers, bakers, cartmen, or river pilots—had reason to feel otherwise, most felt that neither wages nor prices sought a natural level, and the failure of the authorities to regulate such matters seemed to leave the question in the hands of those with a disproportionate amount of economic power.[10]

Although some scholars stress a broad middle-class "consensus" among Americans of the late eighteenth century concerning the ideas of republican liberty, the course of the movement for colonial independence reveals a spectrum of opinions on the meaning of liberty and its relationship to economic life. On one extreme, a merchant in Revolutionary Philadelphia condemned regulation as "inconsistent with the principles of Liberty" because it interfered with a man's right to the "disposal of his property on such terms and for such considerations as he may think fit." Another protested that "no law can be framed to limit a man in the purchase of disposal of property, but what we might infringe those principles of liberty for which we are gloriously fighting." Even the Council of Censors in Pennsylvania finally declared regulatory action to be an unconstitutional "invasion of the rights of property." "Like him who owned the goose that laid golden eggs," warned another critic, "you will cut off the source of all further supplies, and like him too, when you repent, you will repent in vain."[11]

On the other hand, some of the more plebeian rebels clearly thought a definition of liberty as the unrestrained ability to invest wealth to be of dubious value for those who had none. Working citizens might well think that the concept of liberty as an unfettered right to make a profit invited all sorts of nonproductive ways to make money, like speculative investments; thinking of themselves and their own labors rather than the entrepreneur as "the goose that lays golden eggs," they saw the emerging market, defined exclusively in terms of profit potential rather than productivity, to be a threat to their own meager resources, as a resulting polarization of wealth expropriating the property of small scale owners. Finally, concentration of economic power also implied the concentration of political power. Thus, the Committee of Privates, based upon the artisans of Philadelphia, had sought without success to include in Pennsylvania's Revolutionary Bill of Rights, an article stating: "An enormous proportion of property vested in a few individuals is dangerous to the rights, and destructive of the common happiness of mankind; and therefore, every free state hath a right to discourage possession of such property."[12]

While white Americans may well have universally extolled the value of liberty and the importance of the right to property within it, a divergence of meaning overshadowed the importance of their consensus in terminology. Significantly, different positions within society carried the seeds of different and often conflicting ideas of ownership and human liberty. The larger merchant-investor ultimately tended to argue for an idea of ownership based on legal acquisition and aimed at maximizing the return on investments. In contrast, the poorer manual craftsman's idea of ownership generally grew from a relationship to his tools, his work, and his peers.

The late eighteenth-century debate over the nature of liberty with regard to property, ownership, and popular regulatory activities provided the seedbed for a rudimentary labor ideology. Usages of a previous generation of craft militants informed the attitudes of many like Lecount about human nature, the social contract, and liberty. The organization they built in many ways represented to their opponents an institutionalization of the Revolutionary artisans' "mob . . . assembled to regulate prices."

II

As union printers pursued their regulatory course, they justified their efforts with the rhetoric of Anglo-American republicanism with which their craft had given them a unique familiarity. Thus, the language of an embryonic labor movement reflected an understanding of human nature that implied the need for a social contract or government within which certain natural rights would remain inalienable. This rhetorical justification for their self-organization not only posed every different definition of liberty but also established the general terminological framework within which the labor movement grew through subsequent years.

Some early unionist rhetoric on the subject of human nature clearly echoed the prevailing Anglo-American religious and philosophical expressions of the age. "The great volume of creation is open before you—look ot the instructive page of nature," John Welwood Scott told his audience. "How the earth smiled with animated beauty when this new tenant surveyed its luxuriant productions," he said of human innocence in Eden. "How delightful is the contemplation of this primeval scene! but alas!" Adam ate of the forbidden fruit, and human virtue "spread her spotless wings and soared to heaven, leaving the earth subject to the control of misery." Churchill also began his address with the premise of a "fallen and guilty" human nature."[13]

What journeymen read on that "instructive page of nature" depended in great part on the deciphering of their religious faiths, and there existed a wide spectrum of doctrines among them. Although Methodism may have played a very decisive role in the development of a labor consciousness in Britain or in particular localities like Baltimore, no one denomination shaped the thinking of urban American craftsmen.

Available information on the religious affiliations of early unionists is scarce but intimates that they reflected the religious life of the wider community, dominated by various currents within Protestantism. Union membership included Episcopalians, Congregationalists, and—in Pennsylvania—Quakers and Presbyterians like Scott or James Winnard. Some unionists did join one or another of the newer and more evangelical faiths as did Wands, who distributed tracts proclaiming the imminence of Christ's "Second Coming," and Nathaniel Willis, whose neighbor brought him to a revival meeting.[14] Josiah Ball became a Methodist circuit rider and, as we have seen, Southwick later promoted the evangelicalism of the early nineteenth-century Awakening in upstate New York.

Some unionists practiced less common faiths. Timothy

Byrne, John Binns, Michael Duffy, and some other Irish printers were Roman Catholics. George and David Bruce were active freethinkers. Samuel Woodworth, the New York union's chief poet, became a founder of the Church of the New Jerusalem, whose members were disciples of Emanuel Swedenborg, the Scandanavian mystic. A circle of Philadelphia printers practiced an even more arcane, Germanic variety of occultism.[15]

It is highly significant that adherents of such a wide variety of faiths embarked together on their secular, unionist course. If some spoke of a sinful and degraded human nature, they could nevertheless imbue the entire discussion with their own distinctive meanings. One could, for example, accept and echo the standard doctrines of innate wickedness while mediating its practical implications for the human potential. "Though perfection is not attainable in this world," explained Churchill to his fellow unionists, "yet the condition of man is susceptible of almost infinite improvement" despite its "vices and follies." "Posterity will probably view the present age in the same light in which we behold the nations of antiquity," he suggested. "The period, I trust, is rapidly approaching, when the recital of many events which are now taking place, will excite the surprize and indignation of the world." Even a devout Protestant and an ardent Federalist like John W. Scott could argue that humanity, "however degraded by crime, has still a claim to mercy."[16]

Workingmen could also introduce the concept more even-handedly, pointing out the degraded nature of their "betters" as well as themselves. Understood in such a way, the rhetoric of a sinful human nature combined with a recognition that the depravity that really threatened society as a whole was less that of the powerless commoners than of the powerful, wealthy, and well-born.

So, too, references to human depravity by unionists might be coupled to a newer evangelical willingness to see the spark of the divine in all. Religious faith, in part, inspired early unionists to admire American Indians, work against slavery, and advocate an end to the political institution of warfare. The zeal for social justice accompanied the spiritual and theological leveling. The road to a Christian perfectionism was clear, even though the Second Great Awakening of the early nineteenth century had yet to reach the peak of its influence.[17]

Other modifications of orthodox pronouncements on the subject of human nature, its depravity, and acquisitive greed also emerged during these years. Some unionists, including not a few churchgoers in the secularizing society, probably regarded the whole question as an abstract matter of little or no consequence in the day-to-day world of the marketplace.

Finally, some influential early labor leaders espoused a rationalism that carried pragmatic secularism to its logical argument that demonstrable human depravity grew not from innate characteristics rooted in our being but from a culturally determined conditioning capable of change. John I. Johnson—probably the individual later active in the New York Typographical Society—argued against an "unchangeable sameness, invariable conformity" in the human condition. Johnson defined man as "the creature of impression, of accident and of *circumstance,*" touched by "everything around him," with "the moral atmosphere he breathes shaping his mind." Nowhere "in the midst of departed centuries," in "the gloomy and sullen records of the dead," he argued, had "the malignant influence of unfortunate institutions" not "disguised and degraded" humanity. Although it is "customary with the rulers of mankind to attribute the evils of society to some inherent defect in the human constitution," men like Johnson—or the Bruce brothers or Philadelphia's union cabinetmaker Charles Christian—claimed that man "comes pure from the hand of nature," and "his vices, his disposition, and his propensities, flow from the nature of the government he is under."[18]

Regardless of their religious beliefs, or their pronouncements on human nature, practitioners of "the art preservative" of science and learning were generally disinclined to primitivist idealizations of the noble savage. In discussing humanity's "native state of ignorance," in which people worshiped "the Supreme Being through the medium of image," Burdick permitted "a kind of pity" to enter his discourse; he prized "the majesty of superior knowledge, refinement, and virtue" of the eighteenth century. "Happily for mankind," Scott explained, "the ties of consanguinity, mutual wants, and the sympathies of congenial souls, in the earliest stages of the world gave rise to patriarchal, feudal, and social institutions" after the Fall of Adam.[19]

Asbridge also referred those interested in the evolution of humanity—from "the rude uncultivated creation" at Eden, over "the ages of barbarity," to civilized society—to the work of "far more abler pens." He frankly acknowledged that his discussion of the matter would "lose or mislead both myself and you" in "my blind and erring way through this gloomy chaos" and "do it gross injustice in the attempt." He nevertheless assured his audience that civilization softened "the disposition of man," a creature already "formed for society."[20]

Printers had a particularly good opportunity to see the work of those "far abler pens" who had established the framework of Anglo-American ideas of the social contract. Thomas Hobbes had explained how individuals' instincts for self-preservation had early at the dawn of civilization declared to each other in effect, *"I authorize and give up my right of governing myself, to this man, or this assembly of men, on this condition, that thou give up thy right to him, and authorize all his actions in like manner,"* thereby becoming "united in one person. . . . a COMMONWEALTH, in Latin CIVITAS." John Locke had added that such an arrangement required *"a sufficient Declaration of a Mans Consent"* in order to make him "a perfect Member" of the body politic. In their Declaration of Independence, the American rebels, of course, had claimed the right of withdrawing that consent, dissolving the social contract, and freely reconstituting a new social order among themselves. The journeyman Asbridge summarized such ideas when he told his peers that "we have willingly deposited a small proportion" of our "heaven-gifted" liberties "for the salutary purpose of checking the depredations of wild extravagance and vicious inclinations" among men in a state of nature.[21]

That journeymen echoed ideas of the social contract settled little about its parameters. What were these heaven-gifted liberties? How small was the portion ceded to society? Most importantly, perhaps, at what point would a new arrangement be justified?

Unionist practice as well as rhetoric indicate that hired men approached such problems with two important assumptions. First, they began with the egalitarian premise that they should be treated as their employers' equals, repeatedly expressing their desire to act "as men towards men" or as, commonly, "men professing an ingenious art." Like the New York City masons, they chose organization and action rather than "hereafter be considered a poor spiritless set of beings." As a whole, early unionists would have agreed with the cordwainers of that city in their determination to be regarded as brother craftsmen by their employers, rather than as "humble instruments that fill their cellars."[22]

Secondly, journeymen made none of the facile distinctions made by "abler pens" between political liberty and economic security. Their condemnation of conditions in the Old World, however inaccurate or chauvinistic, reveals an economic criterion by which early American workingmen measured American liberty. Ringwood urged his listeners to look "to Europe—the happiest spot of devoted Europe!" There, he argued, a "hell-born DESPOTISM reigns in iron sway. Ambition, with giant tred, stalks o'er the fields, spreading desolation around, and drenching the earth with blood." Such enthusiastic warfare, argued Clough, constituted an essential aspect of the European plight that could "no longer afford the bread of comfort to her once industrious manufacturers," while, in contrast, as Brudick explained, "commerce stores our tables with the harvests and products of every clime." Ringwood spoke "whilst the plains of poor afflicted Europe have been drenched with human gore; while the devastation hath been spreading itself even to the fruitful shores of the Nile; and while, in Ireland, numbers have experienced all the horrors of famine."[23]

Conversely, these same speakers sought to show the presence of that "guardian goddess of Columbia" in terms of economic prosperity and opportunity. Liberty, according to one printer, appeared among the American colonists "when poverty and want darkened around them" to dispel "the fiend Despair" to grant them the justice of their sitting "beneath their own vines and their own fig trees, with none to make them afraid." Freedom made its home in the "harmony and plenty within our peaceful inhabitations" of the New World "where nought but the exertions of honest industry is necessary, to insure the *comforts*, ay, some of the *luxuries* of life" to the laborer.[24] Hired mechanics linked liberty to the banishment of "poverty and want," the assurance of "harmony and plenty," and the remittance of a fair return to "the exertions of honest industry" on their part.

With the achievement of American independence, optimistic craftsmen may well have anticipated greater personal freedom, mobility, and security in the rapid expansion and prosperity of those old trades. They had not bargained for the complete structural transformation of their craft as an integral feature of that growth. As a result, they found a declining freedom of action and fewer opportunities.

The journeymen of the early national period experienced a process whereby their employers, a decreasing proportion of the craft, expropriated to themselves exclusively the privilege of establishing standards for the quality of work, the hours and conditions of labor, and the level of wages. Wage-earning printers shared the growing resentment of hired craftsmen in other trades against the masters, "as they are called after the slavish style of Europe." The employers sought to "be tyrants if they could" by claiming the "right to limit us at all times, and whatever may be the misfortunes of society, the change in the value of necessaries, the encrease or decrease of trade," or other considerations. Workers protested when the masters not only asserted that they had "a right to determine for us the value of our labor; but that we have no right to determine for ourselves, what we will or will not take in exchange for our labor." The intolerable avarice of their employers would "introduce into this free country that system of opression and disorganization which European mechanics labour under," charged the Philadelphia shoemakers. Such "ungenerous conduct justly merits our contempt," complained the New York carpenters. The development of prices and wages based simply on the will of "evil disposed and selfish" employers pushed hired craftsmen to ponder again the meaning of American liberty.[25]

The relations of work, like social relations in general, grew from the consent of the governed, and the craftsmen in a trade, like the citizens in society, always retained what Asbridge termed "a natural right of inquiry into the conduct and measures of men, with whom, as a sanctuary" they had rested their heaven-gifted rights. In doing so, the New York cabinet- and chairmakers in particular found "something overbearing" in their employers' exercise of power over such matters "without deigning to consult us." Carpenters there found the "haughtiness and overbearance" of their masters more suited to those who "give laws to slaves . . . depriving free men of their just rights."[26]

A unionist practice carried journeymen beyond the framework of the institutionalized interpretations of nature, the social contract, and liberty. By conjuring "a sense of their original rights and privileges as men," their efforts at self-organization could be logically woven into a "fabric in imitation of the superstructure of nature, as erected by the Great Architect of worlds!" Hired craftsmen, too, independently "assembled together in a peaceable manner for our common good," in order "to promote the happiness of the individuals of which our little community is composed. . . . "[27]

The language journeymen used to justify their activities implied a republicanism of the workplace. Indeed, an 1809 statement by New York City's striking carpenters, modeled on the American Declaration of Independence, offered an excellent argument that human liberty also existed in the "social compact" governing their working lives. "Among the inalienable rights of man," they explained, "are life, liberty, and the pursuit of happiness. By the social compact every class of society ought to be entitled to benefit in proportion to its usefulness, and the time and experience necessary to its qualification." Individuals had social duties, such as that of "single man to marry and married men to educate their children." "Among the duties which society owe to individuals," they insisted, "is to grant them compensation for service sufficient not only for the current expences of livelihood, but to the formation of a fund for the support of that time of life when nature requires a cessation from labor."[28] Such a definition of duties and individual rights differed greatly from that shaped by "abler pens" in both America and Britain.

In their effort to secure these rights, early unionists formulated several measures that became important to the later labor movement. One of the key points of the agreement won by journeymen in 1796 and published in *The Cabinet-Makers' Philadelphia and London Book of Prices* specified that "whenever the necessaries of life, house-rent, &c shall rise above that what they are at present, the Employers agree to advance the per centum to what shall be agreed on: And in like manner, the Workmen do agree to reduce the prices in the same proportion as the said necessaries lower" over time.[29] Probably the most logical solution to rising prices predated by almost a century and a half the efforts of the Congress of Industrial Organizations to secure what would later be called the escalator clause or a cost of living agreement (COLA).

Other early efforts focused on reducing the hours of labor. Workers in the building and waterfront trades seemed to have pioneered efforts to limit the workday to ten hours in the early 1790s and had victories by 1805, but printers, too, raised the issue. In battling for a minimum weekly wage, the typographical societies sought also to define the work week. The early national period saw the first battles over the length of the workday.[30]

In pursuit of such rights, early journeymen recognized the traditional social compact of labor as dissolved. They then gave their own organizations names like the *United* Journeymen Tailors Society, the *Federal* Society of Journeymen Cabinet and Chair-Makers, or the *Union* Society of Journeymen Cordwainers; printers, too, appealed directly to the legacy of recent American developments by naming several of their organizations after Franklin. The decision to organize a trade union of hired men required the beginnings of an ideological revolution as well as a psychological declaration of their independence by hired workers.

An even better analogy to the eighteenth-century model of

revolution was the journeymen's withdrawal from their employers' businesses to establish cooperative workshops, marking the
beginnings of what became perhaps the greatest preoccupation
of the nineteenth-century labor movement.[31] Such efforts mir-
rored workers' growing perception of a distinction between
themselves as producers and the "idlers" who employed them.
In an age when individual struggles to rise to a genuinely
independent status and the formation of flexible business part-
nerships were commonplace, they naturally enough extended
older practices, such as mutual aid and a reliance upon their
own "houses of call" in some crafts by pooling their meager
resources and, collectively, opening a workshop. Through much
of the nineteenth century, the practice remained the journeymen's solution to new conditions.

Fully a generation before the more well-known experiments
of the 1820s and 1830s, wage-earning cabinet-makers, carpenters,
cordwainers, and tailors established their own cooperative workshops in the United States. After a stirring and successful use
of such an association by the cabinet- and chairmakers in
Philadelphia during their 1796 strike, the New York City trade
clashed with employers and resorted to such a tactic. Walking
off their jobs during the slack season in the winter months of
1802–03, the journeymen's society charged the employers with
attempting to "deduct at least 15 per cent. from our former
wages," to coerce those old fashioned masters who retained any
"love of justice and humanity" into accepting the dictates of
an employers' association, and to "not employ any workmen
except according to the prices which they themselves have laid
down in their new fashioned book." Journeymen saw no choice
but to accept what their masters "from time to time, conde-
scended to allow us, or to shift for ourselves." Since they could
not afford to remain idle during a turnout, they therefore chose
to open their own "Ware-Room" at No. 49 John Street in early
December.[32]

The union printers expressed such far-reaching concerns in
their own cooperationist proposal. Asbridge argued that a cooperative print shop organized by the union could achieve "at
least three laudable purposes." First, it could enable the union

to keep all of its members employed, saving money otherwise going to their relief. Secondly, it would "give an importance and respectability to the society," creating "an interest for its welfare among its members," and "be the enticing standard around which the society will eagerly rally." Finally, it might help raise funds for the support of the needy and distressed members.[33]

The seemingly anachronistic demand for escalator clauses and the shorter workday and the organization of cooperative workshops grew from an understanding of the social compact unique to working craftsmen. Their rudimentary sense of distinctiveness also justified united efforts by hired men from different trades and had particularly far-reaching implications for the course of a labor movement.

III

The emerging postrevolutionary circumstances failed to immediately erode certain preindustrial sensibilities like the impulses to mercantilist and self-regulatory activity in the crafts. Another important example was the survival of old distinctions between producers engaged in constructive manual labor and idlers who, by virtue of birth or wealth, were not productive and merely enjoyed the fruits of others' industry. As in Britain, Philadelphia workmen frequented a tavern called the Four Alls, which announced its presence with a large painted signboard portraying a mansion with four appropriately dressed figures standing on its steps and an explanatory inscription below reading: "1. King—I govern all. 2. General—I fight for all. 3. Minister—I pray for all. 4. Laborer—And I pay for all."[34] In the changing social order of the new republic, such older distinctions had serious contemporary implications.

Through the rest of the nineteenth century, those workers who articulated a sense of their own distinctiveness used a criterion of class based on labor, not on modes of production nor on means of payment. Like journeymen, the surviving small-scale, independent artisan worked and was hence part of the producing classes. Indeed, well into the early twentieth century, even the most militant of American labor radicals adhered to an idea of class consciousness not confined to industrial workers as a discrete group, but rather embracing workers in different trades and industries and never completely excluding the laboring small proprietor. This self-conception had evolved from that of the broad eighteenth-century community of mechanics and laborers. As the work force expanded numerically, the idea of class socially narrowed to slough off progressively the larger manufacturers among the masters.

The efforts of producers in various trades to collaborate for their mutual support clearly reflects this appreciation of eighteenth- and early nineteenth-century society. From the beginning, union printers could scarcely have helped but notice that the friends or enemies of one journeymen's society tended to be the friends or enemies of labor organizations in general. Walter Franklin, the lawyer who helped defend the Federal Society of Journeymen Cordwainers, also performed legal services for the Philadelphia Typographical Society, refusing to accept payment. The Philadelphia cabinet- and chairmakers found a printer for their price book of 1795 in Ephraim Conrad, a man also involved from time to time in unionist activity in his own trade. Conversely, Bartholomew Graves, the Philadelphia master driven from the ranks of the local Typographical Society, eagerly printed the transcript of the cordwainers' trial of 1806 with the ominous warning that "it is better that the law be known and certain than that it be right."[35]

Both participants and contemporaries understood the obvious implications of the struggle of workmen in one craft for their peers in other trades. New York City tailors, in organizing themselves, made a special point of noting that theirs was a fight against "impositions" common "on every mechanical branch." A hostile commentator on the Philadelphia strike of 1791 warned that should "customs productive of idleness and dissipation introduced by the journeymen carpenters" prevail, "the contagion will soon be communicated to other artificers" of the city. When their craft brothers in New York City turned out in 1795, they did so along with the masons, and that city's strike of 1810 sparked a great deal of concern among employers that painters, glaziers, and still other craftsmen in the building trades might join in the demand for higher wages. Similarly, the architect engaged in the construction of New York's new city hall refused a wage increase for the stonecutters for fear that it would be "the means of raising the wages for all persons connected with the building line."[36]

At times, the success of hired men in one craft seems to have directly inspired efforts in another. Baltimore's United Journeymen Cordwainers Society formed by June 1795 in the wake of activities by the local United Journeymen Tailors Society. So, too, in the following year, Philadelphia's Federal Society of Journeymen Cordwainers organized in the wake of a strikingly successful campaign by the Federal Society of Journeymen Cabinet and Chair Makers.

The trials of the shoemakers' societies shook the early journeymen's associations in other crafts. The New York City society, when facing prosecution in 1809-10, not only issued public statements but sent a special memorial to the various other unions in the city requesting funds to appeal any conviction. The Typographical Society discussed the matter at four meetings and assigned Asbridge and two other leading members to study the issue and confer with the shoemakers' leaders. They finally responded, "expressing the good wishes of this Board for the success of their Cause and stating, that from the recent exhaustion of our funds in assisting our own members who had stood out for wages, it was totally out of our power (at present) to render them the assistance desired." Sharing the printers' meeting place in a "second-rate tavern" called Harmony Hall, the carpenters' union, which had also just been on strike, probably responded similarly.[37]

The most important example of such concerted activity involving more than a single craft came in 1796, after several clashes between journeymen and masters in Philadelphia's furniture trades. The Federal Society of Journeymen Cabinet and Chair-Makers began in the spring of 1794, and, a year later, had to have Conrad print its revised edition of their price book due to "different constructions being put on them both by employers and journeymen, which has been the cause of frequent disputes between them." The union urged all to be particular in their attention to the agreements, but tensions within the craft escalated through 1795.[38]

During the winter's slack in 1795–96, as they later explained, unionists acutely felt "the rapid advance of price in every article of life," driving them toward "a scanty subsistence, produced by the sweat of our brow and the exertion of genius," and appointed a committee to review wage levels. With "all the respect which is due from man to man," the society submitted a new book of rates to their employers. After requesting some time to study the question, these masters, "in open violation of all honor and justice, dispatched delegates to the different cities of the Union, to form a coalition with employers." Their delegates probably tried to recruit other workmen to come to the city, a common tactic to undermine a strike or a threatened strike. More seriously, they sought "to prevent us procuring Employment in any" of these other cities, initiating the first instances of blacklisting unionists on such a scale. In Philadelphia itself, masters united "against employing us as Members of [the] Society" in one of the most blatant attacks on an early American workingmen's organization.[39]

The first weeks of 1796 saw intense discussions among the journeymen. Their most radical spokesmen began to hold sway. One of them was Charles Christian, a locally well-known freethinker. The men chose to publicize their employers' campaign. They charged their masters with "monopolizing the profits of an ingenious branch of the arts," trying "to introduce into this Free Country that system of oppression and disorganization which European mechanics labour under," and preventing "the improvement of Mechanism in America, by destroying the liberty of its Professors." As "Citizens of a Free Country, where the Laws insure to every one the full enjoyment of his natural rights," the journeymen declared, it would be "highly criminal if we permitted the smallest infringement of them without using every means in our power to prevent it." The union's public appeal appeared on the 17th of February.[40]

Explaining their position, the workers later issued a historic call to other trade societies of journeymen. "We hope and entreat that a union of the respective mechanical branches in this city, and throughout America, will immediately take place, in order to repel any attack" on the developing trade unions. "We feel that the united efforts of all the societies, must produce a more permanent establishment of the independence of each, than the individual exertion of a single one. Hasten, then, fellow citizens, to declare yourself ready at any time to assist one another, in a cause which will determine the independence of so useful a body as the working citizens of America."[41]

This appeal "to the respective Mechanical Societies of this City for assistance" resulted in "their generous contributions," enabling the striking cabinet- and chairmakers, under Christian's supervision, to open "A WARE ROOM, in Market-street, Supported by the Society." Hopeful that "THOSE WHO HAVE TRIUMPHED OVER TYRANNY in its most formidable appearance, will also discountenance it in the shape it has attacked us," the journeymen presented their case to the public again, urging it to patronize their cooperative workshop.[42]

The project of Christian and his peers depended directly on "those Societies who have assisted us in this crisis; in particular the respectable and independent Societies of Hatters and Shoemakers," referring to what yet remained a secretive and probably semi-clandestine association, organized after the fashion of the English hatters, and to the Federal Society of Journeymen Cordwainers, organized two years before by a core of workmen who had first tried to unionize in 1792. The cabinet- and chairmakers also thanked committees of "other Mechanical Societies, viz. House-Carpenters, Tailors, Goldsmiths, Saddlers, Coopers, Painters, Printers, &c &c. . . ." Clearly, a wide variety of different craft organizations had responded to the February appeal, cooperated in the defense of a society under attack, and received its call "to meet at MYER tavern, 5th and Race streets," on the first Monday of May 1796 "in order to digest a plan of union, for the protection of their mutual independence."[43]

Unions in at least ten different crafts had combined in this struggle to aid the cabinet- and chairmakers' union which, in turn, offered a "plan of union" to maintain the solidarity originally generated by its own plight. Written sources do not reveal whether Philadelphia labor, at its conference of May 2, 1796, digested this proposal fully. Not only did the strikers emerge victorious, but they then linked their employers' agreement on a wage increase to that extraordinary escalator clause, mandating the automatic adjustment of wages to match future changes in the cost of living.[44]

This pioneering effort to build a city-wide federation of workers apparently involved John McIlvaine, a journeyman printer who, seven years later, gained a certain prominence as an advocate of militant trade regulation by the Philadelphia Typographical Society. McIlvaine probably also participated in the association of journeymen printers then actively aiding the cabinet- and chairmakers. His undated *Address to the Journeymen Cordwainers L.B. of Philadelphia* probably appeared during those same years, offering yet another historic plea for the solidarity of local labor organizations.[45]

> *Cordwainers! Arouse! The time has now come*
> *When our rights should be fully protected;*
> *And every attempt to reduce any one*
> *By all should be nobly rejected.*
>
> *Fellow-Craft-men! Arouse! We united should be*
> *And each man should be hailed as a brother,*
> *Organized we should be in this hallowed cause,*
> *To love and relieve one another.*
>
> *Speak not of failure, in our attempt to maintain,*
> *For our labor a fair compensation;*
> *All that we want is assistance from you,*
> *To have permanent organization.*
>
> *A commencement we've made, associations we*
> *have,*
> *From one to thirteen inclusive,*
> *Come join them my friends, and be not afraid,*
> *Of them being in the least delusive.*

Regardless of the exact role of the Federal Society of Journeymen Cordwainers in formulating the cabinet-makers' plan of union, their response to McIlvaine's undated address and the actual outcome of the events of 1796 remain and probably will always remain uncertain. Perhaps the shoemakers, flushed by their own success, drifted from the proposal after their own strike in May 1796, and McIlvaine's address sought to win them back to an earlier course. Possibly, too, McIlvaine's effort represented a distinctively different attempt to unite the various craft societies of the city. Nor is it inconceivable that some sort of federation of the trades actually lasted for some months, or even for a few years. After all, at least some of the journeymen's societies likely to have participated, like those of the tailors or hatters, had organized in secret and would have probably insisted that any unified body adopt similar measures for the defense of their own craft security. (See appendix B.) In any case, the ability or inability of Philadelphia workingmen to digest a particular plan pales before their actual achievement.

During the early national period, organized printers at Philadelphia participated in a successful campaign of solidarity behind striking cabinet- and chairmakers. At least ten unions—or "from one to thirteen inclusive," according to McIlvaine—acted in concert, at least for a time. Even by the most rigidly institutional criteria of traditional labor history, a united movement of hired workers from various crafts began not with the formation of the Mechanics' Union of Trade Associations in December 1827, but a generation earlier in April 1796.

This level of self-organization and the incipient labor ideology it articulated emerged within the framework of an ongoing dialogue among English and American thinkers on the relationship between republicanism and wealth. The classic antidemocratic writings of the English political philosophers Richard Trenchard and Thomas Gordon had defined "the first principle of all Power is Property; and every Man will have his Share of it in proportion as he enjoys Property." Since property could not be made equal or be owned collectively, they argued, "the Phantome of a Commonwealth must vanish, and never appear again but in disordered Brains." Some writers to American newspapers made a similar link between property ownership and the exercise of political power, arguing that a genuine republic in the New

World would be impossible given "the great distinctions of persons, and difference in their estates or property, which cooperates strongly with the genius of the people in favour of monarchy."[46]

Not all, however, accepted the inevitability or desirability of the unregulated wealth. "Where great property is," wrote "The Watchman" to Boston's *Independent Chronicle*, "there generally is influence. Whatever therefore tends . . . to vest in a few so great a quantity as to make the distribution vastly and extravagantly unequal" must also weaken republican values. "Where *wealth* is hereditary, *power* is hereditary," noted "A Farmer" in a Maryland paper. The presence or absence of a formal title would be "of very little, or no consequence," for the rich, in reality, constituted a *"nobility:* and the *poor, plebian* in all countries—And on this distinction alone, the true definition of aristocracy depends." "A True Patriot" argued in the *New Jersey Gazette* that the greatest threat to liberty would be "the unequal division of property in the space of so short a time." Another predicted that the profiteering of Revolutionary years had indicated a trend which, "if not carefully counteracted, will one day, produce a revolution." "Hunger will break through stone walls and the resentment excited by it may end in your destruction," warned yet another writer to the newspapers.[47]

Two yankee veterans of the Revolution made particularly acute observations about the emerging American society. William Manning, a former Minuteman and innkeeper at Billerica, Massachusetts, argued that "the Causes that Ruen Republicks" might be found in *"a Conceived Difference of Interests Between those that Labour for a Living & those that git a Living without Bodily Labour,"* which caused "the grate shuffel between the few & the many" evident in such events as the Shays Rebellion. So, too, an itinerant cobbler from Bethlehem, Connecticut, saw the greatest threat to American republicanism as "an eternal struggle between the laboring part of the community and those lazy rascals that invented every means the Devil has put into their heads, to destroy the laboring part of the community," an idea not entirely silenced by his own prosecution under the Federal Sedition Law of 1798. Such radical critics of postrevolutionary American development felt strongly that securing liberty required that the majority of the population have some independent means of support, either in a small farm or an artisan workshop.[48]

Some of the urban hired men involved in trade union activities shared the concerns of Manning and Brown. Theophilus Eaton, one of the Flatbush members of the New York Typographical Society, expressed much of the frustration his peers must have felt in his slender volume of verse. Constructing a dialogue between a rich man and a poor laborer named Albert, Eaton placed words in the former's mouth which he himself must have heard frequently, advising the poor to be sober, frugal, and industrious to pick up wealth along life's way. The answer, however, was all his own.

> *Albert replies, "Just tell me now,*
> *When to pick up, and where and how.*

His rambles through New York City caused Eaton to wonder at

> *What boundless wealth, and us'd how ill!*
> *Collected by inhuman will,*
> *From needy folks and abject poor,*
> *Whose wants compel them to endure.*[49]

Eaton found an American city polarized between the wealthy class and the needy, whose lack of property compelled them to sell their labor for wages. Anticipating the radically Agrarian critique that came to dominate the political concerns of antebellum labor, he asked his fellow citizens

> *. . . who owns the land*
> *Whereon your noble buildings stand?*
> *I'll answer too—the wealthy class,*
> *Who let no chance of winning pass.*
> *These call the poor to occupy,*
> *And never fail to charge them high*
> *Enough for taxes, wear and tare [sic],*
> *With interest and carriage hire.*

Mockingly, he lampooned the Lawyer, the Lady, the Modern

Gentleman, the Landlord, and other representative figures of the New York City elite, warning them:

> *No fear have I, nor favour crave,*
> *But each his proper due shall have.*
> *To meddle with the rich, I know*
> *Is brittle business to do;*
> *And irksome to defend the poor,*
> *With false intent or motive pure,*
> *Because "none but the poor will steal,"*
> *Or rich uneasy make me feel;*
> *And yet I venture heedless on,*
> *And bid my diffidence begone.*[50]

Men like Manning and Brown drew conclusions from this realization. The former understood the nation's course after independence as one charted by the few for their own betterment at the expense of the many. If wages could be halved, he explained, "rents fees & salleryes" would double, increasing the dependence of the many upon "a few for favours & assistance in a thousand ways." Brown portrayed a similar policy by the few who, "having consumed a large portion" of the nation's total wealth, sought "to engross the remainder, and to *reduce* the people to abject poverty." He denounced the government as the agent of the wealthy and declared that the "real occupation of government is to plunder or steal as will best answer their purposes," while "the business of the people is to secrete their property by fraud or give it peaceable up," leaving "the name of liberty and equality . . . like the sounding brass and a tickling symbol [sic]." Thus, government policies and the rights of the majority of Americans "are so opposite that they have eternally been at war with each other." Soon, he predicted, the propertyless working people will "become miserable through idleness to avoid the mortification of laboring for them they hate and detest."[51]

Eaton's verses, too, also expressed the hostility of a producer. Nowhere do the rich and powerful fare so poorly as when compared to the honest workingmen who

> *. . . a present living get,*
> *Through perseverance, toil, and sweat,*

> *With carpenters and teachers too,*
> *And authors, printers, and a crew*
> *Of other able useful men*
> *Who wield the tool, the type, or pen,*
> *It fares the same—these lay the plan,*
> *For greatness in some other man—*
> *Nor do the bugs of greatness know,*
> *To whom they all their greatness owe,*
> *Or will not own the fact for they*
> *Alike upon the people play*
> *The monkey tricks of* brag *and* prate,
> *As though they did themselves create.*[52]

More prominent thinkers also shared these concerns. Of particular importance to later labor militants and radicals was the legacy of Thomas Paine, the staymaker-preacher turned editor and Revolutionary pamphleteer, who had helped chart the remarkably democratic course of the American Revolution in Philadelphia. Sections of Paine's *Rights of Man* and *Agrarian Justice* clearly argued that a man accumulating riches reached "a prohibitable luxury" beyond which his property would be so great as to overwhelm access to property ownership by others. Paine believed that a certain regulation of wealth would be indispensible to the survival of a republic. According to his version of republican theory, the earth "in its natural uncultivated State" would have remained "the *common property of the human race*," a status which changed only with the development of civilization and, ironically, "those advantages which flow from agriculture, arts, sciences, and manufactures." He argued that those dispossessed of property had lost what would have been theirs in a state of nature and had a natural right to compensation. Paine specifically recommended that republican governments provide financial aid to educate the children of the poor, to couples upon marriage, to the aged, and to the young upon reaching the age of legal maturity, and advocated free public burials and public works projects to make jobs for the unemployed.[53]

Paine came to enjoy considerable popularity among some mechanics, particularly after his moving to New York City late in 1803. There, he had close ties to some wage-earning crafts-men, at least a few of whom were engaged in the pioneering effort to organize unions. Born at a time when Paine's agitation for national independence had shaken the country, Jacob Frank of Philadelphia moved to New York the same year as Paine, married, and became president of the Franklin Typographical Association. Four years later, Paine began writing for Frank's new publication, the *New York Aurora and the Public Adver-tiser*, and Frank himself penned a touching tribute to his mentor upon Paine's death in 1809. Other acquaintances and publishers of Paine whose activities included membership in a labor organ-ization included Jonas Humbert, a baker; Charles Christian, the cooperationist and cabinetmaker; and printers like Southwick, Conrad, David Bruce, Richard Folwell, and Alexander Ming, probably a participant in the earliest New York City efforts. Of these, Frank, Humbert, Christian, Bruce, Conrad, and Ming appear to have been cothinkers and protégés of sorts.[54]

Such individuals began to pose the need for far-reaching political changes in order to secure and sustain what they viewed as the original purity of American civic life. Their concerns covered a wide range of issues, from slavery to John W. Scott's suggestion that government funds be used to encour-age the development of literature and the arts, and even included Eaton's speculation that if society should grant to poor individuals

> . . . *one hundred dollars each,*
> *United they might forward reach,*
> *To bu'ness good within their call,*
> *'Till they were useful people all.*
> *If I judge right, two million serve,*
> *Just twenty thousand to preserve,*
> *By giving dollars ten times ten*
> *To ev'ry poor and needy man.*
> *It were a little heav'n below,*
> *To see the rich such mercy show—*
> *And never more should fashion be*
> *The awful seeming thing to me,*
> *Which now it is, if it would bring*

> *To practice such a noble thing.*
> *But woe is me—thus doom'd to see*
> *That such a thing will never be.*
> *The poor may look in vain to find*
> *A regulation of this kind....* [55]

Within a generation of American independence, radically minded workingmen like Christian or Eaton expressed distinctively labor-oriented grievances in the language of eighteenth-century republicans like Paine to formulate a social and economic critique of the new nation's course.

IV

Union printers drew upon their own legacy as craftsmen in their efforts to regulate trade matters, and upon the rhetoric of their betters for ideological justification. In employing the ideology of natural rights, unionists, with varying degress of consciousness and subtlety, transformed the meaning of "life, liberty and the pursuit of happiness" and shaped an innovative and original interpretation of human rights. This approach not only explained and sustained self-organization for better wages and working conditions (and the tactics and institutions of modern unionism), but also encompassed cooperative production and other innovations usually attributed to much later stages in the growth of labor organizations. In the struggle to attain such goals, union printers periodically battled alongside their peers in other trades on behalf of the general rights of the working citizens of America.

Hired craftsmen composed the charter of the labor movement in the early national period. This new interpretive framework fostered the growth of a broad spectrum of ideas, some of which began to appear almost immediately. These germinated for a generation before erupting in the practice of the workingmen of the late 1820s and 1830s, in the upheaval usually cited by scholars as the inception of a genuine movement of American labor. The dynamic achievement of that forgotten generation of organized printers and their peers in other crafts set the course for the subsequent, more easily discernible activities of the later labor movement.

Epilogue

To Digest a Plan

*The Implications of
an Early American
Labor History*

In 1810 a young journeyman named Samuel Huestis won admission to the recently formed New York Typographical Society. Although he traveled frequently out of town, Huestis had settled into the local trade and its organization by 1816. A few years later, he participated in the first distinctively socialist organization in American history, the New York Society for Promoting Communities, founded by Dr. Cornelius Camden Blatchly and, after 1824, closely allied to the efforts of Robert Owen. Within the craft, the old Typographical Society had long since gained incorporation and withdrawn from active trade regulation, so Huestis joined with John Windt and other free-thinkers, Owenites, and radicals in the craft to launch a new Typographical Association as a genuine trade union in 1831. Such associations also imply his support of the newly formed independent Workingmen's Party of the city, which ran Blatchly for the state assembly in 1829.[1]

The craft that had shaped the thinking of Huestis and his peers differed radically from that of Franklin's day. The American craft had grown from perhaps a score of printers operating out of shops in half a dozen communities to well over a thousand, with hundreds of shops scattered in virtually every community larger than a few thousand. The eighteenth century was no golden age for the trade, but its rapid expansion took place within a persistently small-scale workplace that had made possible the sort of mobility basic to the career of an individual like Franklin. In response to the structural transformation of the trade, the hired workers began to think and act differently, and Huestis's career dramatized the crystallization in the 1820s and 1830s of ideas predating 1815.

By then, the economic expansion of printing had polarized the craft between the owners of the relatively large and prosperous enterprises and the disproportionately growing segment of hired men. While many printers remained in small workplaces and the line between journeymen and small masters still remained somewhat permeable, precious few of the employed who were without some peculiar connections to the political or denominational elites could retain ownership of an office long enough to rise into the ranks of the truly secure and successful.

Amidst these changes, artisans continued to cling to the older values that grew from a centuries-old legacy of craft self-organization. These older practices, along with the politics of the Revolution, gave rise to formal and informal associations of mechanics, but economic and social development had also polarized the traditional moral economy of craftsmen. Such regulatory bodies of craftsmen in general did not formally assist members in distress, and mutual aid clubs did engage in regulatory activities. More importantly, the different circumstances of the employing and employed mechanics forged differing interpretations of that legacy. Employing artisans, for example, often established a mutual fund to protect what was particularly important to them, their shops and equipment; the increasingly precarious state of the hired mechanic, however, placed a renewed importance on a joint treasury from which they or their families might draw in the event of their illness, injury, or death. The regulatory legacy justified employers' frequent agreement among themselves about the prices to be charged for their products and the wages to be paid their journeymen, while also providing an initial line of defense for the growing proportion of hired men.

Within their own organizations, journeymen struggled to define human liberty, natural rights, and republicanism with reference to their working lives. The prosecuted union shoe-makers of Philadelphia spoke the language of natural rights when they argued through their attorney "that every man being the sole owner, and master of his own goods and labor, had a right to affix the price of them; leaving to those who were to purchase, the right to accept or reject as they might think proper."[2] The essence of unionism became the right of hired men to act in concert to shape their economic and social cir-cumstances. In this, their ideas could not have clashed more sharply with the concept of property rights institutionalized by the young republic.

So, too, official policy placed trade-regulating bodies of hired men in a precarious position. On the one hand, as a warning to others, the authorities in the early national period conducted five trials of shoemakers' unions: at Philadelphia in 1806, Baltimore in 1809, New York City in 1810, and Pittsburgh in 1814 and 1815.[3] On the other hand, legislative bodies also offered unions a chance to purchase legal security as mutual aid clubs at the price of forsaking regulatory activities. The option of selectively repressing particularly defiant workers' organiza-tions and of regulating others provided important precedents for the later legal constraints on American labor organizations.

Clearly, the civic policing of labor activism played no role in the partisan political debates of the day, for Republican work-ers pursued unionist goals no more eagerly than their Federalist brothers. For example, the internal battles in the Philadelphia Typographical Society during 1803–04 aligned militant advocates of regulation like the Federalist William W. Wands against the more conservative leadership of Republicans like Bartholomew Graves, and the factionalism of 1806–07 brought the Republican Lewis C. P. Franks into conflict with the Republican Joseph Gales, Jr. Significantly, the early trade unions as organizations scrupulously avoided the very appearance of partisan align-ments. When several members of Baltimore's Union Society of

Journeymen Cordwainers tarred and feathered a non-union Federalist co-worker for political reasons, the union quickly disavowed their act. Even in the midst of the War of 1812, the New York Typographical Society refused to join either the pro-war Republican Tammany Society or the anti-war Federalist Washington Benevolent Society for a patriotic celebration of the Fourth of July; rather, it held its own, separate gathering.[4]

The unwillingness of either political party, as such, to address workers' concerns generally created little tension in an age when property requirements still barred many wage earners from voting. Nevertheless, the old artisan practice of fielding independent mechanic tickets still retained a certain appeal, as evidenced in two letters to the New York City press.[5] "Real American" charged in 1810 that wealthy office-holding "placemen" had grown rich while their mechanic electors "work and toil from year to year without advancing one step forward to prosperity." Four years later, "Poor Mechanic" argued that he and his peers faced a choice between two parties dominated by the interests of the wealthy in "oppressing the poorer classes." The War of 1812 had encouraged a spirit of monopoly among entrepreneurs, while an apathetic ill-humor "pervades almost all the ranks of married men," enabling the former to make the national crisis "the harvest of the rich, and the destruction of the poor." The rich of both parties acted "as a band of brothers" against the laboring poor, and he urged his peers: "let us then, among ourselves, discard the question, 'are you a democrat or federalist?' Let our question be are you for THE POOR, PEACE AND COMMERCE, or THE RICH, WAR AND SPECULATIONS?" He suggested a pragmatic alliance with the Federalists to "obtain a peace" with Britain before the wealthy of that party, lured by "the sweets of monopoly, desirous of continuing to reap its advantages," switched to support of the war. This sort of suggestion came to naught because the more successful and influential sort of artisan who had spearheaded the campaigns of the 1780s had already achieved a political niche among the respectable and powerful of the city and because the disproportionate increase among the more disenfranchised wage earners also weakened the potential of independent political action by the crafts as a whole.

Of course, pragmatic necessity had inspired the activism of organized craftsmen in the early national period. Only in this sense was historian David Saposs correct in arguing that labor organizations "prior to 1827" had "as yet no 'labour philosophy,' whether of co-operationism, agrarianism, socialism, or class struggle."[7] Nevertheless, the essence of a labor philosophy had clearly evolved.

The organizers of the earlier unions correctly doubted their ability to gain or retain what they regarded as their rights in the changing world around them without the power of self-organization. Such convinced unionists found the events after 1815 a confirmation of their worst fears about the course of economic and social development charted by their social betters. Depending on the area, the War of 1812 and the subsequent Panic of 1819 both seriously affected the state of American printing. Decreased demand and intensified competition dispossessed more small-scale masters, further swelling the proportion of hired men within the craft and entrenching the larger, more profitable shops that could weather hard times more easily.

Under such circumstances, the prospects for unionism faded. No new organizations of hired printers emerged between 1815 and 1827 and the older societies at Baltimore, Boston, Albany, and New Orleans seem to have simply collapsed. The Philadelphia Typographical Society, despite its possible involvement in an 1816 protest by local pressmen, contined to disavow regulatory concerns and shriveled in size and influence. After establishing a uniform wage scale in 1815, the New York City union, too, decided to seek the refuge of incorporation which it attained in 1818. Only the Columbia Typographical Society successfully sustained itself as a trade union, avoiding a resolution to apply for incorporation in 1821 by one vote that enabled it to survive as the oldest trade union in the United States, a local of the international Typographical Union.[7]

During the great labor upsurge that began in 1827, a new wave of unionism swept the craft. Between 1830 and 1838, journeymen printers from New England to Mississippi organized new local unions which, in turn, united into a National Typographical Society. When Huestis and his peers established their new union at New York in 1831, they reflected on "the conditions of the printing business for some years past" and the fate of the older Typographical Society. The craftsmen of 1809, they explained, had started their group "for the purpose of sustaining a uniform scale of prices, and of affording pecuniary relief to the sick and distressed of its own members, their widows and orphans," but, with its incorporation, it had become "merely a mutual benefit institution." Almost immediately, conditions in the trade deteriorated "until, instead of a uniform scale of prices, every man was compelled to work for what he could obtain."[8] Before the collapse of these unions in the depression that closed the 1830s, these new unions generally had begun to echo the concerns that had inspired the movement of forty years before, differing from their predecessors primarily in the explicit rejection of an exclusive focus on mutual aid and the strategy of incorporation by the state.

Historians have dated modern trade unionism from the revival of labor organizations around 1850. In that year, local unions of printers, generally reorganized only a few years earlier, began holding annual conventions that resulted, three years later, in the establishment of the National Typographical Union, which later admitted a few Canadian locals and became the International Typographical Union. Its first generation paid tribute to its pioneers. In June 1859 the Boston local that hosted the convention of the NTU sponsored a festival, to which they invited Nathaniel Willis, who had entered the craft seventy years earlier and participated in early efforts to unionize the trade; gratified, he nonetheless excused himself because of his "age and infirmities." Within weeks, the old New York Typographical Society, then a mutual aid club that existed alongside the existing local unions, held its Semi-Centennial Anniversary, and obtained autographs and remarks from three of its early members, David Reins, Daniel Fanshaw, and George Mather; they even convinced Reins to sit for a portrait to hang in the Printers' Free Library.[9]

As the example of Huestis indicates, the intervening half-century had dealt a succession of serious blows and had battered the traditional civic deference of such men. First, financial panic severely shook both the economy in 1819, 1837, and 1857 and the confidence of workers in the virtue of their own passivity; conservative estimates that the first of these threatened a tenth of New York City with outright starvation hint at an even broader impoverishment. Second, literate workingmen in the large cities found a wealth of new literature attacking the idea that the social order represented the inevitable extension of an immutable human nature. Finally, the reform of state suffrage laws opened the way for workingmen to act in concert politically.

In 1826, Philadelphia craftsmen renewed their efforts of thirty years before to form a broad front of working citizens in the city and throughout the nation. Toward the end of that year, they formed the Mechanics' Union of Trade Associations, which in turn launched the Workingmen's Party of Philadelphia in 1828. Among its key activists were craftsmen like John J. Dubois, a leader of the shoemakers' union since the 1790s, and John Thompson of the old Typographical Society.[10]

Shortly thereafter, when New York City workingmen began building their own movement, veterans of earlier labor organizations also played an important role. These included: Jonas Humbert, a baker; Robert Townsend, Jr., a carpenter; and printers like Huestis, Ephraim Conrad, and George Bruce. In the spring of 1829, the workers of that city established a Committee of Fifty at a series of mass meetings. The Committee embraced the most radical sort of antimonopolist politics, articulated in *Rights of Man to Property!* by Thomas Skidmore, an advocate of an Agrarian revolution of the propertyless and near-propertyless to seize and redistribute the wealth of society. That fall the Committee launched the Workingmen's Party of New York City[11]

The Jacksonian labor upsurge that erupted with the Mechanics' Union in 1827 and lasted until the Panic of 1837 extended the early trade unionists' protest against the loss of the autonomy they associated with craft labor. Like their predecessors, the later Workingmen appealed to the first principles of social organization and government. Skidmore's means, for all of their peculiarly revolutionary implications, aimed at an egalitarian society rooted in a vision shared by both his less overtly radical opponents within the contemporary labor movement and his predecessors in earlier workers' movements. The former came to think that their goals might be more easily attained through such measures as free public education and a more judicious distribution of the public lands. Twenty years before, striking carpenters, under Townsend's leadership, had explained their own reading of the Declaration of Independence as enumerating the hired workers' right to an income sufficient to support a family, to subsist in old age, and to afford a reasonable opportunity to rise in the world to the ownership as well as use of productive property.

The idea of a political labor movement, sustained by some veterans of these Workingmen's parties like George Henry Evans, reappeared in 1844 as the National Reform Association began its renewed Agrarian agitation, which was aimed at a more equal distribution of the public lands as a step toward a more generalized redistribution of wealth and property and breaking down concentrations of economic power. After a reconciliation with the New York Typographical Society so warm that he tried to make it the executor of his will, Daniel Fanshaw not only had clear credentials as an advocate of labor organization but joined in petitioning against slavery in the District of Columbia, and fostered the political movement for land reform. The memory of the most famous of Agrarian spokesmen, Horace Greeley, inspired one of the last acts by a veteran of the labor movement. In 1873 Samuel Williams, "the oldest printer in the State of New York," heard that union members in the city had agreed to set a certain amount of type to raise money for a monument to Greeley, the first president of their existing union; the eighty-four-year-old printer, who had joined the old Typographical Society sixty-three years before, "put on an apron and went to work, completing the full amount stipulated."[12] Clearly, the first modern trade unionists were aware that their efforts, in politics as well the workplace, were rooted in earlier struggles.

The dynamic of self-organization precludes a simplistic characterization of the earliest efforts of journeymen as preindustrial or reactionary, for any impulse they had to defend mechanics' privileges led directly to conflicts over new issues like wages, working conditions, and the shorter working day. This dynamic is evident in the case of the Philadelphia house carpenters who had been fighting to win a ten-hour day since 1791; their continued efforts, including a strike in 1827, sparked the organization of the Mechanics' Union, the Philadelphia Workingmen's Party, and, ultimately, the 1835 general strike. Their New York City peers had attained the ten-hour day, at least from some employers, by 1805, but faced annoying problems in enforcing the innovation and collecting their full wages; by 1829, when their struggle inspired the development of the New York City Workingmen's Party, "petitions had been tried in vain for twenty or thirty years, and even more."[13] Older goals required new strategic and tactical applications.

Even more clearly, perhaps, the establishment of cooperative workshops reveals the deep roots of concerns that became central to the nineteenth-century American labor movement. These originated not in the utopian experimentation of men like Robert Owen or Josiah Warren in the 1820s but in the practical needs of an earlier generation of journeymen who sought to support themselves during long strikes by collectively managing production, marketing their wares, and dividing the profits. The artisan defense of their personal autonomy and liberty moved hired craftsmen to strategies and tactics with a logic of their own.

What is usually seen as the first movement of American labor, lasting from 1827 into 1837, represented the culmination of half a century of labor struggles. Ideologically, David Saposs's assumption that no labor philosophy existed prior to 1827 fails to acknowledge that many journeymen had, for a generation, formulated, held, and expressed their belief in the necessity of their own organization as propertyless producers to defend themselves from the unfettered control of those employers who owned the larger shops in which most of them labored.

The institutional criterion of Helen Sumner also failed to distinguish clearly between the two periods of labor activism.

The movement of 1796 had transcended craft lines as surely as that of 1827. Nor did the later associations of the 1820s and 1830s prove to be more capable of securing a stable existence than did their predecessors.

Neither ideological beliefs nor institutional practices distinguished these efforts. Rather, the circumstances of the 1820s and 1830s required the more vigorous application of standards and practices already developed. A full generation of experience further convinced workers that the mere clarification of the meaning of liberty would not suffice to readjust American economic life and ensure better wages and more equal opportunity. Having a better grasp of the dimensions of the problems, they also made more detailed analyses and elaborate proposals. So, too, recognizing that their concerns were more than a matter of passing importance, these nineteenth-century craftsmen left often substantial histories of their efforts and ideas. In contrast, the earliest founders of American unionism lacked the perspective that only time could give.

Indeed, the pioneers of American trade unionism left no indication that they saw their movement as one that would touch and improve the lives of millions of their later peers. Nor did they think that their efforts would seem important enough after two centuries to attract serious study. Their motives were quite simple. "Let none be deterred from doing good, by a distrust of his own abilities, or by a fear of disappointment," suggested one union orator.

> *What though no golden boxes nor ornamental swords should be presented to us for our services—what though no ringing of bells, no roaring of cannon, no brilliant and gorgeous illuminations, should proclaim the public approbation of our conduct—what though no monumental marble should relate to posterity, that we had successfully labored [against tendencies] to increase the miseries of the human race, and augment the number of widows and orphans— what though our names be not, like Cromwell's "damn'd to everlasting fame"—yet a far greater, a far*

nobler reward will await us:—the approbation of our own consciences, the gratitude of posterity, and the smiles of approving Heaven![14]

They simply did not realize the importance of what they had begun.

Appendix A.

Clandestine Labor Organizations in Early American History

Workers in the United States have frequently resorted to the organization of secret societies to pursue unionist goals. The largest American labor organization in the nineteenth century, the Knights of Labor, originated in a clandestine society of Philadelphia tailors, and, as the presence of its contemporary Brotherhood of the Union among printers or the Knights of St. Crispin among shoemakers indicates, such a legacy was deeply rooted in the American crafts.[1] Nevertheless, preconceived ideas about the relative lack of repression in the United States, along with the inherent problems of sources, provide major obstacles to serious study of the subject.

In the early national period, references to associations of workers are often very brief, like the offhanded notice of a society of Philadelphia printers that aided striking cabinetmakers in 1796. No doubt, various early unions formed and collapsed without having left documentary evidence of their existence. One wonders whether participants wished to keep their activities hidden from the vigilant eyes of their employers. It is difficult to understand the intentions of men whose very activities remain undocumented. An important key to this puzzle is the development of unionism among American tailors.

Oral traditions existed among the older craftsmen of the late nineteenth and early twentieth century that, although since closed to us, found some reflection in the work of some of the pioneering historians of American Labor. George E. McNeill, for example, found that tailors in the early United States kept an affiliation with the English General Society of Taylors formed at London in 1760. The Colorado Commissioner of Labor Statistics, drawing upon the memories of old timers in the Denver local, identified the first American union of that trade as a Philadelphia society, organized and incorporated in 1806. Other sources reveal that, in the same year, journeymen formed associations at New York City and Boston. Despite earlier activities under the auspices of the British society, tailors in three cities moved toward an independent, public existence, apparently as benevolent clubs—an incorporated one in the case of Philadelphia—in the very year in which authorities in this country first brought to trial leaders of a trade union, that of the Philadelphia shoemakers.[2]

Practices among the English tailors make this coincidence all the more enticing. There, the Parliament passed laws in 1796, 1799, and 1800 to eradicate combinations of hired workmen seeking to influence wages and working conditions. Nevertheless, at the turn of the century, master tailors petitioned the Home Office about a journeymen's group "general throughout the trade." The "very basis and foundation" for this organization were local houses of call. These "divisions of the Society at large" would "keep up a correspondence with each other" to sustain a loose network of more than fifteen thousand of Britain's journeyman tailors. An 1801 trial unveiled the continued functioning of the London houses that provided members with jobs based on their length of residence in the city, and coordinated the efforts of the "honourable men" or "flints" to exclude the "dungs," men working under scale from the local shops.[3]

These men responded to prosecution not by dissolving their union but by going further underground with these activities. By 1810 eight houses of call functioned in London alone. They developed a sophisticated practice of meeting at different houses "under pretence of their being Clubs or Societies, denominated Provident Institutions," that is, mutual aid or benevolent societies. These meetings would then send representatives who, two nights later, gathered to get a watchword at a second location, and to use the password to gain admission to a third house. There, "with CLOSED DOORS they proceed to business, a sentinel being placed at the door, a slate, being the only thing upon which they mark their proceedings." There, the representatives elected a Select Committee of five or seven men to discuss wages and working conditions, and to formulate resolutions in "a short hand (of their own understanding) on the slate," which would, in turn, be shown to delegates who reported back to the "provident" societies later.[4]

American tailors were among the "15,000 and upwards" workingmen in the illegal and secretive General Society. A Combinations Act by Parliament would not have directly affected their already discrete activities here, but the successful prosecution of the Federal Society of Journeymen Cordwainers at Philadelphia would have moved the tailors to take precautionary measures, logically starting in the city that had witnessed the trial.

Union tailors at Philadelphia seem to have been very well prepared when the courts moved against them in 1827. The trial introduced considerable evidence to demonstrate a tightly knit and secretive organization. After the court obtained the book in which the journeymen kept the constitution, bylaws, and minutes of the society, the prosecution complained that the book "abounds so much with alterations, interlineations, and erasures, with here and there a missing leaf" that it would be of little value. The minutes also ended months before the strike for which the society was on trial. The journeymen claimed that no dates had appeared on the subpoena requiring them to produce the minutes and that the missing pages had been earlier used for purposes other than the minutes. The president of the union, explaining that such records as minutes were no longer kept, testified that the written request for the proceedings of the special general meeting that had called the strike could not be honored since the records had been destroyed. Claiming to be a benevolent society, the tailors' leaders successfully defied the prosecutions' efforts to find written evidence of "the shop rule, the pitcher rule, or the rule of honour," requiring journeymen to join the society or be scabbed. This was, according to the prosecuting attorney, "the life and soul of the society—the means by which they attain the chief ends of their combination." Such a rule, society members responded, was a shop concern on which their society, as such, took no action. Flustered, the prosecution won conviction on only one of the eight counts in the indictment.[5]

The Philadelphia society, incorporated in 1806—although legally barred from trade regulation—could have nevertheless functioned as a union, as might those other loose associations formed elsewhere that year. More likely, perhaps, their presence implies a parallel trade union organization composed of the same members. Two of the members of the Philadelphia society prosecuted in 1827, for example, held membership in no less than three organizations of local tailors, two of which even met at the same tavern.[6] The similarity to the English pattern seems quite obvious.

Moreover, journeyman tailors were active in the United States prior to 1806. A New York City society clashed with employers in 1804, and a militant body at Baltimore waged a series of strikes starting in 1795. The oral tradition in the Denver local may not have been wrong, however, in describing the Philadelphia group as the oldest, for some sort of association existed there as early as 1796 and may well have antedated the Baltimore efforts. Taken as a whole, the evidence indicates that early unionists involved in these campaigns left no record of their own, in large part, as a matter of policy.

The tailors maintained their clandestine practices for decades, and had a major impact on the broader labor movement. For example, James L. Wright, who entered his apprenticeship at Philadelphia during the 1827 trial of the local union, remembered its lesson well. After organizing the Garment Cutters Association in 1862 and experiencing its collapse, he argued that its failure had been due to its break with the craft's long tradition of clandestine unionism. He, along with six other local tailors, then formed the Noble and Holy Order of the Knights of Labor, a body he helped to lead until his death in 1893.[7]

These early efforts of tailors to organize in secret implies that journeymen in other trades may have done so as well. McNeil, again drawing upon the oral traditions of a craft, explained that American hatters also kept their early affiliation with the English societies. Home Office reports on their activities in Britain reveal obviously delegated committees, of which one report complained, "so secretly are they conducted that it is difficult to find them out." Organizations of American hatters so successfully avoided documenting their demands, struggles, and activities that only brief notices survive that Baltimore had a society during 1809 and that Philadelphia had one in 1796 and at least two in 1811.[8]

No group of American craftsmen would have been more justified in organizing secretly than the shoemakers. Each of the five known prosecutions of trade unions in the early national period aimed at the destruction of their organizations. Such prosecutions did not necessarily dissolve the societies, which simply took legal precautions similar to those of their peers in other Anglo-American trades. In September 1807 over a year after the successful prosecution—and assumed dissolution—of Philadelphia's Federal Society of Journeymen Cordwainers, the Baltimore union noted receipt of "a letter from the Society in Philadelphia . . . requesting a correspondence between the two" on conditions in the trade. Baltimore journeymen realized the risks they faced and committed themselves in writing to defend and financially support any member "prosecuted for performing any duties required by the articles of this Society," if "in such defense he acts conformable to the instructions of this Society." The Pittsburgh union, after being threatened with prosecution in 1814, rewrote sections of its constitution, deleting written evidence of its trade regulating features with no apparent intention of abandoning them, and assumed what it hoped would be the protective legal coloring of a benevolent associations.[9]

Although much more likely to have published some record of their presence, unions of journeymen printers had no guarantee that their organizations would be any more secure from legal action than those of shoemakers, hatters, or tailors. Historian Ethelbert Stewart hinted at organized printers' use of such defensive measures when he wrote, in 1905, "that whatever livery of charitable clubs they wore in public, in their hall rooms they were labor organizations."[10] The possibility of such efforts by printers' societies to conceal deliberately their existence and objectives intimates that self-organization in the trade may have been more widespread and deeply rooted than the available information indicates, as it most certainly was in most of the early American crafts.

Appendix B.

A Directory of Known Participants in Early American Associations & Combinations of Journeymen Printers Prior to 1816

Sources cited in this study yield the following list of 617 instances of participation in an early printers' association by 590 individuals. (A few additional individuals joining at New York in 1816–18 account for the additional journeymen used in the foregoing look at the problem of their mobility on p. 49.) Names sometimes appear with different spellings even within the same source, and only the most common is given here.

Other materials further revealed an almost equal number of contemporary unionists in other early American crafts. New York materials included the names of 204 shipwrights and, with the Philadelphia data, of nine cabinet- and chairmakers, four carpenters, and a tailor. Materials from these two locations, together with Baltimore, Pittsburgh, Lexington (Kentucky), and Chester County (Pennsylvania), account for 271 shoemakers. All together, the names of almost 1100 early trade unionists have survived.

ABERCROMBIE, THOMAS B.
Philadelphia

ADAMS, CHARLES CHAUNCEY
New York City

AITKEN, ROBERT SKEOTCH
Philadelphia

AKERMAN, SAMUEL
Philadelphia

ALBRIGHT, JOHN
Philadelphia

ALEXANDER, JOHN
Philadelphia

ALEXANDER, WILLIAM
Philadelphia

ALLEN, CORNELIUS
New York City

ALLEN, FRANCIS D.
New York City

ALLEN, J. D.
New York City

ALLEN, JOHN
New York City

ALLEN, JOHN
Washington

ALLEN, JOHN W.
Philadelphia

ALLEN, ROBERT
Washington

ANDERSON, WILLIAM I.
Philadelphia

ANDERSON, WILLIAM J.
Baltimore

ANDREWS, SYDNEY W.
New York City

ASBRIDGE, GEORGE
New York City

AUSTIN, JOHN MORSE
Philadelphia

AVERY, THOMAS
Philadelphia

AYLES, SILAS
Philadelphia

BACCHUS, G. W.
Baltimore

BACK, HENRY
New York City

BALL, JOSIAH
New York City, Boston

BANCROFT, OLIVER
New York City

BARBER, JOSEPH
New York City

BARBER, ROBERT
New York City

BARNHILL, GEORGE
Philadelphia

BATES, ISAAC
New York City

BEACH, CYRUS
New York City

BEAMONT, SAMUEL
New York City

BEASLEY, ———
Philadelphia

BEDFORD, JOSEPH
Philadelphia

BEEBE, LEWIS
New York City

BEEK, W.
New York City

BELCHER, JOSHUA
Boston

BELL, GEORGE
New York City

BELLAMY, EDWARD T.
New York City

BENJAMIN, EDWIN
New York City

BERESFORD, ROBERT H.
Philadelphia

BERNARD, JOHN
Philadelphia

BERRIMAN, JACOB M.
Philadelphia

BERTRAND, PETER
Philadelphia

BICKERTON, BENJAMIN
Philadelphia

BINNS, JOHN
Philadelphia

BLACKMAN, NATHAN L.
New York City

BLACKWELL, LEWIS
Philadelphia

BLAIR, WILLIAM
Philadelphia

BLAUVELT, J.
New York City

BLAUVELT, THOMAS
New York City

BLOOD, ———
New York City

BOATE, HORATIO
Philadelphia

BOLAND, ALEXANDER
Philadelphia, Baltimore

BOWEN, JOSIAH
New York City

BOWMAN, ABRAHAM
Philadelphia

BOWMAN, GODFREY
New York City

BOYD, JOHN
Philadephia

BRACKEN, HENRY
Philadelphia

BRADBURY, SAMUEL B.
Boston

BRADY, GEORGE
New York City

BRODERICK, JOHN
New York City

BRODERICK, JOSEPH
New York City

BROWN, JOHN
New York City

BROWN, JOHN JR.
New York City

BRUCE, DAVID
New York City

BRUCE, GEORGE
New York City

BRUCHOLTZ, BERNARD
Philadelphia

BRYSON, JAMES W.
Philadelphia

BUDD, HENRY
Philadelphia

BUELL, WILLIAM S.
New York City

BURBRIDGE, WILLIAM H.
New York City

BURDICK, WILLIAM
Boston

BURKE, FRANCIS
Washington

BURR, LEVI W.
New York City

BURTON, JAMES B.
Washington

BUSHELL, JOHN
Philadelphia

BUSK, JOHN
Baltimore

BUTLER, ABLE N.
New York City

BUTLER, A. J. W.
New York City

BYRNE, CHRISTOPHER
Washington

BYRNE, TIMOTHY
Philadelphia, New York City

CALLOW, GIRARD
New York City

CARLE, WILLIAM
Philadelphia

CARLL, SAMUEL P.
Boston

CAROTHERS, WILLIAM
Philadelphia

CARPENTER, ———
New York City

CARR, ROBERT
New York City

CARTER, JAMES B.
Washington

CARTER, THEOPHILIS
New York City

CHANDLER, ADONIRAM
New York City

CHATTERTON, PETER
New York City

CHEEVE, JAMES A.
New York City

CHILDS, JOHN
Philadelphia

CHURCHILL, GEORGE
Albany

CLAPP, AMOS
Boston

CLARK, CALVIN
New York City

CLARK, HORACE
Philadelphia

CLARK, LEMUEL E.
New York City

CLARK, MOSES
New York City

CLARKE, JOHN C.
Philadelphia

CLAYPOOLE, JOHN C.
Philadelphia

CLAYTON, EDWIN B.
New York City

CLAYTON, HENRY W.
New York City

CLAYTON, W. H.
New York City

CLINTON, JOHN
Philadelphia

CLOUGH, JOHN
New York City

COLBREATH, JOHN C.
New York City

COLBY, LUTHER
Boston

COLE, JOHN ORION
Albany

COLERICK, ARTHUR
Philadelphia

COLES, WILLIAM
Philadelphia

COLLECT, ISAAC
New York City

COLLIER, ———
New York City

COLLINS, ———
Philadelphia

COLLINS, JOHN
New York City

COLTON, JEDUTHAN
New York City

CONNELLY, ———
Philadelphia

CONRAD, EPHRAIM
Philadelphia

COOK, JOHN
Philadelphia
COOPER, ———
Philadelphia
COOPER, HENRY
Philadelphia
COOPER, JOHN
Philadelphia
COPLAND, JARED W.
New York City
CORBIN, CHARLES
New York City
CORNELY, WILLIAM
Philadelphia
CORRY, WALTER A.
Philadelphia
COSSART, THEOPHILIS
Philadelphia
COVERLY, JAMES C.
Philadelphia
COWAN, JOHN
New York City
COWDERLY, BENJAMIN
  FRANKLIN
New York City
COYLE, FRANCIS
Washington
CRAB, THOMAS
Philadelphia
CREE, DAVID
Philadelphia
CRISSY, JOHN E.
New York City
CROCKETT, WILLIAM D.
Boston
CROOKER, THOMAS G.
New York City
CROSSFIELD, JEHIEL
Philadelphia

CROSSIER, JOHN
Philadelphia
CUMMINGS, ENOCH
Philadelphia
CUMMINGS, THOMAS W.
New York City
CURTIS, JONATHON
New York City
DALTON, THOMAS F.
Philadelphia
DANN, JOHN
Philadelphia, New York City
DAVIES, SAMUEL H.
New York City
DAVIS, R.
Philadelphia
DAVIS, WILLIAM
Philadelphia
DAVISON, WILLIAM
Philadelphia
DAY, CALVIN
Baltimore
DEAN, THOMAS
Boston
DEAN, WILLIAM E.
New York City
DECKER, C. C.
New York City
DEGRUSHE, WILLIAM S.
New York City
DEJEANE, JOSEPH
New York City
DELANO, BENJAMIN
New York City
DEMING, ANSON N.
New York City
DENHAM, PETER
Philadelphia

DENNY, DANIEL
Philadelphia

DICKINSON, DAVID
Philadelphia

DICKINSON, SAMUEL
New York City

DICKSON, WILLIAM,
Philadelphia

DIXEY, WILLIAM
Philadelphia

DOBLEHOWER, CHARLES
Philadelphia

DODGE, ANDREW
New York City

DODGE, DANIEL
New York City

DONNINGTON, JOHN WICKLIFF
New York City

DOUGHERTY, WILLIAM
Washington

DOUGLAS, JOHN
Philadelphia

DOUGLAS, RICHARD
New York City

DOW, JOHN
Philadelphia

DOWELL, ALAN
Philadelphia, Baltimore

DOWNS, MILES G.
Philadelphia

DOYLE, JOHN
Philadelphia

DOYLE, JOHN B.
Philadelphia

DUFFEY, WILLIAM D.
Philadelphia

DUFFIE, DANIEL D.
New York City

DUFFY, MICHAEL
Philadelphia

DUHY, CHARLES W.
Philadelphia

DUKE, JAMES
New York City

DUNCAN, WILLIAM
New York City, Washington

DUNHAM, SILAS
New York City

DUSCOMBE, JOHN
New York City

EARLE, MORRIS F.
Philadelphia

EASTBURN, THOMAS
New York City

EATON, THEOPHILUS
New York City

EBNER, HENRY W. J.
Philadelphia

EDES, BENJAMIN
Baltimore

EGBERT, JOHN
New York City

ELLIOTT, JOHN M.
New York City

ENGELS, SILAS
Philadelphia

ERSKINE, JOHN
Washington

EUSTICE, GABRIEL
New York City

EVANS, JOHN
New York City

FAGAN, AUSTIN
Philadelphia

FAITHFUL, WILLIAM
Philadelphia

FANSHAW,[1] DANIEL
New York City

FANSHAW, JAMES
New York City

FANSHAW, WILLIAM
New York City

FARR, CHARLES W.
New York City

FARR, JOHN
New York City

FARWELL, J. H.
Boston

FEENEY, PATRICK
Philadelphia

FINDLAY, JAMES
New York City

FINK, CHARLES
Philadelphia

FINK, NICHOLAS
Philadelphia

FISH, ELIAKIM
Boston

FITZ-NEWCE, JOHN
Philadelphia

FLANAGAN, MICHAEL
New York City

FLETCHER, JOHN R.
New York City

FOLWELL, RICHARD
Philadelphia

FORBES, JOHN
New York City

FORCE, PETER
New York City

FOSTER, CRAWFORD
Philadelphia

FOSTER, THOMAS G.
Washington

FRANCIS, GEORGE
New York City

FRANK,[2] JACOB
New York City

FRANKS, LEWIS C. P.
Philadelphia

FRASER, ANDREW
New York City

FREEMAN, JOHN
Philadelphia

FREYMUTH, BENJAMIN F.
Philadelphia

FRITEZ, PETER F.
Philadelphia, Baltimore

FRYER, WILLIAM
Philadelphia

FULLERTON, S.
New York City

GALES, CHARLES
New York City

GALES, JOSEPH JR.
Philadelphia

GARRISON, ———
New York City

GARSON, HENRY
Philadelphia

GAVIN, GEORGE W.
Philadelphia

GIBBS, HANCE H.
Philadelphia

GIBBS, JOHN W.
Philadelphia

GIDEON, JACOB JR.
Washington

GILL, HENRY W.
Boston

GIRD, HENRY JR.
New York City

GLEASON, JOSEPH W. JR.
New York City

GOODRIDGE, J.
New York City

GRAHAM, ALEXANDER
Washington

GRAHAM, WILLIAM S.
Philadelphia

GRAVES, BARTHOLOMEW
Philadelphia

GRAY, EDWARD JR.
Baltimore

GRAY, NATHANIEL
New York City

GRAYSON, JOHN
Philadelphia, New York City

GREACEN, JOHN T.
Philadelphia

GREEN, NEAL
Philadelphia

GROWARD, G. H.
New York City

GULLEN, RICHARD
New York City

GUMBLETON, ROBERT
New York City

GUYON, ———
New York City

GUYON, JAMES
Philadelphia

HAGERTY, JOHN
Baltimore

HALL, ANDREW
New York City

HALL, SERJEANT
New York City

HAMILL, HENRY R.
New York City

HAMILL, JOHN
Philadelphia, New York City

HAMMOND, JOHN
New York City

HAND, SILAS B.
Philadelphia

HANDLEY, ———
New York City

HANLEY, JOHN H.
Philadelphia

HANNA, ANDREW
Baltimore

HANNUM, ISAAC G.
Philadelphia

HANSHAW, ———
New York City

HARDCASTLE, JOHN
New York City

HARDCASTLE, THOMAS
New York City

HARDIE, JAMES B.
New York City

HARMER, JOSEPH
New York City

HARRINGTON, WILLIAM
Philadelphia

HASWELL, THOMAS
Philadelphia

HAUPTMAN, JACOB
New York City

HAYDEN, SELIM
New York City

HAYDEN, SILAS
New York City

HAYES, PHILY, JR.
New York City

HAZEWELL, C. C.
Boston

HEDGERS, JEREMIAH
New York City
HENRY, PETER
Philadelphia
HENRY, THOMAS
New York City
HERRING, JAMES
Philadelphia
HEWES, JOHN
Baltimore
HEYER, WALTER W.
New York City
HILTON, JOHN
New York City
HINCKLEY, WILLIAM
Washington
HINES, JOHN
Washington
HIRLEY, JAMES
New York City
HITNER, GEORGE
Philadelphia
HOGAN, ANDREW
Philadelphia
HOLLOCK, ISAAC A.
New York City
HOLMES, JAMES
Baltimore
HOLT, JESSE
New York City
HOOD, NATHANIEL
Philadelphia
HOPKINS, ELLIOT
New York City
HOPPOCK, JOHN LAMBERT
Philadelphia
HOUGHTON, THEOPHILIS
Albany

HOWELL, CHARLES
New York City
HOWLAND, ———
Boston
HOYT, ICHABOD
New York City
HUESTIS, SAMUEL
New York City
HULL, SAMUEL P.
New York City
INGERSOLL, JONATHAN JR.
New York City
INNET, EDWARD
Philadelphia, New York City
IRVINE, BAPTIS
Philadelphia
JANSON, BENJAMIN G.
New York City
JANSON, T. B.
New York City
JENKINSON, JAMES N.
New York City
JOHNSON, JOHN I.
New York City
JOHNSON, RICHARD
Philadelphia, New York City
JOHNSON, SAMUEL B.
New York City
JONES, IRA
Philadelphia
JOYNER, NATHANIEL
New York City
JUSTICE, JOSEPH
Philadelphia
KAUFFELDT, NICHOLAS
Philadelphia
KENNEDY, ANDREW
Philadelphia

KENNEDY, JAMES
Baltimore

KENNEDY, THOMAS
Philadelphia, New York City

KEYSER, JOSEPH
Philadelphia

KING, GEORGE I.
New York City

KINSLEY, JOHN
Philadelphia

KNORR, HENRY
Philadelphia

KONKLE, PETER C.
Philadelphia, New York City, Washington

LANE, WILLIAM P.
Philadelphia

LANG, WILLIAM
Philadelphia

LATHAM, JOHN P.
New York City

LAUDER, FRANCIS
Philadelphia

LAWRENCE, ALEXANDER J.
Washington

LAWRENCE, DANIEL
Philadelphia

LEAKIN, SHEPPARD CHURCH
Baltimore

LEAKIN, THOMAS
Baltimore

LEARNED, WILLIAM
Boston

LEBRING, CORNELIUS C.
New York City

LECOUNT, SAMUEL
Philadelphia

LEE, CHARLES
Philadelphia

LEONARD, STEPHEN BANKS
Albany

LEWIS, HENRY L.
Washington

LEWIS, LEWIS
Philadelphia

LINCKE, GEORGE
New York City

LINTZ, JOHN
New York City

LITTLE, WILLIAM
Philadelphia

LIZZARD, SAMUEL
Philadelphia

LOEFLER, CHRISTIAN
New York City

LONGCOPE, SAMUEL
Philadelphia

LOOKER, JOHN M.
New York City

LORING, THOMAS
New York City

LOVE, ROBERT
Philadelphia

LOWER, BROOK W.
Philadelphia

LUCAS, J. D.
New York City

LUCIEN, ——
Philadelphia

LUCY, WILLIAM
New York City

LUND, HANS
New York City

MACK, EBENEZER
New York City

MAFFET, SAMUEL
Philadelphia

MARSELL, JOSEPHUS
Philadelphia

MARTIN, HENRY
Washington

MARTIN, JOHN N.
Philadelphia

MASSEY, JAMES
Baltimore

MATHER, ANDREW
New York City

MATHER, GEORGE
New York City

MAXWELL, ――――
New York City

MAXWELL, ROBERT
Philadelphia

MCBRIDE, WILLIAM
New York City

MCCALL, THOMAS
Philadelphia

MCCANN, ――――
Philadelphia

MCCLASKEY, JAMES
Philadelphia

MCCLASKEY, RICHARD
New York City

MCCONNELL, WILLIAM
New York City

MCDONALD, ――――
Philadelphia

MCDOUGALL, JOHN
New York City

MCDOUGALL, WILLIAM
New York City

MCELROY, JAMES P.
Philadelphia

MCELWEE, WILLIAM
Washington

MCGLASHAN, DANIEL
Albany

MCGLASSIN, GEORGE
Philadelphia

MCILVAINE, JOHN JR.
Philadelphia

MCKAY, JOHN
New York City

MCKAY, WILLIAM F.
New York City

MCKEE, HENRY
New York City

MCKENNA, DAVID
Washington

MCKENNAN, WILLIAM
Albany

MCKENZIE, ALEXANDER
Philadelphia

MCKENZIE, DANIEL
Philadelphia

MCKIBBON, JAMES
Philadelphia

MCLAUGHLIN, GEORGE
Philadelphia

MCLAUGHLIN, NATHANIEL
Philadelphia

MCNEIL, ――――
New York City

MCPHATRIDGE, THOMAS
Philadelphia

MEAD, H. G.
Philadelphia

MEARNS, JAMES
Philadelphia

MEEHAN, JOHN
New York City

MERRILL, OTIS B.
Philadelphia

MERRIT, SAMUEL
Philadelphia

MESIER, JAMES W.
New York City

MILLER, HENRY
Philadelphia

MILLER, JOHN
New York City

MILLER, PHILIP
Philadelphia

MILLER, WILLIAM A.
New York City

MITCHELL, ———
New York City

MOFFAT, JOHN
New York City

MOORE, DAVID
New York City

MOORE, E. N.
Boston

MOORE, SETH H.
Boston

MORRIS, JOHN A.
Philadelphia

MORRISON, JOHN
Washington

MORSE, EVANDER
New York City

MORTON, JAMES
Philadelphia

MULHOLLAN, JOHN
Philadelphia

MULLIGAN, PATRICK
Philadelphia

MUNROE, OTIS
New York City

MUNSON, JOHN
New York City

MURDEN, JOSEPH T.
New York City

MURPHY, ———
Philadelphia

MURRAY, ———
New York City

MYERS, WILLIAM
New York City

NASHEE, GEORGE
Philadelphia

NEIL,[4] WILLIAM
Philadelphia, New York City

NEILSON, R.
Baltimore

NESBIT, THOMAS
Philadelphia

NICHOLS, HENRY,
Philadelphia, Boston

NORTON, WILLIAM L.
Philadelphia

NORVELL, JOHN
Baltimore

NOWLAND, WILLIAM T.
Washington

OLIVER, AARON
New York City

O'NEIL, THOMAS
New York City

PACKARD, ROBERT
New York City

PALMER, JOHN P.
New York City

PARKE, WILLIAM R.
Philadelphia

PARKER, ———
New York City

PASTEUR, JOHN I.
New York City

PATER, STEPHEN A.
Philadelphia, New York City

PATTERSON, SAMUEL
New York City

PECHIN, WILLIAM
Baltimore

PECK, JOHN O.
New York City

PELL, JOHN
New York City

PENFORD, NICHOLAS B.
New York City

PERRIAM, J.
Philadelphia

PERRY, DAVID
New York City

PERRY, DAVID JR.
Philadelphia

PETERS, J. J.
New York City

PETTIGREW, JAMES
Philadelphia, Washington

PHILLIPS, GEORGE
Philadelphia

PIERSON, CALEB
New York City

PIGEON, JOHN
Philadelphia

PINKIND, MICHAEL
Philadelphia

PITMAN, ISAAC
Philadelphia

POLE, JOSEPH
New York City

POLLARD, CHARLES
New York City

POMROY, R.
New York City

PORTER, ———
Philadelphia

POTTER, ROBERT K.
Boston

PRIMROSE, JAMES
New York City

PRITCHARD, ———
New York City

PUDNEY, JOSEPH
New York City

PULHEMUS, JAMES
New York City

QUEAREAU, PHILIP F.
New York City, Boston

RASER, MATHIAS
Philadelphia

RAY, JOHN T.
Philadelphia

RAYSDALE, EDWIN
New York City

REA, SAMUEL
Philadelphia, Washington

REDMAN, BARNABAS
Philadelphia

REED, ALEXANDER
Philadelphia

REEDER, JESSE
Philadelphia

REINS, DAVID H.
New York City

REVELL, JOHN
Baltimore

REYNOLDS, JAMES R.
New York City

RIGHTER, WILLIAM
Washington

RILEY, HENRY
New York City

RILEY, PETER
New York City

RILEY, WILLIAM
Philadelphia

RINGWOOD, THOMAS
New York City

RIPLEY, HEZEKIAH
New York City

ROBERTS, THOMAS H.
Baltimore

ROBINSON, HOWARD S.
Boston

ROBINSON, JOHN
Philadelphia, New York City

ROBINSON, PATRICK L.
New York City

ROBINSON, WILLIAM
Philadelphia

ROGERS, THOMAS J.
Philadelphia

ROLLACK, ISAAC A.
New York City

ROSS, JOHN
Philadelphia

RUCKEL, SAMUEL
New York City

RULAND, EBENEZER
New York City

RUST, JOHN C.
New York City

SAGE, HARRIS
New York City

SAUNDERS, JOHN
Philadelphia

SCHNEIDER, ———
Philadelphia

SCOTT, ALEXANDER
Philadelphia

SCOTT, JOHN
Philadelphia

SCOTT, JOHN WELWOOD
Philadelphia

SEARING, AUGUSTUS P.
New York City

SEELY, ROBERT G.
Philadelphia

SEWALL, STEPHEN
Philadelphia

SEYMOUR, JOSEPH W.
New York City

SHERIER, FRANCIS
New York City

SHERMAN, JOHN H.
New York City

SICKLES, HENRY
New York City

SIDMAN, SAMUEL S.
Philadelphia

SIMONTON, ROBERT
New York City

SIMPSON, THOMAS G.
New York City

SINCLAIR, JAMES
Philadelphia

SINGLETON, GEORGE
Baltimore, Boston

SISK, JOHN
Philadelphia

SITCHER, ANDREW
New York City

SKINNER, WHITING
Philadelphia, Baltimore

SLADE, EDWARD
New York City

SLATER, JOEL
New York City

SLAUSEN, RUFUS
New York City

SLOTE, PETER
New York City

SMALL, PIERCE G.
New York City

SMITH, ———
New York City

SMITH, JAMES
New York City

SMITH, JOHN G.
New York City

SMITH, JOHN HARTLEY
Philadelphia

SMITH, NATHAN D.
New York City

SMITH, WILLIAM JR.
Philadelphia

SNOWDEN, THOMAS
New York City

SNYDER, ANDREW
Philadelphia

SOUTHWICK, HENRY COLLINS
New York City

SPRINGER, JOHN H.
New York City

STACY, MAHLON
Baltimore, New York City

STAHLY, CHRISTIAN
Philadelphia

STARR, SAMUEL
Philadelphia

STEED, HENRY
Philadelphia

STEEMER, ANTHONY
Philadelphia

STEINBERGH, JOHN P.
Albany

STEWART, JOHN B.
Philadelphia

STEWART, THOMAS
Philadelphia

STONE, SAMPSON
New York City

STORER, E. GILMAN C.
New York City

STORES, ROGER
New York City

SUTER, JOHN
Washington

SWAIN, E. C.
Baltimore

SWAINE, MORTINES
New York City

SWITZER, JOHN
Philadelphia

TATE, ANDREW
Washington

TEN EYCK, ABRAHAM
New York City

THAW, WILLIAM
Philadelphia

THEIL, HENRY
Philadelphia

THIELD, ———
New York City

THOMAS, WILLIAM
New York City

THOMPSON, GEORGE
Philadelphia

THOMPSON, HENRY
New York City

THOMPSON, JAMES
Philadelphia

THOMPSON, JOHN
New York City

THOMPSON, RICHARD
New York City

TILLGHMAN, JOHN W.
New York City

TINKER, JAMES
New York City

TOMAS, JOHN
New York City

TOMLIN, GEORGE
Philadelphia, Baltimore

TOMPKINS, WILLIAM
New York City

TOTTEN, NOAH
New York City

TOWN, THOMAS
Philadelphia

TREE, ROBERT
New York City

TURNER, JAMES
New York City

TURNEY, JAMES
New York City

VAN PELT, PETER
New York City

WADE, JOHN H.
Washington

WALKER, J. W.
New York City

WANDS, WILLIAM W.
Philadelphia

WANE, JOHN
Baltimore

WARNER, ERASMUS
New York City

WATT, ROBERT
New York City

WELDEN, JOHN W.
New York City

WEST, THOMAS
New York City

WHITE, GEORGE
Philadelphia, Albany

WHITELY, EDWARD
Philadelphia

WHITELY, JOHN
Philadelphia

WILKIE, JOHN J.
New York City

WILIAMS, ———
New York City

WILLIAMS, C. C.
New York City

WILLIAMS, JOHN H.
New York City

WILLIAMS, SAMUEL
New York City

WILLIAMS, WILLIAM B.
New York City

WILLIS, NATHANIEL JR.
Boston

WILSON, DANIEL
New York City

WILSON, GEORGE MOYES
Philadelphia

WILSON, JAMES
Philadelphia

WILSON, JOHN
Philadelphia

WILSON, SAMUEL
Philadelphia

WINNARD, JAMES
Philadelphia

WISE, F. A.
Baltimore

WOOD, W.
New York City

WOODS, JOHN
New York City

WOODWARD, THOMAS GREEN
New York City

WOODWORTH, SAMUEL
New York City

WOODWORTH, I.
New York City

WRIGHT, DAVID
Philadelphia

WRIGHT, JOHN
Philadelphia

Wrigley, Francis
Philadelphia

WYETH, GEORGE
Philadelphia

WYLIE, NATHANIEL
Baltimore

YARD, PEARSON
Philadelphia, New York City

YOULE, TIMOTHY
New York City

YOUNG, BENJAMIN
New York City

YOUNG, JAMES
Philadelphia

YOUNG, JOHN
New York City

YOUNG, WILLIAM
New York City

YOUNG, WILLIAM PRICE
Philadelphia

YUNDT, LEONARD
Philadelphia

Notes

PROLOGUE. The Art Preservative

1. Carl Van Doren, *Benjamin Franklin* (New York: Viking Press, 1938), 216.

2. The best single source on the colonial craft remains Isaiah Thomas, *History of Printing*, 2 vols. (Worcester, Massachusetts: printed by Isaac Sturtevant, 1810). Thomas, a printer and publisher, built a vast collection of rare materials that formed the basis for the impressive library of the American Antiquarian Society, which he founded in 1812. The corrections and comments sent to Thomas by other printers included "William McCulloch's Addition to Thomas' 'History of Printing'," *American Antiquarian Society Proceedings*, ed. Clarence S. Brigham, n.s. 31 (1921): 140; and "[Charles] Goddard's Contributions to Thomas' History of Printing," in *Journals and Journeymen: A Contribution to the History of Early American Newspapers*, ed. Clarence S. Brigham (Philadelphia: University of Pennsylvania Press, 1950), 99–107. Thomas's planned revision remained incomplete at his death in 1831, but Joel Munsell, an Albany printer who shared Thomas's interest in the history of the craft, published a new annotated edition in 1874. The American Antiquarian Society issued a new, reorganized one-volume edition in 1970. Although the recent edition is quite suitable for discussing the early establishment of printing in America, it lacks some of his and Munsell's curious data on postrevolutionary printers in the 1874 edition. Therefore, in this study, references to Thomas's study that lack a volume number refer to the reorganized 1970 edition,

while citations with a volume number refer to the more anecdotal Munsell edition. For other references used here, see: George Parker Winship, *The Cambridge Press, 1638-1692* (Philadelphia: University of Pennsylvania Press, 1945); Thomas, on the Cambridge press (43–45), on James Printer (90–93), and on Green (55, 66); and William C. Kissel, "The Green Family: A Dynasty of Printers," *New England Historical and Genealogical Register* 104 (April 1950): 81–93.

3. Thomas, 79–81, 81–82, 105–10, and on Salem and Newburyport, 176–77, 179; and Carl Bridenbaugh, *Cities in Revolt: Urban Life in America, 1743–1776*, 2d ed. (London, Oxford, New York: Oxford University Press, 1971), 291.

4. Thomas, 340–42, 343–55.

5. Thomas, 457–58, 461–64.

6. Thomas, 335–56.

7. Thomas, 387–89. See also the section on Ephrata in Julius Friedrich Sachse, *The German Sectarians of Pennsylvania: A Critical and Legendary History of the Ephrata Cloister and the Dunkers*, 2 vols. (Philadelphia: printed for the Author, 1899–1900), vol. 2.

8. See Table 1. This data is from Evans's *American Bibliography.*

9. Thomas, 379–80, 390–91; and McCulloch, 137–38, 140.

10. See Table 2.

11. Thurlow Weed Barnes, *Memoir of Thurlow Weed* (Boston: Houghton, Mifflin and Co., 1884), 5.

12. John W. Francis, *Old New York; or, Reminiscences of the Past Sixty Years* (New York: W. J. Widdleton, 1865), 364; *Walt Whitman's New York, From Manhattan to Montauk*, ed. Henry M. Christman (Freeport, New York: Books for Libraries Press, 1972; originally published 1963), 48; on Hartshorne's membership, New York Typographical Society minutes for 1809–1818, MS, Special Collections, Milton S. Eisenhower Library, Johns Hopkins University, Baltimore, May 28, June 1, 1816, (hereafter NYTS); and Thurlow Weed's description of Jonathan Seymour's paternalism, *Autobiography of Thurlow Weed*, Harriet A. Weed, ed., (Boston: Houghton, Mifflin and Co., 1883), 57.

13. Quoted in Paul W. Conner, *Poor Richard's Politicks: Benjamin Franklin and His New American Order*, 2d ed. (London, Oxford and New York: Oxford University Press, 1969), 215.

14. See Rollo Silver, *Typefounding in America, 1787–1825* (Charlottesville, Virginia: published for the Bibliographical Society of the University of Virginia, 1965).

15. An excellent guide to the development of this machine is James Moran, *Printing Presses: History and Development from the Fifteenth Century to Modern Times*, 2d ed. (Berkeley and Los Angeles: University of California Press, 1978).

16. Alfred Lawrence Lorenz, *Hugh Gaine: A Colonial Printer-Editor's Odyssey to Loyalism* (Carbondale and Edwardsville, Illinois: Southern

Illinois University Press, 1972), 4; and Milton W. Hamilton, *The Country Printer: New York State, 1785–1830* (New York: Columbia University Press, 1936), 45.

17. Letter from Henry D. Barron, quoted in *The History of Waukesha County, Wisconsin* (Chicago: Western Historical Company, 1880), 563.

18. Quotes from Rollo G. Silver, *The American Printer, 1787–1825* (Charlottesville, Virginia: published for the American Bibliographical Society of the University of Virginia by the University Press of Virginia, 1967), 4; and Weed, 22. See also David Brody's discussion of "Time and Work during Early American Industrialization," *Labor History* 30 (Winter 1989): 5–46.

19. The older men include Charles Pierce, Samuel Williams, Thurlow Weed, Theophilus Cossart, George Mather, Francis Wrigley, and William Hartshorne. Joel Munsell, *Typographical Miscellany* (Albany: J. Munsell, 1850), 84; Weed, 44, 48; McCulloch, 216, 140; *Columbian Centinel*, October 7, 1829; and Whitman, 46–47. See also the obituaries for Thomas G. Woodward, William E. Dean, Charles McDevitt, William Wood, and Samuel Williams in the *Printers' Circular* 7 (March 1872): 19, and (January 1873): 402; 11 (September 1876): 188; 12 (May 1877): 64; and 13 (July 1878): 106. On Theophilus L. Houghton, see M. W. Hamilton, 278. On McDevitt, see *Tribute to the Memory of Charles McDevitt, who was nearly Sixty Years a Member of the New York Typographical Society* (New York: F. Hart & Co., Printers, 1877). The *Printers' Circular* noted some of the activities of his final years with formal testimonials, 2 (November, December 1867): 319, 337–39; his speech at the anniversary of Franklin's birthday, 2 (February 1868): 391–92; and his continued participation in the New York Typographical Society, 6 (May 1871): 115–16. For obituaries of the younger men, see the *Columbian Centinel*, as follows: Alexander Boland (died at age 48) November 9, 1808; Elliot Hopkins (41) March 11, 1815; John Morrison (24) January 10, Samuel Bradbury (33) May 18, Thomas Abercrombie (36) August 10, James Mearns (43) 14, 1816; John Revell (30) April 29, 1818; John Moffat (38) December 8, 1819; Henry C. Southwick (45) February 3, 1821; Eliakim Fish (33) February 28, Henry Nichols (33) March 6, 1822; Samuel Fullerton (42) March 5, 1823; James Pettigrew (39) February 4, 1824; Philip F. Quereau (36) May 13, 1826; William Neil (40) June 6, 1827; John P. Latham (38) July 22, 1832; William Kerr, Jr. (42) April 6, George Nashee (40) November 13, 1833; and Edward S. Bellamy (39) March 28, 1835. The Philadelphia Typographical Society also marked the graves of three early members in its plots: James McKinnon (47) in April 1828; Francis "Wrigly" (86) September 1829; and John "McIlvane" (57) August 1836. See Charles R. Barker, "Inscriptions in Ronaldson's Cemetery, Philadelphia," from *Pennsylvania Genealogical Magazine 9*, in *Pennsylvania Vital Records*, 3 vols. (Baltimore: Geneaological Publishing Co., 1983), 3:515. Early

mortality has been a hotly disputed point between the discontented in the craft and its promoters. In the middle of the nineteenth century, for example, Charles Turrell, defended "The Longevity of American Printers" at a New York City Printers' Festival, Munsell, 81–84. The life expectancy estimate given here is reprinted from Gilbert Vale, *Independent Beacon* 1 (July 1850): 355.

20. Weed, 53, 54.

21. Seymour Martin Lipset, Martin Trow, and James Coleman, *Union Democracy: The Internal Politics of the International Typographical Union*, 2d ed. (Garden City, New York: Anchor Books, Doubleday & Co., 1962), 137, 139.

22. *The Autobiography of Horace Greeley, or Recollections of a Busy Life. To Which are Added Miscellaneous Essays and Papers* (New York: E. B. Treat, 1872), 84; and John Bach McMaster, *A History of the People of the United States: From the Revolution to the Civil War*, 2d ed., 8 vols. (New York: D. Appleton & Co., 1895–1913), 1:97. See also John K. Alexander, "Poverty, Fear, and Continuity: An Analysis of the Poor in Late Eighteenth Century Philadelphia," in *The People of Philadelphia: A History of Ethnic Groups and Lower Class Life, 1790–1840*, ed. Allen F. Davis and Mark H. Haller (Philadelphia: Temple University Press, 1973), 17; and Frank Monaghan and Martin Lowenthal, *This Was New York, the Nation's Capital in 1789* (Garden City, New York: Doubleday, Doran & Co., 1943), 50–59.

23. Henry Rosemont, "Benjamin Franklin and the Typographical Strike of 1786," *Labor History* 22 (Summer 1981): 401–02.

24. Thomas Cooper in *The City in American History*, ed. Blake McKelvey (London: George Allen and Unwin; New York: Barnes and Noble, 1969), 132; Monaghan and Lowenthal, 81, 77; Weed, 53–54; and Gaillord Hunt, *Life in America One Hundred Years Ago* (New York and London: Harper & Bros., Publishers, 1914), 218.

25. Rodman Gilder, *The Battery: the Story of the adventurers, artists, . . . who played their parts during full four centuries on Manhattan island's tip* (Boston: Houghton, Mifflin Co., 1936), 132, 141; John F. Watson, *Annals of Philadelphia and Pennsylvania, in the Olden time; Being a Collection . . . Intended to Preserve the Recollection of Olden Times, and to Exhibit society in its change of Manners and Customs. . . .*, 2 vols. (Philadelphia: Carey, 1845), 1:405–07; and J. H. Powell, *Bring Out Your Dead: The Great Plague of Yellow Fever in Philadelphia in 1793*, 2d ed. (New York: Times Inc., 1965), 47, 57. See also Sidney I. Pomerantz, *New York, An American City, 1783–1803: A Study in Urban Life* (New York: Columbia University Press, 1936), 216–17.

26. Ethelbert Stewart, "A Documentary History of Early Organizations of Printers," U.S. *Department of Commerce and Labor Bulletin* 11 (November 1905): 944, 951.

27. M. Dorthy George, *London Life in the Eighteenth Century*, 3d ed. (London: Lund Humphreys, 1951), 200, and quoted 199.

28. *Recollections of the Life of John Binns: Twenty-Nine Years in Europe and Fifty-Three in the United States. Written by Himself, with Anecdotes, Political Historical and Miscellaneous* (Philadelphia: printed by Parry and M'Millan, 1854), 341; and Weed, 54.

29. Washington Irving, quoted in Gilder, 128, 108–09; on Wood Charles McDevitt, "Reminiscences of the Typographical Society," *The Printer* 5 (February 1864): 51–52.

30. See Watson, 1:485–89; and Weed, 52.

31. J. Thomas Scharf and Thompson Westcott, *History of Philadelphia*, 3 vols. (Philadelphia: L. H. Evarts & Co., 1884), 2:982–92.

32. Weed, 59.

33. Silver, *The American Printer*, 38–40.

34. Thomas, 1:104, 105.

35. *Mechanick Exercises, on the Whole Art of Printing [1683–84]*, ed. Herbert Davis and Harry Carter, 2d ed. (London: Oxford University Press, 1962). Weed noted that old drinking practices were "not yet reformed" in the New York City craft during 1815 and 1816. Pp. 58–59.

36. John Clough, *An Address, Delivered on the Fourth of July, 1801, Before the Franklin Typographical Society of New-York, and a Select Company* (New York: George F. Hopkins, 1801), 15; "History of the Philadelphia Typographical Society," *Printers' Circular* 2 (April 1867), 195n.

37. George Churchill, *An Address, Pronounced before the Albany Typographical Society, November 6, 1813; on the Advantages Resulting to Mankind from the Invention of Printing* (Albany: n.p., 1813), 4; William Burdick, *An Oration on the Nature and Effects of the Art of Printing. Delivered in Franklin-Hall, July 5, 1802, Before the Boston Franklin Association* (Boston: Munroe and Francis, 1802), 15; Weed, 59; and Binns, 18, 19. Other crafts claimed similar traditions. Cordwainers, for example, enjoyed a reputation for literacy and intelligence. An early nineteenth-century commentator noted that the craft, "being a sedantary and comparatively noiseless one, may be considered as more favourable than some others to meditation," and to "literary productiveness" among its practitioners. Also, as "a trade of light labor," it attracted "persons in humble life who are conscious of more mental than bodily strength." *The Book of the Feet: A History of Boots and Shoes, . . . Also Hints to Last-Makers, and Remedies for Corns, Etc. by J. Sparks Hall. With a History of Boots and Shoes in the United States, . . .* (New York: William S. Graham, 1847), 4; Graham, the American printer who used the second London edition for his work and probably wrote the section on boots and shoes in this country, may

have been the William S. Graham who had joined the Philadelphia printers' society over forty years earlier.

38. "Wanted—A Printer," *The Printer: A Monthly Newspaper devoted to the interests of the "Art Preservative of all Arts"* 6 (April 1866): 165. A glimpse at the sort of material to which they were exposed can be obtained by comparing the names of the known participants in early labor activities to those in Roger P. Bristol, *Index of Printers, Publishers and Booksellers Indicated by Charles Evans in American Bibliography* (Charlottesville, Virginia: Bibliographical Society of America, 1961), referring to Charles Evans, *American Bibliography: a Chronological Dictionary of All Books, Pamphlets, and Periodical publications . . . down to and including the year 1920 . . .*, vol. 14 (Chicago: printed by Blakely Press, 1903–1959). This, of course, indicates only works printed in shops belonging to former or future members of journeymen's printers' societies, and fails to represent the scope of works on which they were employed. The American printers of this period offer the most unavoidable illustration of E. P. Thompson's point that "the working class did not rise like the sun at an appointed time. It was present at its own making." *The Making of the English Working Class* (New York: Vintage Books, 1963), 9–11. Other studies of labor in the Old World particularly helpful in formulating this study were C. B. Dobson, *Masters and Journeymen: A Prehistory of Industrial Relations, 1717–1818* (London: Croom Helm, and Totowata; New Jersey: Rowman and Littlefield, 1980); and William H. Sewall Jr., *Work and Revolution in France: The Language of Labour from the Old Regime to 1848* (Cambridge, London, and New York: Cambridge University Press, 1980).

39. David Bruce, Jr., "Reminiscences of Thomas Paine," *The Truth Seeker* 6 (February 8, 1879): 87; Francis, lxxxiii, 141–42; NYTS, May 18, June 1, 1816; *Walt Whitman's New York,* 47; Freneau's *New Year Verses;* and "Still Another," an obituary of William Bradford, "the oldest printer in New Jersey" who died at Trenton at the age of eighty. *The Printer* 1 (March 1859): 249.

40. See also McCulloch, 140; on Robert Carr as Franklin's messenger, see his obituary in the *Printers' Circular* 1 (March 1866), 11; and Scharf and Westcott, 1: 460–61. The father of Nathaniel P. Willis, the Boston trade unionist was also a printer and had served his apprenticeship in the same shop as Franklin. See the obituary for his son, the famous poet, in the *Printers' Circular* 1 (February 1867): 165.

41. Burdick, 24, 25–26, 27. Not only did such Americans hail Franklin as "the patron of our art," but others—even the printers of Paris in the midst of the French Revolution—claimed him as one of their own. Van Doren, *Benjamin Franklin,* 781.

42. Ebenezer Mack, *An Oration, Delivered Before the New-York Typographical Society, on the Fifth of July, 1813, In Celebration of the*

Thirty-Seventh Anniversary of American Independence, and Fourth of the Society (New York: S. Woodworth and Co., 1813), 5–6.

43. Mack, 11, 13–14.

44. Churchill, 7, 8.

45. By his death in 1790, Franklin knew that hard work alone was insufficient to rise in the world. To his will, he added a long codicil establishing funds in Boston and Philadelphia for loans to "such young married artificers, under the age of twenty-five years, as have served an apprenticeship in the said town, and faithfully fulfilled the duties required in their indentures, so as to obtain a good moral character from at least two respectable citizens who are willing to become their sureties." Van Doren, Benjamin Franklin, 762. See also, 762–64; and Rosemont's "Benjamin Franklin and the Typographical Strike of 1786."

ONE. Birds of Passage

1. Clarence S. Brigham, *History and Bibliography of American Newspapers*, 2 vols., consecutively paged (Worcester: American Antiquarian Society, 1947), 1485; Stevens, 36, 37–38; Hamilton, 89n, 299; and *Half-Century Souvenir and First Historical Year-Book of the Albany Typographical Union Number Four*, ed. Charles H. Whittemore, et al, (Albany: J. B. Lyons Co., 1905), 11. Weed recalled Southwick's "great talents, popular manners, and munificent . . . hospitalities and charities" but noted that he had believed "himself to be both a practical farmer and a Christian, while in face he was simply a theorist in agriculture and an ethusiast in religion," 43–44, 46. During one of his stays in New York City, Southwick joined the old General Society of Mechanics, probably during an interlude as a master printer. *Annals of the General Society of Mechanics and Tradesmen of the City of New-York, From 1785 to 1880*, ed. Thomas Earle and Charles T. Congdon (New York: Published by Order of the Society, 1882), 411. See also M. W. Hamilton, 182; and Southwick's obituary in the *Columbian Centinel*, February 3, 1821. He and his family were particularly good friends of Joel Munsell, the Albany publisher, journalist, and historian of the craft.

2. See Table 3.

3. U.S. Department of Commerce and Labor, Bureau of the Census, *A Century of Population Growth: From the First Census of the United States to the Twelfth* (Washington: Government Printing Office, 1909).

4. *New York Herald*, February 6, 1802. See also *New York Gazette and General Advertiser*, January 28, 1802; and *Commercial Advertiser*, January 20, 1803. Bruce Laurie offers a useful, if brief, look at developments during the early national period in his synthesis of recent work in *Artisans into Workers: Labor in Nineteenth Century America* (New York: Hill and Wang, 1989).

5. Lawrence C. Wroth, *The Colonial Printer* (Portland, Maine: Lakeside Press, 1973; originally published 1911), 84; cited in Silver, *The American Printer*, 40, 44, 46–49; and on early experiments with small cylinder presses, 42–44, 45.

6. Silver, *The American Printer*, 33, 30.

7. Edwin Wolf II, *The Annual Report of the Library Company of Philadelphia for the Year 1965* (Philadelphia: Library Company of Philadelphia, 1966), 40–41; *The Constitution of the Company of Printers* (Philadelphia: printed by William W. Woodward, 1794), reprinted in E. Stewart, 861–63n; and Silver, *The American Printer*, 83–89.

8. Charles L. Nichols, "The Literary Fairs in the United States," in *Bibliographical Essays: A Tribute to Wilberforce Ames* (Cambridge: printed by the Harvard University Presses, 1924); and Francis, 353.

9. *The Constitution, Proceedings &c. of the Philadelphia Company of Printers & Booksellers* ([Philadelphia]: printed by Daniel Humphreys, 1793); cited in Silver, *The American Printer*, 84. The company met on Mondays, April 1, July 1, and October 7, 1793, and, despite its inability to muster a quorum on January 6 of the new year, on April 7, 1794. Humphreys printed these proceedings, first as broadsides and later as part of a second edition of the *Constitution, Proceedings &c. of the Philadelphia Company of Printers & Booksellers* that appeared in 1794.

10. Silver, *The American Printer*, 78–81 and, on Philadelphia, E. Stewart, 862n–63n.

11. *Mercantile Advertiser*, January 15, 1802.

12. See Table 4, based on Harry B. Weiss, *The Number of Persons and Firms Connected with the Graphic Arts in New York City, 1633–1820* (New York: New York Public Library, 1946), 13. This work based its calculations primarily on the extensive compilation of entries in the city directories published in *A Register of Artists, Engravers, Booksellers, Bookbinders, Printers and Publishers in New York City, 1633–1820*, comp. George Leslie McKay (New York: New York Public Library, 1942). See also H. Glenn Brown, "Philadelphia's Contribution to the Book Arts and Book Trade," *Papers of the Bibliographic Society of America* 37 (1943): 275–92.

13. Compare the signatures reproduced in E. Stewart, 865, to James Robinson, *The Philadelphia Directory, City and County Register, for 1802*. (Philadelphia: printed by William W. Woodward, 1802); and *The Philadelphia Directory, City and County Register, for 1803* (Philadelphia; printed by William W. Woodward, 1803). It should also be remembered that the compilers and printers of city directories may have been more likely to list their fellow printers than hired workmen in other crafts. For estimates that roughly half of Philadelphia craftsmen had their own shops, see Thomas Smith, "Reconstructing Occupational Structures: The Case of the Ambiguous Artisans," *Historical Methods Newsletter* 7 (June 1975): 137; Stuart H. Blumin, "Mobility

and Change in Antebellum Philadelphia," in *Nineteenth Century American Cities*, ed. Stephen Thernstrom and Richard Sennet (New Haven: Yale University Press, 1969): 37. Billie G. Smith makes a similar case in "The Material Limits of Laboring Philadelphia, 1750 to 1800," *William and Mary Quarterly*, 3d ser. 38 (1981): 197, but the time span covered makes the argument more plausible, at least for the earlier years; the implications for upward mobility of a high proportion of masters to journeymen would also contradict somewhat Smith's balanced assessment of "The Vicissitudes of Fortune: The Careers of Laboring Men in Philadelphia, 1750–1800," in *Work and Labor in Early America*, ed. Stephen Innes (Williamsburg: Institute of Early American History and Culture, 1988), 221–51.

14. Thomas, 1:154–55, 249, and for Elizabeth, the sister of John Bushell, one of the 1786 strikers, see p. 358. Bushell learned his craft in a shop which employed "an African" named Primus. Thomas, 1:130–31. McCulloch also referred to women in the trades, 194, 217, and to blacks, 175.

15. NYTS, December 22, 1810, March 16, April 6, November 30, December 17, 1816, February 1, and November 1, 1817. For Hardcastle, see *The New-York Directory, and Register, for 1792. Illustrated with a New and Accurate Plan of the City, and part of Long-Island. . . . By William Duncan* (New York: printed by Thomas and J[ames] Swords, 1792); the same publisher's *New-York Directory, and Register, for 1793, 1794, 1795; Longworth's American Almanack, New-York Register, and City Directory* (New York: printed by Thomas and J[ames] Swords, 1797); and Longworth's for 1798. On McKenzie, see the proceedings of October 7, 1809, in the Philadelphia Typographical Society minutes for 1802–[1804/1806]–1810, MS, Special Collections, Milton S. Eisenhower Library, Johns Hopkins University, Baltimore (hereafter PTS). Early unions usually acknowledged apprenticeships served abroad, but, as late as 1818, the Washington printers hotly debated the acceptability of John Fleming's Irish training, and only the president's deciding vote in his favor admitted him to membership. E. Stewart, 892. See, too, the *Constitution of the Columbia Typographical Society. . . .* (Washington: Columbia Typographical Union, 1866), 55.

16. In seeking information on the hundreds of participants in these societies, I rarely found men who clearly fit those categories. On the Aitken family, see Thomas, 1:266–67, McCulloch, 96–97, and, Scharf and Westcott, 3:1973. Other active unionists like Henry C. Southwick learned the trade from his father. Robert Maxwell, James W. Mesier, and John Collins may have been related to prominent printers of the previous generation like Hugh Maxwell, Peter Mesier, and Isaac Collins. Thomas, 1:88–91, 186–91, 321–22, and 196–201.

17. Charles Brockden Brown, *Arthur Mervyn; or, Memoirs of the Year 1793*, 3d ed., 2 vols. (Philadelphia: D. McKay, 1887), 1:22; and "Circular:

To the Master Printers of the City of New York," in NYTS, July 13, 1811.

18. Arthur Colerick, William Fryer, and Joseph Gales, Jr. served British apprenticeships, according to the records of their admission to the union in PTS. On Gales, Samuel Lecount, and Francis Wrigley's English backgrounds, see *Stationers Company Apprentices, 1701–1800*, ed. D. F. Mackenzie, *Oxford Bibliographical Society Publications* 19 (1978): 124, 263, 290. On the Irish apprenticeships and backgrounds of Nathaniel Hood, James Winnard, John Binns, Timothy Byrne, and John Fleming, see Binns, 14–28; Boland's obituary in the *Columbian Centinel*, November 9, 1808; Stewart, 892; and the appropriate admission notices in the PTS. On George and David Bruce, sons of an Edinburgh tanner, see three pieces in *The Printer:* the untitled biographical sketch of David Bruce on which he had collaborated; George Bruce's "Art of Type Founding," and "George Bruce: A Sketch of His Life," 1 (March, April, 1859): 257–59, 281–82, and 6 (October, 1866): 177–80, the basis of the account in Stevens, 38, which included their pictures opposite pp. 36 and 38. John Albright, a striking printer of 1786, was Johann Albrecht. His comrade Leonard Yundt had come from Basel, Switzerland, and Henry Ebner, one of their successors in the Typographical Society formed in 1802, was from Dusseldorf. See McCulloch, on Yundt, 184, 233, 237, 246, and on Albrecht, 175. A. Rachel Minick, *A History of Printing in Maryland, 1791–1800* (Baltimore: Enoch Pratt Free Library, 1949) discusses Yundt's career in Baltimore; and Charles R. Roberts, *History of Lehigh County, Pennsylvania*, 3 vols. (Allentown: Lehigh Valley Publishing Co., 1914) 1:278, notes Ebner's background. See also Goddard, 102. Mearns's obituary is in the *Columbian Centinel*, August 14, 1816. On Doublebower, see "The Printers of Philadelphia." John Gracean gained admission as simply having served an apprenticeship in Europe, PTS, May 28, 1808.

19. Weed, 58; and Francis, xix. While a journeyman, Francis probably had some connection to the old New York Typographical Association or to the Franklin Typographical Society, for the New York Typographical Society, formed in 1809, held him in high esteem. For its sponsorship of a speech on his life and accomplishments by Charles McDevitt on February 9, 1861, see pp. cxviii–xcix, and, for its participation as a group at his funeral, p. cxxxv.

20. On Churchill, see *Centennial History of Madison County, Illinois and Its People, 1812 to 1912*, ed. Wilbur T. Norton (Chicago: Lewis Publishing Co., 1912), 54, 85, 101, 135–38, 140, 163, 167, 200, 202–03; Munsell, 121, 122–23; and J. T. Hair, *Gazetteer of Madison County* (Alton, Illinois: J. T. Hair, 1866), 286–89.

21. One does periodically catch glimpses of union printers moving westward. George Nashee reached Columbus, Ohio; John M. Looker and Elliot Hopkins, Cincinnati; and Nathan Blackman, Vincennes,

Indiana. Like Norvel, Benjamin Delano sought success in Detroit. After Churchill's appearance in Madison County, Illinois, Hezekiah Ripley arrived at Belvidere, Sergeant Hall at St. Louis, and Garrit W. Ryckman in distant San Francisco. William Tompkins and Peter Bertran turned up in Kentucky, the latter moving on into Alabama where Joseph DeGeane also strived to secure a shop. Eliakim Fish went to Baton Rouge; Robert Packard, the West Indies; and Charles Pollard, Havana. For their Latin American adventures, see below, chapter 3. Also, Charles W. Duhy, Thomas Woodward, Ichabod Hoyt, William Neil, and Alvan Munroe reached New Orleans, where the influx of printers no doubt contributed to their organization of the New Orleans Typographical Society, discussed in PTS, June 30, 1810. See also Frederick Follett, *History of Printing in Western New-York, from the Beginning to the Middle of the Nineteenth Century* (Rochester: printed by Jerome & Brothers, Daily American office, 1847), 33, 39, 52. On these individuals, see: on Blackman, Henry S. Cauthorn, *History of the City of Vincennes, Indiana from 1702 to 1901* ([Vincennes?]: M. C. Cauthorn, 1902), 58–59; on Delano, Joel Andrew Delano, *The Genealogy, History, and Alliances of the American House of Delano, 1621 to 1899* (New York: n.p., 1899), 437; on Ripley, Follett, 39; on "Rykeman," NYTS, February 1, 1817, and Weed, 49–50; on Hoyt, McDevitt's "Reminiscences of the Typographical Society," 51; on the locations of their newspapers, Brigham, 1372, 1378, 1401, 1406, 1424, 1459; and on the locations of their deaths, the obituaries in the *Columbian Centinel* for August 9, 1800, March 11, 1815, May 3, 1820, July 7, 1821, August 28, 1822, September 24, 1823, June 6, 1827, and November 13, 1833.

22. Weed, 58. The conclusion about unionists upstate comes from a comparison of the known participants in early labor organization to the names in "Appendix I: Printers, Editors, and Publishers of Country Newspapers, New York, 1785–1830," in M. W. Hamilton, 253–309.

23. On Wrigley, see McCulloch, 140. For some of the ages of unionists, see the various obituaries cited above, as compared to their initial participation in trade organizations. Biographical data on a few additional members are in the New York City Jury Lists for 1816 and 1819, Historical Documents Collections, Queens College, New York City.

24. Quoted by Silver, *The American Printer*, 13.

25. Weed, 57, 59. See also Barnes, 5. For wage scales, see Stevens, 58; E. Stewart, 865; and the sources cited in the course of discussing various labor disputes in chapter 2.

26. Monaghan and Lowenthal, 73, 72.

27. Watson, 2:420–21; Thomas A. Javier, *In Old New York* (New York: Harper & Brothers, 1894), 201, and quote from 48; Monaghan and Lowenthal, 35, 31; J. H. Powell, *Bring Out Your Dead*, 21; Alexander, 11; and James Ford, *Slums and Housing, with Special References to New York City: History, Conditions, Policy*, 2 vols. (Westport,

Connecticut: Negro Universities Press, 1971; originally published 1936), 64.

28. Powell, *Bring Out Your Dead*, 10; and Binns, 284.

29. Ford, 74, 66, 62, 64–65; Monaghan and Lowenthal, 37; Weed, 53; and Javier, 48.

30. Javier, 49, 53–54; Monaghan and Lowenthal, 36–37; Gilder, 126; and Powell, *Bring Out Your Dead*, 13.

31. Quoted Ford 79, 80, 63. See also Christopher Tunnard and Henry Hope Reed, *American Skyline: The Growth and Forms of Our Cities and Towns*, 3d ed. (New York: Mentor Books, 1956), 64.

32. Powell, *Bring Out Your Dead*, 45, 234; Alexander, 18, 32; Sam Bass Warner, *The Private City: Philadelphia in Three Periods of Its Growth* (Philadelphia: University of Pennsylvania Press, 1968), 15, 56; and his "If All the World Was Philadelphia: A Scaffolding for Urban History, 1774–1930," *American Historical Review* 74 (1968–69): 33.

33. See *Pennsylvania 1800 Census*, ed. Ronald Vern Jackson 2 vols. (Salt Lake City: Gend-ex, 1972); and *Philadelphia Directory, City and County Register, for 1802*.

34. Tunnard and Reed, 67; George Rogers Taylor, "The Beginnings of Mass Transportation in Urban America: Part I," *Smithsonian Journal of History* (Summer 1966), 38; Alan Kulikoff, "The Progress of Inequality in Revolutionary Boston," *William and Mary Quarterly*, 3d series, 18 (July 1971): 375–412, 384; Howard B. Rock, *Artisans of the New Republic: The Tradesmen of New York City in the Age of Jefferson* (New York: New York University Press, 1979), 72; and Ford, 61, 62. Rock's title, together with Charles G. Steffen, *The Mechanics of Baltimore: Workers and Politics in the Age of Revolution, 1763–1812* (Urbana: University of Illinois Press, 1984) offer considerable new information about early American workers' organizations through a relatively thorough exploration of the available sources. Their achievement in this contrasts with that of studies that embrace the early national period but cover a longer and later period, like Sean Wilentz, *Chants Democratic: New York City & the Rise of the American Working Class, 1788–1850* (New York: Oxford University Press, 1984); Bruce Laurie, *The Working People of Philadelphia, 1800–1850* (Philadelphia: Temple University Press, 1980); or Laurie's general synthesis of new scholarship in *Artisans into Workers*. The relative abundance of later sources naturally tended to draw the attention of such historians toward the later period at the expense of the early national period. The work of Rock and Steffen arguably went much further in addressing Sanford Cohen's complaint that "much that is vague about the formation of the first labor organizations in the United States, and labor historians have yet to work out a totally satisfactory explanation." *Labor in the United States* (Columbus, Ohio: C. E. Merrill Books, 1960), 71–72.

35. Powell, *Bring Out Your Dead*, 15–16; Ford, 61; and quote from Monaghan and Lowenthal, 32, 37.

36. Quoted from Ford, 64, 65, 62, 89–90. For similar hovels on a grand scale, see George, 85–91.

37. McDevitt's "Reminiscences of the Typographical Society," 51.

38. Weed, 52.

39. Quoted in Ford, 89–90.

40. Rock, 252–53, based on the account in the *American Citizen,* April 10, 1809. For an account of such costs in an earlier period, see Main, 115–18.

41. Silver, *The American Printer,* 9, 93.

42. Munsell, 91.

43. Weed, 55.

44. See Rosemont, 406–10; *A Documentary History of American Industrial Society,* ed. John R. Commons, et al. 2nd ed., 10 vols. (New York: Russell and Russell, 1958) 7:113, 114, a source representing an estimated tenth of the sources compiled by this team in their unprecedented Labor Collection now at the Historical Society of Wisconsin, Madison; the published collection, however, represents almost all of the items gathered for the period prior to 1820. Also, "R. M. Poer's Remarks" in "The Printers' Union—Mass Meeting in the City Hall Park," *The Printer* 4 (September 1864): 135.

45. Silver, *The American Printer,* 64–65.

46. Brigham, 1367–1508. Josiah Ball is an example of the failure of the newspaper publishers' list to include all of the "successful" men, having issued a magazine, the *Columbian Museum,* from his Boston office. See Benjamin M. Lewis, *A Register of Editors, Printers, and Publishers of American Magazines, 1741–1810* (New York: New York Public Library, 1957), 9.

47. *Trial of Twenty-Four Journeymen Tailors, Charged with a Conspiracy: Before the Mayor's Court of the City of Philadelphia, September Session, 1827* (Philadelphia: n.p., 1827), in *Doc. Hist.* 4:204.

48. Allen C. Clark, "Joseph Gales, Junior, Editor and Mayor," *Records of the Columbia Historical Society* 23 (1920): 5, 98–101, 123, 139; Brigham, 1377, 1416; and Binns, 2, 196. Other "successful" men also had brief encounters with journeymen's associations. Charles Chauncey Adams, shortly after joining the New York society, moved to Poughkeepsie, where he established a series of newspapers that lasted until his death in 1814. William Alexander, after briefly participating in the 1802 wage dispute in Philadelphia, left town to publish the *Carlisle Herald,* which survived into 1815, assuming George Phillips, another participant in that 1802 conflict, as his partner in 1807. Brigham, 1367, 1368, 1467; and M. W. Hamilton, 255.

49. See the *American,* March 25, 1805; *Evening Press,* March 25, 1805; and *Federal Gazette,* March 25, 1805, August 26, 1806, and

January 1, 1807. On the Baltimore Typographical Society, see the *Baltimore Telegraphe*, July 17, August 7, 17, 1802, October 18, 1803; and PTS, December 24, 1803. See also Billie G. Smith's "The Vicissitudes of Fortune."

50. For sources on the Bruce brothers, see those cited above, note 19. On Wrigley, *The Philadelphia Directory for 1806. By James Robinson* (Philadelphia: printed for the publisher, 1806) and the same publisher's directories for 1808 and 1811.

51. John Bushell operated the "Cross Keys" tavern on Philadelphia's Front Street; Thomas, 1:357–58. Bartholemew Graves kept the Lemon Tree near the outskirts of Philadelphia; Scharf and Westcott, vol. 3, 1985. Arthur Colerick of that city not only ran an inn but tried simultaneously to work as a tailor; *The Philadelphia Directory for 1802* and 1811. Hezekiah Ripley tried to conduct a public house at three locations in upstate New York after deciding to leave the printing business; Follett, 39. Yet another printer, after the failure of his short-lived newspaper, explained in his last number that he had been "hitherto baffled in all his exertions to attain a decent competence, owing to the freaks and vagaries of 'outrageous fortune,' had at last resolved to court her smiles in the humble vocation of a tavernkeeper"; quoted in Scharf and Westcott, 2:989.

52. Francis, xxix–xxx; Silver, *The American Printer*, 9, 93; *Constitution of the Franklin Society (Printers) of the City of Philadelphia, Instituted March 8, 1788* (Philadelphia: printed by Stewart & Cochran, 1792). See also Ira Jones, *A New Treatise on the Consumption Containing an Attempt to Investigate its Real Nature. To Which is Annexed a Systemmatic Mode of Treatment. By an Advocate of Universal Improvement* (Newfield, Connecticut: printed by Lazarus Beach, 1796); and "Dr. John Wakefield Francis," *The Printer* 3 (February 1861): 200. For other healers: Stephen Sewall, a participant in the 1802 wage dispute, who became a practitioner of Thomsonian medicine, a physician practicing botanic and herbal healing. Frederick Gadiner Fassett, Jr., "A History of Newspapers in the District of Maine, 1785–1820," *The Maine Bulletin* (November 1932), 100–01; and Russel B. Nye, *Society and Culture in America, 1830–1860* (New York: Harper and Row, 1974), 345, 347–49. For the clergymen: Josiah Bowen as a Methodist minister in the letter from the Methodist Historical Society to the American Antiquarian Society, October 2, 1948, cited in the latters' Printers' Authorities File, American Antiquarian Society, Worcester, Massachusetts; and John Welwood Scott as a Presbyterian minister in his own *An Historical Sketch of the Pine Street, or Third Presbyterian Church in the City of Philadelphia* (Philadelphia: Bailey, 1837), 47, 50, 55.

53. *The History of America, abridged for the Use of Children of all Denominations* (Philadelphia: printed by Wrigley & Berriman, 1795).

When William McCulloch sought to gather information for Isaiah Thomas on the history of the Philadelphia trades, he interviewed Wrigley. McCulloch, 140; Weed, 45; Binns, 271–73; [Philip M. Freneau,] *New Year Verses, Addressed to those Gentlemen who have been pleased to Favor Francis Wrigley, News Carrier, January 1, 1783*, broadside (Philadelphia: printed by Hall & Sellers, 1783). See also, for Samuel Woodworth, Stevens, 82–94. Works by John W. Scott and David Bruce may be found in the appended sources. On Theophilus Eaton: Brigham, *History*, 1407; M. W. Hamilton, 270; and *Longworth's American Almanack, New-York Register, and City Directory* for 1809, 1812, and 1813. He eventually returned to upstate New York and died in Bethlehem. See his obituary in the *Albany Register*, May 12, 1820. While in the New York City area, his residence in Flatbush caused some difficulties with the society, See NYTS, October 30, December 16, 23, 30, 1809, January 6, March 3, 24, 31, April 7, 14, 21, 1810, July 18, September 5, 1812. His *Review of New-York, or Rambles through the City*, 2nd ed. (New York: John Low, 1814) is discussed below. Other workers like John Bradford wrote similar pieces; his *Poetical Vagaries of a Knight of the Folding Stick of PASTE CASTLE, to which is annexed the History of the Garret, &c., translated from the Hieroglyphics of the Society by a Member of the Order of the Blue String* ([Newark:] printed for the author, 1813) is discussed in Rock, 269–72, 300–01. This is to say nothing of their encouragement and support of literary work by friends and relatives. An officer of the Boston Franklin Society—Nathaniel Willis, Jr.—was the father of the Yale graduate and popular Anglo-American poet, Nathaniel Parker Willis. See *Boston Printers, Publishers, and Booksellers: 1640–1800*, ed. Benjamin Franklin V (Boston: G. K. Hall & Co., 1980), 415–17; and Henry A. Beers, *Nathaniel Parker Willis* (Boston and New York: Houghton Mifflin and Co., 1885), 6–13.

54. For Ellis Lewis the jurist, Stevens, 82–94, 100–02. On John Morse Austin, another lawyer, see F. B. Dexter, *Biographical Sketches of the Graduates of Yale College* (New York: H. Holt and Company, 1885–1919), 90–91. On Weed and Force, Stevens, 94–100; on Gales, Clark, 101–04. On Leonard, see Brigham, 1443; Hamilton 282; and [Henry B. Pierce,] *History of Tioga, Chemung, Tompkins, and Schuyler counties, New York. With Illustrations and biographical sketches of some of its prominent Men and Pioneers* (Philadelphia: Evarts & Peck, 1879), insert between 170 and 171. On Leakin, see J. Thomas Scharf, *History of Baltimore*, 2 vols. (Baltimore: Regional Publishing Co., 1971; originally published 1881), 174, 187; on Mack, E. M. Treman, *The History of the Treman, Tremaine, Truman family . . .*, 2 vols. (Ithaca: Press of the Ithaca Democrat, 1901), 1:368–76, 394–97; and, on Norvel, Floyd Benjamin Streeter, *Political Parties in Michigan, 1837–1860: An Historical Study of Political Issue and Parties in Michigan for the*

Admission of the State to the Civil War (Lansing: Michigan Historical Society Commission, 1918), 25, 27, 37, 41–42; and Silas Farmer, *History of Detroit and Wayne County and Early Michigan: A Chronological Cyclopedia of the Past and Present,* 3d ed. (Detroit: S. Farmer, 1890), 88, 100, 102, 176–77, 187, 880, 883. Reading voters also sent to the Pennsylvania legislature Jacob Schneider, apparently the "J. Schneider" in the Philadelphia Typographical Society. Morton J. Montgomery, *History of Berks County in Pennsylvania* (Philadelphia: Evarts, Peck & Richards, 1886), 394–95; and James B. Nolan, *The First Decade of Printing in Reading, Pennsylvania* (Reading: Reading National Bank and Trust Co., 1930), 12, 45–49. See also Binns, 196. John Orton Cole of the Albany Typographical Society won election to several local offices, and Henry W. J. Ebner of the Philadelphia society gained similar honors at Allentown, Pennsylvania, where he had started a small mercantile business. Ithaca voters sent Mack to the New York assembly, and George Churchill later represented a Madison County constituency in the Illinois legislature. Gales and Force served as mayors of Washington, D.C., and Leakin of Baltimore. See: on Cole, George R. Howell, *History of the County of Albany* (New York: W. W. Munsell & Co., 1886), 655–56; Joel Munsell, *Annals of Albany,* 10 vols. (Albany: J. Munsell, 1853–1859), 5:338, 7:156, 8:130, 142, 9:1, 112, 209, 222, 240, 333; on Ebner, Roberts, 278; and on Churchill, Munsell, *Typographical Miscellany,* 122–23, and *The History of Madison County, Illinois. With Biographical Sketches of many Prominent men and Pioneers* (Edwardsville, Illinois: W. R. Brick & Co., 1882), 82, 135, 140, 167, 202–03. These, of course, do not include lesser, appointive offices like John Hewes's post as a Baltimore customs inspector in 1808. Minick, 74–87.

55. *The Printer,* 3 (April 1861): 250.

56. *The Following is copied from the journal kept by Mr. Jacob M. Berriman, . . . As many persons, perhaps, will doubt the truth of the above account, they may satisfy themselves by calling at Mr. Peck's Museum in Philadelphia, where the skin was presented,* broadside (Suffield, Connecticut: printed by Edward Gray, 1799); *The Philadelphia Directory, By Francis White* (Philadelphia: printed by Young, Stewart, and McCulloch, 1785); and Robinson's *Philadelphia Directory* for 1802 and 1803.

57. *The Philadelphia Directory for 1797. By Cornelius William Stafford* (Philadelphia: printed by William W. Woodward, 1797); the same publisher's directory for 1798; and the *Philadelphia Directory* for 1802 and 1803. In 1810, the Philadelphia Typographical Society accepted the resignation of John B. Stewart after a membership of two years, reporting that he planned to leave the craft for another business. Circumstances apparently drove him back into printing by 1817 when he joined the Columbia Typographical Society at Washington; PTS,

December 17, 1808, March 31, 1810; and *Constitution of the Columbia Typographical Society*, 77.

58. Thurlow Weed, who wrote little about his days as a journeyman, mentions knowing and working with various members of trade societies, including, Henry C. Southwick, Samuel Williams, Gerrit W. Ryckman, Daniel Fanshaw, William E. Dean, Samuel Wood, Thomas Kennedy, George Mather, Adoniram Chandler, John W. Donnington, and John O. Cole. See Weed, 31, 43–44, 48–49, 56, 57. Other indications of these personal ties are readily available in two manuscript sources. Mary Kugler Sweitzer's account book, 1808–1816, shows the financial relations between her husband, a striker of 1786, Francis Wrigley, and Jacob Schneider. The account books for Matthew Carey's Philadelphia shop include the payment of wages to journeymen in the early national period; an excellent old index prepared by the Works Projects Administration indicates that most of the Philadelphia Typographical Society passed through his shop at one time of another during these years. Both of these are at the American Antiquarian Society in Worchester, Massachusetts.

59. John Welwood Scott, *A Discourse before the Provident Society, April 3d, 1811, the Eighteenth Anniversary of the Institution* (Philadelphia: n.p., 1811), 9; on Mack, Treman, 270–75; and on Collect, see William Moseley, *Freemasonry in Staunton, Virginia. . . .* (Staunton, Virginia: n.p., 1949).

TWO. All As One

1. A scholarly understanding of the early emergence of these workers' associations has developed very slowly. Richard T. Ely's pioneering work on *The Labor Movement in America* (New York: Thomas Y. Crowell & Co., 1886) had asserted that the hired worker before the 1820s had "no thought of organization occured to him, and if there had been any reason for organization, his isolation, and the unsteady character of his employment, would have rendered it well-nigh impossible"; pp. 36, 38, 39. Ely found no unions outside of New York City, and only "here and there" between 1800 and 1825 did he find "the most primitive form of labor organization . . . the union of one class of employees in a single place with no connection with laborers working in other localities or at other callings." Thirty years later, when Commons, Sumner, Andrews, David J. Saposs, E. B. Mittelmann, H. E. Hoagland, and Selig Perlman collaborated on two volumes of their *History of Labour in the United States*, 2d ed., 4 vols. (New York: McMillan Co., 1946), they described the years before 1827 as the "dormant period" of American labor history. "A continuous and persistent effort of wage-earners is prevalent in but two industries," wrote Saposs, referring to printing and shoemaking. Sumner took great care to

contrast the workingmen's movement of 1827 through 1833 with the previous organizing efforts. In the earlier years, she argued, journeymen "had not learned the advantages of mutual aid, nor had they striven to keep up permanent organizations for aggressive purposes." In her view, an American labor movement "made its first appearance in Philadelphia in 1827" with the formation of the Mechanics' Union of Trade Associations, a city-wide body uniting the craft societies which had earlier confined their activities to their particular trades; 1:111, 169, 185. By the 1930s, Norman J. Ware could acknowledge that the labor movement had originated in the 1790s, "about 140 years" before his *Labor in Modern Industrial Society* (Boston and New York: D. C. Heath and Co., 1935), but he argued that early unionists organized "not because they were peculiarly oppressed but because they were peculiarly advantaged . . . " 123, 126–27. NYTS, September 22, 24, 1810; *Federal Gazette*, September 26, 27, 1810; Baltimore *American*, September 27, 1810.

2. *Rivington's Royal Gazette*, November 14, 1778. E. Stewart, 860, gives the year 1776 and assumed a strike took place, but Rosemont shows the weaknesses of this assumption; pp. 411–12.

3. In general, see the account of this strike by Henry Rosemont, cited above. The incidents of 1778 and 1786 were only symptomatic of a growing discontent among the hired printers. "The devil seems to have got into Journeymen," reported a Boston master in 1792. He complained bitterly to his partner about their insistence upon higher pay for press work and his fears of a general effort by them to increase pay for typesetting as well. Ebenezer T. Andrews to Isaiah Thomas, quoted in Silver, *The American Printer*, 10.

4. Rosemont, 420–27. See also: Silver, *The American Printer*, 82, 83; Thomas, 1:237–38, 238–39; *Constitution of the Franklin Society (Printers)*; and *Aurora*, April 7, 1796. Among the victims of the plague was the president of the Society, Samuel Johnson. Powell, *Bring Out Your Dead*, 276.

5. *New York Diary, or Evening Register*, July 3, 1794; Stevens 35–36; and E. Stewart, 860–63, giving the dates of its existence as 1795–97.

6. *Greenleaf's New York Daily Advertiser*, November 24, 1798, February 4, 1803, May 8, 1804; and *Evening Post*, September 19, 1803; cited in Stevens, 37, 39–40, E. Stewart, 863–64, and Barnett, 3–4, 435. See also the address by Clough; and Thomas Ringwood, *An Address Delivered before the Franklin Typographical Association of New-York, and a Select Company; on the Fifth of July, 1802: In Commemoration of the Twenty-Seventh Anniversary of American Independence, and of the Third of the Association* (New York: Southwick and Crooker, 1802).

7. Bernard Fay, "Benjamin Franklin Bache: A Democratic Leader of the Eighteenth Century," *American Antiquarian Society Proceedings*

40 (1930): 300–02; cited in Silver, *The American Printer*, 114. *Philadelphia Gazette*, December 6, 8, 1800; cited in Silver, "The Book Trade and the Protective Tariffs: 1800–1804," *Papers of the Bibliographic Society of America* 46 (1952): 34; and *The American Printer*, 19. For the 1802 wage schedule, with its signatories, see E. Stewart, 865.

8. On Boston, see Silver, "The Book Trade and the Protective Tariff," 41; and Burdick. On Baltimore, see: *Baltimore Telegraphe*, July 17, August 7, 17, 1802, October 18, 1803, February 27, June 26, 1804; PTS, November 25, 1803; *American*, July 6, 1805, July 8, 1806, July 7, 1807; *Federal Gazette*, July 8, 1806, March 7, July 8, 1807; all cited in Rollo G. Silver, "The Baltimore Book Trade, 1800–1825," *Bulletin of the New York Public Library* 57 (January 1957): 114–25, 182–201, 248–51, 297–305, and 349–57, with the references to the societies on 182 and 120; and also PTS, November 25, 1803. Selig Perlman, *History of Trade Unionism in the United States* (New York: McMillan Co., 1922), 3.

9. On Baltimore, see *Evening Post*, February 19, 20, 26, June 30, July 7, 1808, July 3, 7, 1804, September 26, 27, 1810; *American*, March 26, May 27, 30, June 30, December 20, 1808, June 19, 21, July 4, 8, 1809, September 27, 29, 1810; *Federal Gazette*, May 30, June 30, July 6, 7, 1808, June 14, 21, 30, 1809, September 27, 1810; for its participation in the local celebration of the Fourth of July in 1809, Theodore W. Glocker, "Trade Unionism in Baltimore before the War of 1812," *Johns Hopkins University Economic Seminary Circular* 196 (April 1907): 29; and NYTS, July 27, 1811. On Washington, J. H. Powell, *The Books of a New Nation* (Philadelphia: University of Pennsylvania Press, [1957]), 114; and Silver, *The American Printer*, 23. On Boston, PTS, August 26, September 2, 1809; NYTS, July 27, 1811; and E. Stewart, 869. On New Orleans, PTS, June 30, 1810.

10. Baltimore *American*, May 1, July 31, 1812, February 25, June 4, 1813, February 18, 1814; *Federal Gazette*, October 2, 1813; Glocker, 29; and E. Stewart, 869. On Albany, Munsell, 121; George Churchill's address; and *Scale of Prices Established January 7th, 1815, by the Albany Typographical Society*, broadside (Albany: n.p., 1815) at the Library of Congress; letters dated October 3, November 20, 1816, and February 22, 1817, in NYTS, October 12, November 2, December 7, 1816, and February 22, 1817, the last one of which has been here quoted. Thurlow Weed joined the society when he moved there. Weed, 46. On Boston, the letter of March 2, 1816, declaring March 4 to be their deadline for a new scale, copied in NYTS, March 16, 1816; E. Stewart, 869. This group and/or its predecessor is also discussed and the names of eleven of its participants recalled in *Leaves of History from the Archives of the Boston Typographical Union No. 13: From the*

Foundation of the Boston Typographical Society to the Diamond Jubilee of Its Successors (Boston: Boston Typographical Union, 1923), 3.

11. Alexander Boland, Alan Dowell, Peter F. Fritez, Whiting Skinner, and George Tomlin were Philadelphia printers later active in Baltimore. Philip Quereau and Josiah Ball of the New York printers' union later helped rebuild a Boston society. Among the founders of the Washington union were James Pettigrew and Samuel Rea, former members of the Philadelphia Typographical Society, William Duncan of the New York Typographical Society, and Peter Konkle, who had at different times been a member of both. Together with two former masters and fourteen others, they built the only trade union of the early national period to have survived as such to the present (as Local 101 of the International Typographical Union). See also the early installments of A. T. Cavis's and E. MacMurray's "History of the Columbia Typographical Society," in *Printer's Circular* 3 (October, November, December 1868, January 1869): 229-31, 261-64, 293-97, 325-26, and continuing through 5 (March 1870): 912. Ironically, one of the shops plundered by the British had been that of Joseph Gales, Jr., whose father's republican sedition in Sheffield had not been forgotten by the vindictive officers of the occupying forces.

12. *Baltimore Telegraphe,* October 18, 1803. Certainly this entailed a primitive trade unionist equivalent to the sort of aid urban residents generally extended to other city dwellers in such circumstances. See also Powell, *The Books of a New Nation,* 194, 195, 244; Silver, "The Book Trade and the Protective Tariff," 33-44; the Franklin Typographical Society's proposal for a joint memorial on protectionist legislation, and the Baltimore Typographical Society's proposal for a common address on apprenticeships, PTS, December 11, 1802, and June 18, 1803.

13. PTS August 18, December 24, 1803, the society's advertisement being reprinted in Barnett, 17-18. When journeyman curriers turned out at Philadelphia to win wages comparable to those in New York City, masters also used the same tactic, provoking the strikers to publish a defense of their struggle against what they called an employers' attempt to cut wages "that have been current for twenty years past." *Aurora,* November 9, 1803, cited in Philip S. Foner, *History of the Labor Movement in the United States,* vol. 1, *From Colonial Times to the Founding of the American Federation of Labor,* 2nd ed. (New York: International Publishers, 1972), 77-78. Foner discusses labor in the early national period on 65-71.

14. NYTS, August 19, September 9, 30, October 21, November 1, 1809; and PTS, October 7, 18, 1809. The society also sent continuing notices and updated reports on their attempts to move forward in New York; NYTS, November 11, 1809, May 26, 1810; and Barnett, 359-60. Similar efforts at cooperation from city to city surely existed in other trades. The presence of a Mr. Vanevers in the Baltimore shoe shops

and his application for membership in the local society sparked a considerable debate about the advisability of admitting into their ranks an "unlawful member" of the Philadelphia union. Constitution and By Laws of the Union Society of Journeymen Cordwainers of the City and Precincts of Baltimore [includes MS minutes, 1806–1809], May 17, July 17, 1809, Baltimore County Commissioners, Private Commissioners at Maryland Hall of Records, Annapolis, Maryland.

15. NYTS, November 4, 1815. The Society later proposed a certificate of membership to be honored by the societies of the different cities, a primitive precursor of what became the traveling card of the I.T.U. The idea seems to have been dropped after a letter from the Philadelphia Typographical Society, dated March 17, 1816, explained their legal inability to cooperate; NYTS, February 3, April 6, 1816.

16. NYTS, March 7, 1818.

17. George Bruce, after becoming a master, served on the employers' negotiating team in the New York printing trades. Stevens, 53. John Binns, in Philadelphia, played a major role in a later prosecution of a tailors' union. *Trial of Twenty-Four Journeymen Tailors*, 114, 121, 141. Among the cordwainers, former unionists like William Blair, John McCurdy, and Samuel Logan joined the ranks of the most adamantly anti-union employers in the city. *The Trial of the Boot & Shoemakers of Philadelphia, on an Indictment for a Combination and Conspiracy to Raise their Wages* (Philadelphia: B[artholomew] Graves, 1806), as reprinted in *Doc. Hist.* 3:75–76, 93–94, 98. Another former member, Adam Moreland went to Pittsburgh, where he organized a new society, became one of its central leaders, then, after becoming an employer, united with another former unionist, James Harmon, to spearhead the drive to destroy the union. *Report of the Trial of the Journeymen Cordwainers, of the Borough of Pittsburgh: Had at an Adjourned Court of Quarter Sessions for the County of Allegheny, Holden at Pittsburgh on the first Monday of December 1815* (Pittsburgh: Cramer, Spear & Eichbaum, Franklin Bookstore, 1816), also as reprinted in *Doc. Hist.* 4:25–29, 42–45.

18. Clough, 13–14; and toast no. 18, 16. Ringwood also praised the employers' association, 18.

19. On Thomas, see the financial report in the PTS, November 5, 1810. On the Columbian Press, NYTS, March 30, 1816, and, on Mathers' ink, February 7, March 1, 1817. On the public-house problem, see May 3, June 7, 1817.

20. For the monthly lectures by Force, Mack, Hoyt, David Perry, Reins, Benjamin G. Jansen, and Woodworth, see NYTS, September 4, November 6, December 4, 1813, January 8, February 5, March 5, July 23, 1814. For the latter, see also Stevens, 82–94; NYTS, August 12, December 16, 1809; and the society's awarding him a medal for his verses, April 6, June 15, 29, 1811, February 1, 1812, September 4, 1813.

On Joseph Gleason's oration, see NYTS, June 9, July 4, 7, [Gleason's letter, dated July 8] 21, 23, 1810; his earlier *An Oration pronounced on the thirtieth Anniversary of American Independence July 4, 1806* (Boston: Oliver & Munroe, 1806); Brigham, 1418. The speech he delivered in 1810 must have been Joseph Perkin, *An Oration of Eloquence. Pronounced at the Anniversary Commencement of Harvard University in Cambridge, July 16, 1794* (Boston: Ezra W. Weld and William Greenough, 1794). After 1810, the society's annual addresses were given as follows in the NYTS: George Asbridge, April 27, May 4, June 29, 1811; Samuel Woodworth, undelivered, May 8, June 27, 1812; Ebenezer Mack, May 8, 1813; David H. Reins, undelivered but to be rescheduled, May 7, July 23, 1814; Ichabod Hoyt, June 3, 1815; and Adoniram Chandler, April 6, June 7, July 13, 20, 1816. Orations by Asbridge and Mack were published, and Hoyt's was to be printed by Jonathan Seymour, according to the minutes of August 3, 1815, but neither his nor the others mentioned have been located.

21. E. Stewart, 865; Clough, 14; and Ringwood, 17, 22.

22. A week later, the officers of the Philadelphia society signed the petition and sent it to their representatives in the Congress and the Senate. PTS, December 11, 18, 1802, January 22, February 12, 1803. See, in general, Silver, "The Book Trade and the Protective Tariff," 33–44.

23. *Trial of the Boot & Shoemakers of Philadelphia*, 99; the discussion of the New York Society of Cabinetmakers in Rock, 273, 290 n19. New York's shoemakers may have had a similar association based upon the *Constitution of the Mutual Benefit Society of Cordwainers of the City of New York, Instituted March 1806* (New York: John E. Scoper Co., 1808).

24. NYTS, May 24, 1817; and the report on the expenditures of the PTS, November 5, 1809. The families of non-members were sometimes relieved out of "private contributions" raised by the society from "feelings of humanity." They also engaged in the Old World practice of subsidizing unemployed journeymen stranded in a locally glutted job market to move on. April 5, 1817. For keeping track of members out of work. February 3, 17, May 24, November 9, 1816, May 24, 1817. Clough (p. 12) assured the employers that, in all things, "reasonable procedure" rather than "precipitate inconsideration" would govern the course of the organization.

25. George Asbridge, *An Oration, Delivered before the New-York Typographical Society at Their Second Anniversary, on the Fourth of July 1811* (New York: C. S. Van Winkle, 1811), 21. The evolution of the New York and Philadelphia societies, in addition to being traced in their extant minutes, is briefly summarized in Stevens, 78–80, and E. Stewart, 879–80, 881–82, and on the District of Columbia printers, 892.

26. PTS, August 18, 20, 1803, and the bill received and noted in October 26, 1803. The advertisement ran in the *Aurora,* but the society also paid the *Baltimore Telegraph* and the *New York Advertiser* to run the item; Barnett, 17. Ironically, Robert Carr, a local employer whom the society later admitted to honorary membership, seems to have spearheaded this drive to destroy the society's ability to strike by bringing scores of out-of-town, unemployed journeymen into Philadelphia. "Historical Sketch of the Philadelphia Typographical Society," *Printers' Circular* 2 (April 1867): 195; and George E. Barnett, "The Printers: A Study in American Trade Unionism," as *American Economics Association Quarterly,* 3d ser., 10 (October 1909): 17–18. The three representatives of the independent meeting—identified only as Palmer, Cooper, and Tillman—may have been the men of the same surnames later active in the society; PTS, August 22, 24, December 16, 1803. See, too, NYTS, October 7, November 11, 18, 25, December 2, 1809, March 3, 10, April 7, 21, 1810.

27. NYTS, September 7–December 28, 1811, June 6, 27, 1812, July 11, September 5, October 4, 1812. Also, January 4, 11, 15, February 1, 1812, October 4, 1817.

28. "Death of David H. Reins," *The Printer* 4 (July 1862): 55; and Stevens, 81–82.

29. NYTS, July 29, August 8, 12, 19, 26, September 2, 16, October 7, 14, 21, 1809. For circular, September 20, 23, 27, 30, 1809; and Stevens, 56. For the struggle, see October 28, 30, November 1, 11, December 2, 16, 1809; and *Scale of Prices, Established October 28, 1809. By the New-York Typographical Society,* broadside (New York: n.p., n.d.).

30. *Ibid,* August 18, 1803, for the estimate, and for the officers, November 13, 1802, through January 7, 1804. See also E. Stewart, 885.

31. This account of the factional crisis is based on the PTS, September 12, 1803, through January 7, 1804. On White, see *The Philadelphia Directory for 1805. By James Robinson* (Philadelphia: printed for the publisher, 1805), and those for 1802, 1803, and 1806. Graves first appeared in the directories in 1803 and continued to be listed through the directory of 1809. The timing of his appearance, the stability of his residence, and later charges against him indicate that he became a master. Little was unlisted. On John and Francis Childs, see *The New-York Directory. . . . By David Franks* (New York: printed by S[amuel] and J[ohn] Loudon, 1788) through *The New-York Directory, and Register, for 1796,* and the *Philadelphia Directory of 1803,* et. seq.

32. Graves died on March 14, 1838, at the age of fifty-four in West Chester, Pennsylvania. See American Antiquarian Society, Printers' File. On Little, see Brigham, 1445; and the New York directories of 1808 and 1809. On White's New York career, see Brigham, 1502; Donald H. Stewart, *The Oppositionist Press in the Federalist Period* (Albany: State University of New York Press, 1969), 881; Munsell, *Typographical*

Miscellany, 117–18 and, for his vice-presidency of the Albany union, 121.

33. NYTS, July 27, August 3, 1811. On Sherman, see Brigham, 1481; and, on the Trenton office of George Sherman, David Hacket Fisher, *The Revolution of American Conservatism: The Federalist Party in the Era of Jeffersonian Democracy* (New York: Harper and Row, 1965), 330–31.

34. On Wands, Munsell, *Typographical Miscellany,* 84; Brigham, 1498; M. W. Hamilton, 305, 192, 305; Philadelphia directories of 1799 and, after a gap during which he was unlisted, 1806, 1808, and 1809. On his death, see Munsell, *Typographical Miscellany,* 113; and PTS, October 6, 1810.

35. PTS, December 9, 16, 1803.

36. For examples of such altering of union records, see appendix A on clandestine labor activities.

37. This account of the later factionalism in the society is based on PTS, August 20, 1806 through June 20, 1807. On Konkle, see NYTS, January 26, February 2, March 2, 1811, and *Constitution of the Columbia Typographical Society,* 63. His conflict with Childs during these years is also noted briefly in the "Historical Sketch of the Philadelphia Typographical Society," in the *Printers' Circular* 2:179. John Alexander, whose membership the opposition questioned, may well have been a relatively substantial small employer, given the unusual consistency of his address at 145 Spruce, sustained over the four consecutive previous years. See the *Philadelphia Directory* for 1803 through 1806, and *Longworth's American Almanack, New-York Register, and City Directory* (New York: Old Established Directory Office, Shakespeare-Gallery, 1815) through Longworth's directory for 1820.

38. On Franks, see Scharf and Westcott, 2:1985. He also later published the *Washingtonian* at Towanda, Pennsylvania, from 1816 into 1817. Brigham, 1415.

39. PTS, November 14, 1807, July 30, September 3, October 8, November 26, December 10, 17, 1808.

40. NYTS, November 13, 1813, May 6, June 3, October 7, November 4, 1815; *Scale of Prices, Established October 7, 1815;* and *Constitution of the New-York Typographical Society, passed July, 1809* (New York: C. S. Van Winkle, 1810). See also the letter to the Boston Typographical Society, March 16, 1816, and E. Stewart, 872–83; NYTS, September 29, October 26, November 3, December 22, 23, 30, 1809, January 6, 12, March 16, June 15, July 13, August 24, 31, 1810, January 12, 26, February 2, 1811, January 15, February 5, April 21, 1814. In the process of first assuming their new role as hired men, they permitted members to become masters and retain their membership. An apparent hostility to individual artisans often hid the journeymen's resistance to this

practice. When, for example, the New York Typographical Society rejected the application of John Hardcastle, a former leader of the Franklin Typographical Society, it gave no reason for its decision. But Hardcastle had, since the days of the older society, operated at least four short-lived newspapers, and the board evidently balked at admitting a man who might again become an employer. In 1817 the issue came to a head, and the New York union ejected one of its charter members, Daniel Fanshaw, and amended its bylaws to declare itself exclusively a society of journeyman printers, and to bar employers from membership. NYTS, November 9, 30, 1816; Brigham, 1426; E. Stewart, 878; and Stevens, 41–42.

41. On Ringwood, see NYTS, April 7, 1810, May 25, June 29, 1811. On Gird: Clough, 5–6; Brigham, 1418; and *Longworth's American Almanack, New-York Register, and City Directory* for 1802, and 1807 through 1811; NYTS, May 4, 18, 25, June 1, 8, 22, 29, 1811, April 25, 1812; and the Printers' Files, American Antiquarian Society.

42. Rock, 23–24, 103–04; PTS, March 11, 25, April 1, 1809. Incorporation was no doubt seen as a way to reverse a series of major organizational problems the society faced. Note the failure to muster quorums for December 12, 19, 1807, January 9, April 2, July 14, December 24, 31, 1808, January 14, 21, 28, February 11, 18, 25, 1809.

43. PTS, May 6, 20, June 10, July 1, August 5, 1809. Nevertheless, as late as September 30, 1809, it voted on matters of craft regulation. When Childs balked at circulating a list of local rats to other societies, the Board forced his hand. NYTS, August 19, September 9, 30, October 21, November 1, 1809, and PTS, October 7, 18, 1809. The society also sent continuing notices and updated reports on their attempts to move forward in New York, NYTS, November 11, 1809, May 26, 1810, and also Barnett, 359–60. See also October 7, 28, November 11, December 2, 9, 16, 23, 30, 1809, January 20, March 17, June 16, 30, July 7, August 18, 25, November 10, 17, December 1, 1810.

44. Brigham, 1390; Walter Hugins, *Jacksonian Democracy and the Working Class: A Study of the New York Workingmen's Movement, 1829–1837* (Stanford, California: Stanford University Press, 1960), 212–13; *Annals of the General Society of Mechanics and Tradesmen of the City of New-York,* 87, 89, 92, 95, 97, 98; McDevitt's discussion of Chandler in "Reminiscences of the Typographical Society," 51. For the progress of the incorporation discussion, NYTS, September 4, October 7, November 4, December 2, 23, 1815, January 6, 13, May 4, 1816, January 11, December 6, 1817, March 7, 21, 28, and April 4, 1818.

45. See PTS, August, September, and October, 1810, which lacks any discussion of the strike at all; and the pressmen's statement "To the Employing Printers of the City and County of Philadelphia," dated June 17, 1816, in NYTS, June 22, 1816.

THREE. More Humble Followers

1. Mack, 3. Even "the fair daughters of Columbia," facing "the most rugged toils" in "the field of daily labor" became the "angelic attendants of celestial Liberty." "Few—very few" of that generation remained in 1813, for "their hoary heads are fast blossoming for the grave! they are ripening for eternity!" Their deed, he pledged, "we will record in our bosoms, and cherish them with the warmest gratitude," 6, 7. Other trades also held formal celebrations of the Fourth of July. One of the first acts of the New York Society of Shipwrights and Caulkers in 1815 was to raise funds for an emblem to carry in the Independence Day parade. It sent a committee to meet "the most eminent portrait painters" of the city and chose five representatives "for the purpose of walking in procession with Different Societys on the fourth of July next," carrying the new banner. Society of Shipwrights and Caulkers minutes, 1815–1816, May 22, June 8, 12, 1815, Ms in the volume "Constitution/Members, 1815–1816," Manuscript Room, New York City Public Library. Cabinetmakers and shoemakers also held their own patriotic celebrations. *Independent Mechanic*, June 2, 1811; and *National Advocate*, March 8, 1813; both cited Sean Wilentz, "Artisan Republican Festivals and the Rise of Class Conflict in New York City, 1788–1837," in *Working Class America: Essays in Labor, Community and American Society*, ed. Michael H. Frisch and Daniel J. Walkowitz (Urbana and Chicago: University of Illinois Press, 1983), 51, 73n. 46.

2. Pauline Maier, *From Resistance to Revolution: Colonial Radicals and the Development of American Opposition to Britain, 1765–1776*, 2d ed. (New York: Vintage Books, 1974), chapters 1 and 2. See also Bernard Bailyn, *The Ideological Origins of the American Revolution*, 2d ed. (Cambridge, Massachusetts: Belknap Press of Harvard University Press, 1967) 230; Staughton Lynd, *The Intellectual Origins of American Radicalism*, 2d ed. (New York: Vintage Books, 1969); Gordon S. Wood, "Rhetoric and Reality in the American Revolution," *William and Mary Quarterly*, 3d ser., 23 (January 1966): 3–32; Wilentz, "Artisan Republican Festivals," 37–77.

3. Although much refined since its publication, see Jackson Turner Main's model for *The Social Structure of Revolutionary America* (Princeton: Princeton University Press, 1962), which defined distinctive regional patterns (in New England, the Mid-Atlantic, and the South) and four types of social formations. Both on the frontier and in subsistence farming areas—"a frontier in arrested development"—about one quarter of the adult men worked as unskilled laborers and a bit less than one-tenth as mechanics, mostly farmers earning additional incomes. Commercially viable farmlands supported only a slightly larger proportion of workers, with most of these clustered in some of the larger small towns and villages, 11, 17, 27, 28, 43, 50, 63, 67, 272–

76. Manufacturers and commerce, rather than agriculture, nurtured the craftsmen that flourished in the seaboard cities and larger towns. Only there did the free laboring class attain the size and proportions sufficient to foster a community spirit with a distinctively "mechanical" set of values and consciousness. Unfortunately, of course, there exist even greater obstacles to gauging the extent of localized domestic industry, based particularly upon women workers in the rural areas.

4. For a community of mechanics, see Charles Olton, *Artisans for Independence: Philadelphia Mechanics and the American Revolution* (New York: Syracuse University Press, 1975), 10.

5. For artisans as a bourgeoisie, see Olton, x; and as a group imbued with a proletarian character, Staughton Lynd and Alfred Young, "After Carl Becker: The Mechanics and New York City Politics," *Labor History* 5 (Winter 1964): 218–19.

6. *The Mechanics Lecture* . . . (Philadelphia: printed by John M'Culloch, 1789).

7. On Revere, see Esther Forbes, *Paul Revere and the World He Lived In*, 2d ed. (Boston: Houghton Mifflin Company, 1962).

8. On Macintosh, see George P. Anderson, "Ebenezer Mackintosh: Stamp Act Rioter and Patriot," and "A Note on Ebeneezer Mackintosh," *Colonial Society of Massachusetts Publications* 26 (1927): 15–64, 348–61.

9. On Bushell, Thomas, 1:127, 205–06, 357–58.

10. On Southwick, Thomas, 1:198–99, 199–200, 201–02, 2: 81–82. On Edes, see "December Meeting, 1871," *Procedings of the Massachusetts Historical Society* 7 (1871–73): 179–80; and Edmund S. and Helen M. Morgan, *The Stamp Act Crisis: Prologue to Revolution*, 2d ed. (New York: Collier Books, 1963), 240, which also lists the Loyal Nine, 160–61. A leader of the Boston Typographical Society, Henry W. Gill was apparently the son of John Gill—Edes's partner and another leading Son of Liberty. The elder Gill left printing in 1785, complaining that the new authorities were imposing a stamp tax. *Boston Printers, Publishers, and Booksellers*, 35, 129–31. Silas Engle of the Philadelphia Typographical Society was probably related to the carpenter of that name who served on the radical Committee of One Hundred elected there on August 16, 1775. Richard A. Ryerson, *The Revolution Is Now Begun: The Radical Committees of Philadelphia, 1765–1776* (Philadelphia: University of Pennsylvania Press, 1978), 276.

11. Mack, 4–5; and Ringwood, 8, 10.

12. On Young, "Marriages and Death Notices from the City Gazette of South Carolina," comp. Elizabeth H. Jervey, *South Carolina Historical and Genealogical Magazine* 48 (January 1947): 17; and *Southern Evangelical Intelligencer*, November 4, 1820. On the other printers, *Pennsylvania Archives* (Philadelphia: J. Severns, 1852–56; Harrisburgh Publishing Co., state printers, 1874–1935), 5th ser., 7:834, 854; 6th ser.,

1:41, 239, 245, 274, 582, 592, 924, 935, 966, 970. Bushell may have served in New England before moving on to Philadelphia. See the listing of John "Buswell" and "Buzwell" in the State of New Hampshire, *Rolls of the Soldiers in the Revolutionary War*, ed. Isaac W. Hammon, 4 vols. (Concord, New Hampshire: P. B. Cogswell, state printers, 1885–89), 1:6; 2:267, 268, 270; 3:141, 161, 264, 728. A man named Thomas Allen, possibly the New York City cordwainer who chaired meetings during the 1785 strike there, had served in that state's line of the Continental Army. New York State Comptroller's office, *New York in the Revolution as a Colony and State: A Compilation of Documents and Records from the Office of the State Comptroller*, comp. James A. Roberts, 2 vols. (Albany: Weed-Parsons Printing Co., 1897), 1:237. On Wrigley, see McCulloch, 140; and "Minutes of the Supreme Executive Council of Pennsylvania," in *Colonial Records of Pennsylvania*, 16 vols. (Harrisburg: printed by T. Fenn & Co., 1851–53), 11:31. As late as 1808, an observer at a New York City parade noted the presence of living witnesses to the British occupation marching with the Society of Journeymen Shipwrights. Wallabout Committee, Tammany Society, or Columbian Order, *Account of the Interment of the Remains of American patriots, Who Perished on Board the British Prison Ships during the American Revolution, with Notes and an Appendix by Henry R. Stiles* (New York: privately reprinted, 1865), 117. On Aitken, see Scharf and Westcott, 3:1973; and Thomas, 1:266–67.

13. On Southwick, see Thomas, 1:198–200, 2:81–82.

14. See, on Woodworth, the New York *Daily Sentinel*, August 15, 1830; "The Death of David H. Reins," *The Printer* 4 (July 15, 1862): 55; and on Delano, Delano, 134, 137, 534. The Maryland family of James Geoghegan, an officer of the cordwainers' union in Philadelphia, also played an important local role in the Revolution. Elias Jones, "The Geoghegan Family," in *Revised History of Dorchester County, Maryland* (Baltimore: Reed-Taylor Press, 1925), 315–16.

15. Jackson Turner Main, *The Anti-Federalists: Critics of the Constitution*, 2d ed. (Chicago: Quadrangle Books, 1964) discusses the overwhelming support for the Constitution in the cities on 266–68, 270, and also gives the Philadelphia vote on 190–92. On the New York City vote of 1789, see Rock, 24; and Young, 247. On Lamb, see Lynd, 243.

16. Scott, *A Discourse before the Provident Society*, 9. See also Gleason, 6; and Mack, 4–5.

17. They most often cited the patriotic examples set by John Hancock, James Otis, Patrick Henry, Nathaniel Greene, and Joseph Warren, as well as Thomas Jefferson, and John and Samuel Adams. Mack also praised Richard Montgomery, Horatio Gates, John Stark, John Sullivan, Anthony Wayne, Johann DeKalb, David Rittenhouse, and Benjamin West. He also noted that Thomas Paine, Joel Barlow, and Benjamin Rush "have lately sought the tomb, whose worth—whose

works shall stand recorded to the ages." Asbridge, 19; Gleason, 8–9, 14–15; Ringwood, 12; Mack 14, and 6–14 *passim;* and Burdick, 21, 24–28. John W. Francis, as a young printer, knew men like Rush, Franklin, and Paine who took walks past his door. Francis, lxxxiii, 141–42. William Hartshorne, who joined the New York union in 1816, remembered his experiences as a journeyman and spoke frequently to young Walt Whitman of "the personal appearance and demeanor of Washington, Jefferson, and others of the great historical names of our early national days." *Walt Whitman's New York,* 47; for Hartshorne's membership, see NYTS, May 18, June 1, 1816. Some seem to have had even closer relations with such men. Wrigley and Lecount left London for Philadelphia during Franklin's stay in Britain as the colonial agent, and the former went to work upon his arrival in Franklin's old firm, Hall and Sellers. McCulloch, 140. However, "HEAVEN's CHIEF AGENT in guiding us to the wished-for goal" was George Washington. This man, "the father of our country, our friend, our beneficient friend, has long since been numbered with the silent dead," mourned Clough two years after the great man's death. "Under his banners our fathers fought, under his guidance achieved those inestimable privileges, which we their offspring so dearly prize." Scott recalled how Washington "stood first at the head of our incipient government, till America attained to her proper rank among the nations of the world." Ringwood simply exclaimed of his death, "Looks often are more eloquent than elaborate discourses—would that mine could express the feelings of my heart—my pen is unequal to the task." Similarly, Mack hoped, "where the faltering tongue would fail, the heart may render justice." Ringwood, 13, 14; Clough, 6, 7; Scott, *A Discourse,* 10; and Mack, 7. See also Gleason, 9–10, and Burdick, 21. Direct personal experience often bound even the youngest participants in early trade union activities to this legacy. For example, although only seven or eight at the time of Washington's death in 1799, Judah Delano, a future member of the Columbia Typographical Society accompanied his older sister to the Portland, Maine, procession honoring the fallen statesman. *Constitution of the Columbia Typographical Society,* 52, 38; and his sister's obituary from Ohio's *Kent Courier,* July 10, 1897, reprinted in Delano, 141–42.

18. Mack, 4, 3, 6.

19. Churchill, 5.

20. Hartshorne's work is cited as item no. 1014 in William Matthews, *American Diaries in Manuscript, 1580–1954: A Descriptive Bibliography* (Athens, Georgia: University of Georgia Press, 1974); and Henry Miller's statement is quoted in McCulloch, 213.

21. *The History of Madison County, Illinois,* 85, 202–03; and Munsell, *Typographical Miscellany,* 122–23.

22. Eaton, 40–41, 98–101. Yundt printed the *Letter of Granville*

Sharp, Esquire of London, to the Maryland Society for the Abolition of Slavery (Baltimore: D. Graham, L. Yundt and W. Patton, 1794); and Lawrence printed *A Copy of a Letter from Benjamin Banneker to the Secretary of State, with His Answer* (Baltimore: Daniel Lawrence, 1792); the exchange between the gifted black surveyor and Thomas Jefferson; and William Bell Crafton, *A Short Sketch of the Evidence for the Abolition of the Slave Trade* (Philadelphia: reprinted by Daniel Lawrence, 1792). For Yundt and Hewes, see McCulloch, 246.

23. Steffen, 253–75. Philip S. Foner and some others have discerned evidence of white supremacist sentiments in rhetorical comparisons between the "chattel slavery" of blacks and the "wages slavery" of so-called free wage labor by figures in the antebellum Northern labor movement as an echoing of proslavery apologists. Clearly, though, early unionists began to make such comparisons as early as the 1806 conspiracy trial of the Philadelphia shoemakers who protested that their employers hoped to "reduce the laboring whites to a condition still more despicable and abject than the black slaves." *Aurora*, November 27, 1806.

24. Clark, 88–89, 91–92, 93, 98–99, 123, and 139; the untitled sketch of David Bruce, Sr. in *The Printer* 1:258; and Binns, 28, 40, 54, 143, 168; and for more general assessment of his activities, Thompson, *The Making of the English Working Class*, 139–40, 153–54, 165–66, 169–71. Binns even printed the *Memoir of Dr. Joseph Priestley, . . . And Observations on his Writings, by Thomas Cooper, . . .* 2 vols. (Northumberland, Pennsylvania: printed by J. Binns, 1806). Earlier, Lecount and Wrigley had left their homes in the rougher neighborhoods of old London for Philadelphia. *Stationer Company Apprentices*, 124, 263, 290. Wrigley's neighborhood, known as Alsatia, remained "one of the worst haunts even down to late times" in London and bordered the city's printing district adjacent to Fleet Street. E. Beresford Chancellor, *The Annals of Fleet Street, Its Traditions and Associations* (New York: Frederick A. Stoker, [1912?], 47–52, 317–30. Early societies of London's journeyman printers met in this area, in a tavern known as the Hole-in-the-Wall. *The London Compositor: Documents Relating to Wages, Working Conditions and Customs of the London Printing Trades, 1785–1900*, ed. Ellic Howe (London: Bibliographical Society, 1947), 77. See also the standard work by Clifton K. Yearley, Jr. on *Britons in American Labor: A History of the Influence of the United Kingdom Immigrants on American Labor, 1820–1914* (Baltimore: Johns Hopkins University Press, 1957); and on the developments in Britain itself, Thompson, *Making of the English Working Class*, 17–185; and Gwyn A. William, *Artisans and Sans-Culottes: Popular Movements in France and Britain During the French Revolution* (New York: Norton, 1969).

25. Munsell, *Typographical Miscellany*, 121; J. T. Gilbert, *A History of the City of Dublin*, 3 vols. (Dublin and London: J. Duffy, 1861), 2:

211–14, 216, 220; and Thomas Pakenham, *The Tree of Liberty: The Story of the Great Irish Rebellion of 1798* (Englewood Cliffs, New Jersey: Prentice-Hall, 1969), 78.

26. Churchill, 5; Asbridge 14, 15; and Mack, 12. On journeymen's interest in the revolution, see McCulloch, 131. Sometimes union officer Walter W. Heyer printed Robespierre's *A Report on the Institutions of National Morality and Festival in France. Delivered in the National Convention* . . . (New York: printed by Birdsall and Hyer, 1795). One New York printer could not remain idle "during the agonizing spasms of infuriated man, contending through blood and slaughter, for his long lost liberty." Eleazer Oswald, an English-born New York City artisan sold his small printing office and went to France to join the Revolutionary army. Oswald went into Ireland as a French agent before returning to the United States and dying at the age of forty in New York City's yellow fever epidemic of 1795. See Margaret Woodbury, *Public Opinion in Philadelphia* (Northampton, Massachusetts: Department of History, Smith College, 1920), 30. The original scholarly account of his life is by Scharf and Westcott, who had interviewed Oswald's surviving daughter. It would be interesting to know if he were one of the two sons of John Oswald, the pioneering Scottish Jacobin and socialist who died in 1793 as "Commandant of the First Battalion of Pikes, in service of the Republic of France." James H. Billington, *Fire in the Minds of Men: Origins of the Revolutionary Faith* (New York: Basic Books, 1980), 40; and Francis, lxvii.

27. John Clyde Oswald, *Printing in the Americas*, 2d ed., 2 vols. (Port Washington, N.Y.: Kennikat Press, 1965; originally published 1937), 2:559–60.

28. On Miranda's printers, see M. W. Hamilton, 270–71. See also John H. Sherman's own account of his adventures, *A General Account of the Miranda Expedition, Including the Trial and Execution of Ten of His Officers.* . . . (New York: McFarlane & Long, 1808); and Moses Smith, *The History of the Adventures and Sufferings of Moses Smith, During Five Years of His Life* . . . (Albany: printed by Packard & Van Benthuysen, 1814), 84–85.

29. Asbridge, 9; and Mack, 10. "Thousands are immured in convents without profit to themselves or the world; devouring the rich harvest of the field, and refusing nature an assisting hand in contributing to their support; as if their great creator had not intended them for a nobler purpose, than exhausting a lingering life in digging their own graves, and at last, supinely tumble into them, and mingle with the mother element." Asbridge, 11.

30. Mack, 12, 4; Asbridge, 16; Mack, 8; and Ringwood, 6.

31. Clough, 16; and Mack, 9.

32. Weed, 59, 45. He later attended "the reception of President Monroe, who was met on the Battery," 62.

33. On Folwell, see Williams quoted from *Newark Gazette*, September 4, 1798, in D. H. Stewart, 29, and Brigham, 1504. On Burdick, see *Boston Printers, Publishers, and Booksellers*, 62.

34. Munsell, *Typographical Miscellany*, 84; Brigham, 1498; D. H. Stewart, 880, 882; and Troy, *Farmers' Oracle*, June 6, 1797, quoted in Hamilton, 190–91. Wands later served briefly as a postmaster in Lansingburgh during 1797 before moving on to Philadelphia where he worked as a journeyman and actively participated in the formation of the society there. Taking an aggressively militant stance on the question of trade regulation by wage earners internally, he remained an active member until his death on October 5, 1810. See Hamilton, 305; and PTS, October 6, 1810.

35. [Dues Book] List of Members of the Washington Benevolent Society with Street Addresses and Trades, 1810, Manuscript Collections, New York Historical Society. Like his brother printers, the Washington Benevolent Society had difficulty spelling Huestis's name correctly, recording it as Hustis. Compare D. H. Stewart's political description of the newspapers of the early national period with the newspapers in Brigham, 1369–1494, under the management of participants in trade societies. Fassett, 85–86, and Fisher, 331–31, indicate Pasteur and Sherman probably came from the families of Federalist printers in, respectively, North Carolina and New Jersey.

36. Brigham, 1485; and D. H. Stewart, 879, 888.

37. Binns, 196; and Clark, 98–99, 123, 139. According to Rock, 27, New York City printers, booksellers, and bookbinders, along with curriers, were more likely to be Federalists than were hatters, cordwainers, tailors, or furriers, while the local building tradesmen, unconcerned directly about the tariff issue on which local Republicans appealed to mechanics, seemed divided. Journeymen probably split along similar lines, or, at least, had no real reason for doing otherwise but the gainsaying of their employers' politics.

38. Scharf and Westcott, 2:983, 3:1985. On White, see Brigham, 1502, and D. H. Stewart, 881. Jacob Schneider, possibly the member of the Philadelphia Typographical Society, was publicly horsewhipped at Penn Square in Reading, Pennsylvania, for his conspicuous role in the Fries Rebellion of 1798–99. Montgomery, 394–95, and Nolan, 12, 45–49. In the societies, only a few unionists, like John Pell and John Moffat—or Robert Townsend, Jr., of the carpenter's society—had been members of republican political clubs for some time prior to their involvement in organizing journeymen. Others, like Samuel Patterson, Thomas O'Neil, and Henry Sickels (or another union carpenter, Richardson Ryan) affiliated with Tammany at about the same time they became unionists. Still others, like Asbridge, John Black, Jeremiah Dodge, and David Perry, Jr., joined much later. Significantly, however, none of these men took membership prior to 1805, after the Repub-

licans had secured their hold on the city. Only Walter W. Heyer, later to be briefly active among the Philadelphia printers, became a member earlier, and, at that time, in 1789, the Tammany Society had yet to assume partisan political functions. Membership List, March 9, 1789–July 1, 1924, Tammaniana of Edwin P. Kilroe: Society of Tammany, or Columbian Order in the City of New York, Rare Books Room, Columbia University Library, New York City. One John Forbes, possibly the man later involved in the New York Typographical Society, addressed Tammany on May 12, 1804, cutting "a very sorry figure," according to the hostile account of the *Commercial Advertiser* of two days later. It added, "Very few characters of any kind of respectability were present. Many of our warmed Democrats were ashamed of the business, and prudently declined the honor of mixing with the motley crew." Quoted in Edwin P. Kilroe, *Saint Tammany and the Origins of the Society of Tammany or Columbian Order in the City of New York* (New York: Columbia University Press, 1913), 182. George Snyder of the Federal Society of Journeymen Cordwainers may have belonged to the short-lived Democratic Society of Pennsylvania, as did several close relatives of other unionists. Appendix A in *The Democratic-Republican Societies, 1790–1800: A Documentary Sourcebook of the Constitution, Declarations, Addresses, Resolutions, and Toasts*, ed. Philip S. Foner (Westport, Connecticut: Greenwood Press, 1976), 439–41, which also gives as members Adam Logan, a cordwainer, and two printers, Edmund Hogan and Peter Stewart, possibly relatives of Samuel Logan, Thomas Stewart, and Andrew Hogan, men active in the societies of their respective crafts. Daniel Dodge's father ran a Republican newspaper in New Jersey, and his uncle organized the Essex County Republicans. D. H. Stewart, 10–11, and *Columbian Centinel*, September 7, 1803, and *Spectator*, September 3, 1803. Joseph Gleason, Jr., the printer who later delivered Perkin's oration to the New York journeymen, spoke on behalf of the Young Democratic-Republicans in Boston in 1806.

39. (Stamford, N.Y.: reprinted by Daniel Lawrence, 1805; originally published 1801); and Churchill, 6–7.

40. Asbridge, 17–18; and Burdick, 22.

41. "Naval War with France, 1798–1801," 6; and "Naval War with Tripoli, 1801–1805," 6; in New Jersey Adjutant-General's Office, *Records of Officers and Men of New Jersey in Wars, 1791–1815* (Trenton: New Jersey legislature, 1893–1903). This work also noted the enlistment of Samuel Browning, the New York City cordwainer who joined the artillery in February, 1812, at nearby Governor's Island, leaving the service five years later in Pennsylvania. "War with Great Britain, 1812–1815," 157.

42. Binns, 172–73; and *Poulson's American Daily Advertiser*, October 6, 8, 1810.

43. Gilder, 119, 120–21; and Javier, 235–36. The New York

Typographical Society led seven hundred local workmen to Brooklyn to work on the fortifications there. R. S. Guernsey, *New York City and Vicinity during the War of 1812–15 . . .* , 2 vols. (New York: Woodward, 1889–95), 1:218–20. See also 219–22, 227, 331. Rock estimated that New York artisans of one sort or another contributed a total of 100,000 hours of voluntary labor on the Brooklyn fortifications alone, p. 90.

44. "Death of David H. Reins," 55. Woodworth's song later appeared in accounts about: craftsmen of the period, such as the piece on "George Bruce," in *The Printer*, 178; the war, Benson L. Lossing, *Pictoral Field Book of the War of 1812* (New York: Harper & Brothers, 1868), 970–71; local histories, Guernsey, 1:230–31; labor histories, Foner, *History of the Labor Movement*, 1:94–96; and folk song anthologies, *The Burl Ives Song Book* (New York: Ballantine Books, 1953), 126–27.

45. Mack, 7–8, in which he also cited the work of Stephen Decatur, Isaac Hull, William Jones, and William Bainbridge, and the deaths of James Lawrence, Augustus Ludlow, and Zebulon Pike, just as he and other journeyman orators recalled the heroes and martyrs of the Revolution.

46. *Pennsylvania Archives*, 6th ser., 1:143, 679, 7:425, 428, and 9:148. For "Colonel Cromwell Pearce's Account of the Battle" in which Hoppock fell, see *The Town of York, 1793–1815: A Collection of Documents of Early Toronto*, ed. Edith G. Firth (Toronto: Camplain Society for the Government of Ontario, 1966), 303–06.

47. "George Bruce," 178. Among these were William Carl, formerly of the Philadelphia printers' group and Robert Baird of the New York cordwainers, both of whom enlisted in New Jersey. "War with Great Britain, 1812–1815," in *Officers and Men of New Jersey in Wars*, 24, 37. For examples from among the Boston printers, see William D. Crockett, William Learned, Samuel B. Bradbury, Henry Nichols, and Eliakin Fish in *Records of the Massachusetts Volunteer Militia, called out by the governor of Massachusetts to suppress a Threatened Invasion during the War of 1812–1814* (Boston: Gardner W. Dearson, 1913).

48. Silver, *The American Printer*, 89. Of the third militia brigade, Benjamin Edes and John H. Bell, formerly of the printers' society, served, Edes doing so as a captain. Corporal William Faithful, a former activist in the Philadelphia trade, future member of the Washington union, and probably member of the Baltimore Typographical Association (organized out of the older society in 1812) was also present. Sergeants Abraham Edwards, John Davis, Jon Conners, and Alling Sergeant; Corporals James Darling and Jacob Cable; and Privates Martin Griffin, Alexander McCarthy, Charles Philips, William Randall, Aquila Taylor, Peter Callihan, Thomas Sanders, David Thompson, Thomas Appelby, Robert Boggus, and Levin Tyler had all been active in the old Union Society of Journeymen Cordwainers prior to its successful prosecution five years earlier. William M. Marine, *The British Invasion of*

Maryland, 1812–1815, ed. Louis H. Dielman (Baltimore: Society of the War of 1812, 1913). Nicholson and Key, incidentally, first sought out Edes, the former union officer, at his shop. Silver, "The Baltimore Book Trade," 119–20.

49. See above, note 46. Corry had been a leader of the society for some time prior to the war, signing the group's published reports like those which regularly appeared in the *Aurora.* See, for example, those published in the issues of October 30, 31, November 1, 2, 1804.

50. Rock, 90–97. Victor A. Sapio, *Pennsylvania and the War of 1812* (Lexington: University Press of Kentucky, 1970), points out the lack of direct economic interests residents of that state had in the waging of the conflict.

51. "Historical Sketch of the Philadelphia Typographical Society," *Printers' Circular* 2 (March 1867): 179. For the inability of the printer's society to muster a quorum, see NYTS.

52. Joseph Gales, Jr., followed a similar course in Washington. Their more successful craft brothers in Baltimore joined the Thirty-eighth United States Infantry raised there; Sheppard Church Leakin served among its captains, and Thomas J. Leakin and James Holmes were among its lieutenants. James Massey, another Baltimore printer, became a captain in the local militia. John Lambert Hoppock, before his death at York, achieved a captain's rank in the Fifteenth United States Infantry. David H. Reins, although still only a journeyman, pledged himself in New York City to raise a company of printers as a militia artillery unit. Binns, 232, also 214–19; Clark, 99–101; "Historical Sketch of the Philadelphia Typographical Society," *Printers' Circular* 2 (April 1867), 195, indicating that Robert Carr, the longstanding friend and later honorary member of the society also raised a regiment; Marine; New York Adjutant General's Office, *Index of Awards on the Claims of the Soldiers of the War of 1812,* 2d ed. (Baltimore: Genealogical Publishing Co., 1969; originally published 1860), 392; and Stevens, 81–82. On Hoppock, see "Historical Sketch," *Printers' Circular* 2 (March 1867): 179. To a lesser extent, of course, new masters could take this course to respectability in peacetime as well. Lieutenant Colonel Daniel Dodge commanded a regiment of the city militia by 1808, only a few years after serving as an officer of the Franklin Typographical Society. Wallabout Committee, 73–75.

53. Delano, 534, 137, 138. On Woodworth, see Stevens, 82–94. On the participation of the family of James Geoghan, see above, note 14.

54. Ringwood, 20, 21; Clough, 9; and Gleason, 18.

FOUR. Let None Be Deterred

1. For the use of this symbol by the Charleston Mechanics Society—with the slogan "Industry produceth wealth, 1794"—see Yates

Snowden, "Notes on Labor Organizations in South Carolina, 1742–1861," *Bulletin of the University of South Carolina* (Columbia, South Carolina: University Press, 1914), 43. See also the surviving runs of the *Independent Mechanic*, April 6, 1811, through September 26, 1812, and of the *Mechanics' Gazette*, June 8, 1822, through June 21, 1823. See also *Columbian*, March 14, 1815, cited in Rock, 90–91. A broad spectrum of labor radicals used the sign of the arm and hammer during the following decades. It appeared regularly in the labor press associated with the local Workingmen's Parties of the 1820s and 1830s through the formation of the short-lived Workingmen's Party of the United States in 1876. Its successor, the Socialistic Labor Party, maintained it through its reorganization in the 1890s by Daniel Deleon. The development of the Socialist Party and the Industrial Workers of the World early in the twentieth century did not challenge the Socialist Labor Party's exclusive use of the symbol. After World War I and the formation of Communist Party, some of the most radical of American labor militants chose to import the Russian hammer and sickle.

2. Quoted by Morgan and Morgan, 171, and Jonathon Boucher, *View of the Causes and Consequences of the American Revolution* (New York: Russell and Russell, 1976; originally published 1797), 309.

3. Morgan and Morgan, 244–49. See also Maier, 53–60.

4. For the peculiar course of the Revolution in Pennsylvania, see David Hawke, *In the Midst of a Revolution: The Politics of Confrontation in Colonial America* (Philadelphia: University of Pennsylvania Press, 1961). Richard Ryerson's *The Revolution is Now Begun* provides a more institutional view, and older studies include Charles H. Lincoln, *The Revolutionary Movement in Pennsylvnia* (Cos Cob, Connecticut: J. E. Edwards, 1968; originally published 1901); J. Paul Selsam, *The Pennsylvania Constitution of 1776* (Philadelphia: University of Pennsylvania Press, 1936); and Robert L. Brunhouse, *The Counterrevolution in Pennsylvania* (Philadelphia: University of Pennsylvania Press, 1942). For Pennsylvania's course in the context of the Revolution in other states, see Elisha P. Douglass, *Rebels and Democrats: The Struggle for Equal Political Rights and Majority Rule during the American Revolution* (Chapel Hill: University of North Carolina Press, 1955); and Gordon S. Wood, *The Creation of the American Republic, 1776–1787* (Chapel Hill: University of North Carolina Press, 1969). For the movement in the context of the development of the state's economic policies, see Louis Hartz, *Economic Policy and Democratic Thought: Pennsylvania, 1776–1860* (Cambridge: Harvard University Press, 1948). Eric Foner's study of *Tom Paine and Revolutionary America* (New York: Oxford University Press, 1976) focuses on a key figure in the Philadelphia movement. In contrast to the uniquely democratic course of the Revolution in Pennsylvania, the older British and ultimately victorious system of institutionalized checks and balances

found its ablest American defender in John Adams, whose *Thoughts on Government* circulated widely among the writers of other state constitutions.

5. Brunhouse, 68, 69–70, 72–76; *Pennsylvania Packet*, January 16, 1779; *Colonial Records of Pennsylvania*, 11:664, 665; and Richard B. Morris, "Labor and Mercantilism," *The Era of the American Revolution*, ed. Richard B. Morris (New York: Harper and Row, 1939), 114.

6. *Stationers Company Apprentices*, 124, 263, 290; and *Pennsylvania Archives*, ser. 5, 2: 832, 878, 4: 119. See also Gerald Fothergill, *Emmigrants from England, 1773-1776* (Boston: New England Historic and Genealogical Society, 1913), 144; and *Passengers to America: A Consolidation of Ship Passenger Lists from the New England Historical and Genealogical Register*, ed. Michael Tepper, 2d ed. (Baltimore: Genealogical Publishing Co., 1978), 367; both are cited in *Passenger and Immigration Lists Index*, ed. P. William Filby and Mary K. Meyer, 3 vols. (Detroit: Gail Research Company, 1981), for which a supplementary volume appeared in 1983. On the paper shortage, see Hawke, *In the Midst of a Revolution*, 48. See also Rosemont, 410; and John B. B. Trussell, Jr., *The Pennsylvania Line: Regimental Organization and Operation, 1776-1783* (Harrisburg: Pennsylvania Historical and Museum Commission, 1977), 36–37, 51. After Bergen Heights, the Second Regiment accompanied Major General Anthony Wayne to Hartford to welcome the allied French troops and escort them to Tappan, New York, from which the unit made a forced march to West Point, foiling Benedict Arnold's attempt to betray the post to the enemy, 49–51. Like roughly six in ten of his comrades whose birthplaces can be determined, Lecount had been born outside of the colonies, and, like two in three, he worked at an occupation other than farming. Trussell, 44–45, 49, 249, 253. Also like them, Lecount had enlisted for "three years or during the war," and, after the completion of three years of active duty, including service in most of the major engagements of the war, they faced the refusal of their officers to dismiss them. This deprived them of the more lucrative bounties offered later in the conflict to entice new enlistments. Like the rest of the Line, they had received promises upon joining which, after three years of fighting, seemed no nearer fulfillment by the Revolutionary authorities.

7. Carl Van Doren, *Mutiny in January* (New York: Viking Press, 1943), 42–60, 72–78, 125–27, 211, 217–24. Van Doren wrote that the Second Regiment was "forced to join or else be bayoneted," 46; Trussell, 51, repeated this account. Yet the similar composition of this unit to the others in the Line, their common experiences and grievances, their participation in the Bergen Heights affair, and the apparent support for the revolt by the regiment evident over the next days suggests caution in accepting this evaluation, particularly given its probable

source among the officers of that unit, anxious to minimize the disaffection of the men in their charge. Charles Royster puts the mutiny into the framework of broad popular support for the Revolution in *A Revolutionary People at War: The Continental Army and American Character, 1775–1783* (Chapel Hill: University of North Carolina Press, 1979), 303–08.

8. *Pennsylvania Packet,* May 29, 1781; Van Doren, 234–36, 250–57; Trussell, 51, 261–62; Watson, 2:331–32; Kenneth L. Bowling, "New Light on the Philadelphia Mutiny of 1783: Federal-State Confrontation at the Close of the War for Independence," *Pennsylvania Magazine of History and Biography* 101 (1977): 419–50; Bray Hammond, *Banks and Politics in America: From the Revolution to the Civil War,* 2d ed. (Princeton: Princeton University Press, 1967), 52–53. For Lecount's presence among the reenlistments, see the account kept by one of the officers and reprinted in the *History of Cumberland and Adams Counties, Pennsylvania,* 3 vols. (Chicago: Warner, Baer & Co., 1886), 3:34–35; and John Gibson, *History of York County Pennsylvania* (Chicago: F. A. Battey Publishing Co., 1886), 148.

9. On Lecount's later militia service, see the *Pennsylvania Archives,* 6th ser., 3:1176; and Rosemont lists him among the strikers of 1786. 399, 410.

10. On regulation and the legacy of mercantilism, see also Richard B. Morris, *Government and Labor in Early America,* 2d ed. (New York: Harper & Row, 1965), 1–135; and Rock, 205–34. At times, workers in the municipally regulated trades did act in concert. See Kenneth W. Keeler, "The Philadelphia Pilots' Strike of 1792," *Labor History* 18 (Winter 1977), 36–48.

11. Elias P. Oberholtzer, *Robert Morris* (New York: Burt Franklin, 1963; originally published 1903), 51–56; *Letters to and from Caesar Rodney,* ed. George Herbert Ryden (Philadelphia: University of Pennsylvania Press for the Historical Society of Delaware, 1933), 303; Brunhouse, 71; *Connecticut Courant,* May 12, 1777; and Council of Censors, quoted in Morris, *Government and Labor,* 121, 122. See also 113, 114–15; and Brunhouse, 73.

12. Quoted by Douglass, 266; and Hawke, 190.

13. Scott, *A Discourse,* 15, 5; Churchill, 5.

14. Samuel Huestis, for example, later published John Calvin, *The Institutions of the Christian Religion* (New York: printed by C. S. Van Winkle, 1819). On Winnard, see Moses Auge, *Lives of the emminent dead and biographical notices of Prominent living citizens of Montgomery County, Pennsylvania* (Noristown: Moses Auge, 1879), 412–13; Theodore W. Bean, *History of Montgomery County, Pennsylvania* (Philadelphia: Evarts & Peck, 1884), 461. The Quaker presence was obvious in internal disputes over formal oath-taking, which caused particular problems among the shoemakers of Pennsylvania. See *Trial*

of the Boot & Shoemakers of Philadelphia, 93; and *Report of the Trial of the Journeymen Cordwainers*, 26, 30, 36, 37. See, too, William W. Wand's promotion of the millenarian tract by James Bickeno, *The Sign of the Times; or, the Overthrow of the Papal Tyranny in France, the Prelude of Destruction to Popery and Despotism: but of peace to Mankind*, 2d ed. (Albany: printed by Charles R. and George Webster, 1795) which predicted that the world, formed in 4004 B.C., would end in A.D. 1864. 62–65, and Nathaniel Willis, "A Newspaper Experience of More Than Half a Century," *The Printer* 3 (November 1860): 121–22. See also, Whitney R. Cross, *The Burned-Over District: The Social and Intellectual History of Enthusiastic Religion in Western New York, 1800–1850*, 2d ed. (New York: Harper and Row, 1965). Speaking as a representative of his union, Burdick discussed with pride the role of printing in the Reformation, reflecting the hegemony of Protestantism in the early societies.

15. On the Catholics, see Michael Duffy, *A Short Abridgement of Christian Doctrine. Newly Revised for the Use of the Catholic Church in the United States of America . . .*, 14th ed. (Baltimore: printed by Michael Duffy, 1798); and Binns, 305–10; 339–40. Woodworth's views were common knowledge among his contemporaries and peers and are often mentioned in even the most brief sketches of his life and work. See, for example, the sketch in *American Authors, 1600–1900: A Biographical Dictionary of American Literature*, ed. Stanley J. Kunitz and Howard Haycraft (New York: H. M. Wilson Co. 1938), 836. Anthony Armbruster, one of Franklin's former partners, was a native German, who kept an Old World book which he and his associates used to protect themselves from the "subterranean passages" of the Devil during their frequent treasure hunts near the city. He used the book in rites "of pretended exorcism and divination," which ended in their "describing a circle and uttering some effectual abracadabra." He and his followers often would "arise, at midnight, and spread out a large sheet of whimsical drawings which he possessed, and surround it with four or five candles." McCulloch, 195, 196; and Thomas, 1:250.

16. Churchill, 6, 8, and Scott, *A Discourse*, 11–12. Most Americans of the age faced a similar contradiction between their belief in human depravity and their hope for perfectability of some sorts. See Russel B. Nye, *The Cultural Life of the New Nation, 1776–1830* (New York: Harper & Row, 1963), 20–21, 129–30.

17. One sees the roots of this idea extending back even earlier than the broad popular awakening of the 1790s through the 1830s. The Rev. Samuel Fish, for example, argued as early as 1789 that, although the unfortunate were to be always among us, American Christians must not "bid off the poor at public vendue," retaining slavery and indentured servitude. Despite the Revolution, the nation "is become filthy, the scum remaineth and is not purged out, and we remain a wicked and

unreformed people" facing either "reformation or final ruin" in the near future. The more well-off Americans were brothers in sin with the working poor. "Let us deal our bread to the hungry, and bring the poor that are cast out to our houses," he suggested, "and when we see the naked let us cover them. Let us draw out the soul to the hungry, and satisfy the afflicted soul; then shall though call and the Lord shall answer, here I am." *The Rights of the Poor Defended. In a Discourse on Matthew XXV, 6. Sermon at Lebanon, Connecticut, May 30, 1789* (Norwich, Connecticut: printed by John Trumbull, 1789), 7, 8, 18, 20, 24.

18. *Reflection on Political Society*, 3, 4, 6. On Charles Christian, see Francis, 136; Moncure D. Conway, *The Life of Thomas Paine*, ed. Hypatia Bradlaugh Bonner (London: Watts, 1909), 301; [George Henry Evans,] "A Brief Sketch of the Life of Thomas Paine," in *The Political Writings of Thomas Paine*, ed. George Henry Evans, 2 vols. (Granville, N.J.: G. Evans, 1844), 1:x–xi. Certainly some early unionists thoroughly repudiated this course. In religious New England, the Boston journeymen circulated Burdick's oration, which included a statement of shock at the appearance of "an open and avowedly atheistical paper," Philadelphia's *The Temple of Reason*. This publication, which was actually, of course, a deist rather than atheist paper, helped introduce the heresies contained in writings like those of William Godwin, Mary Wollstonecraft, and Thomas Paine to American readers; Burdick, 14–15. Ira Jones, for example, while operating his own small press in Connecticut, printed and probably wrote *A present to the Unprejudiced. Being an Attempt to Prove that the Soul and Body of Man cannot be seperated;—that when the body dies, the soul dies also;—and that at the Resurrection they both shall rise together. By a Layman* (Newfield, Connecticut: printed by Beach and Jones, 1795). That a layman would write on such a subject reflected the broad interest in such issues. John Thompson printed American editions of Joseph Priestly's deist and rationalist tracts, including *Unitarianism Explained and Defended* (Philadelphia: printed by John Thompson, 1796); *Discourses Relating to the Evidence of Revealed Religion . . . .* (Philadelphia: printed by John Thompson, 1796); and *Observations on the Increase of Fidelity* (Philadelphia: printed [by John Thompson] for Thomas Dobson, 1797).

19. Mack, 3; Burdick, 8, 5; and Scott, *A Discourse*, 7, 11–12.

20. Asbridge, 5, 18–19; and Churchill, 5.

21. Thomas Hobbes, *Leviathon; or the Matter, Forme and Power of a Commonwealth Ecclesiastical and Civil*, ed. Michael Oakeshaft (New York: Collier Books, 1962), 132; John Locke, "The Second Treatise of Government: An Essay Concerning the True Original Extent, and End of Civil Government," sec. 119, in *Two Treatises of Government*, ed. Peter Laslett, 2d ed. (New York and Toronto: Mentor Books, 1965),

392; and Asbridge, 18. Journeymen were also familiar with Jean Jacque Rousseau's arguments. Samuel Longcope, for example, printed his *Eloisa: Or, a Series of Original Letters.* . . . (Philadelphia: printed for Samuel Longcope, 1794).

22. February 22, 1802, statement of Philadelphia printers, E. Stewart, 865. See, too, *The Journeymen Cabinet and Chair-Makers of New York Book of Prices* (New York: n.p., 1796), 3; *New York Evening Post,* May 14, 1809, February 13, 1813.

23. Ringwood, 6; Clough, 10; and Burdick, 18.

24. Mack, 4, 7; Asbridge, 10; and Ringwood, 8.

25. "The Address of the Working Shoemakers," in *The Faith of Our Fathers: An Anthology Expressing the Aspirations of the American Common Man, 1790–1860,* ed. Irving Mark and Eugene L. Schwaab (New York: Alfred A. Knopf, 1952), 335; New York *Independent Journal,* September 21, 1785; and *New York Evening Post,* January 30, 1813. Much of the dispute centered in a broader debate over the actual goals of the American Revolution and the meaning of the Declaration of Independence, see Marjorie S. Turner, *The Early American Labor Conspiracy Cases: Their Place in Labor Law—A Reinterpretation* (San Diego: San Diego State College Press, 1967), 34–36.

26. Asbridge, 16; *Evening Post,* January 5, 1803; and *American Citizen,* May 23, 1810.

27. "The Address of the Working Shoemakers," in *The Faith,* 334; Burdick, 214; and Mack, 13.

28. *American Citizen,* April 10, 1809. Nor was this the only labor organization of the period which directly copied the wording of one of their formal statements directly from that of the Declaration of American Independence. See, for some other examples, the debate between the masters and journeymen cabinet- and chairmakers of New York City in: *American Citizen,* December 22, 1802; *Morning Chronicle,* December 31, 1802; and *Evening Post,* January 5 through 7, 1803. For later examples, see *We, the Other People: Alternative Declaration of Independence by Labor Groups, Farmers, Woman's Rights Advocates, Socialists, and Blacks, 1829–1975,* ed. Philip S. Foner (Urbana and Chicago: University of Illinois Press, 1976).

29. For the "escalator clause," see *The Cabinet-Makers' Philadelphia and London Book of Prices* (Philadelphia: Snowden and McCorckle, 1796), introduction. On the C.I.O.'s efforts, see Art Preis, *Labor's Giant Step,* 2d ed. (New York: Monad Books, 1972), 153–54, 304–05, 308.

30. On the printers, see Barnett, 143. Philadelphia house carpenters turned out in 1791 to demand "compensation extraordinary" for working longer than ten hours. *Dunlap's Daily Advertiser,* May 11, 1791, reprinted almost in its entirety in *The Faith,* 331–34. One observer sneered at their effort, "They will work from six to six—how absurd!" *Federal Gazette,* May 11, 1791. Although local employers apparently

defeated the effort, masters elsewhere were forced to concede. New York City masters, for example, agreed in 1805 to resolve "much irregularity and confusion" by imposing "a uniform regulation, pointing out the proper time to be observed by Carpenters and Masons," seasonally adjusted "to enable them to work ten hours in the long, and nine in the short days." At about the same time, employers in the local shipyards began blacklisting "journeymen ship carpenters, caulkers, and others who were then agitating for shorter hours. Company of Master Builders, *Whereas experience has shewn that much irregularity and confusion has taken place . . . meeting held on the 11th of March 1805 . . .* , broadside (New York: printed by Isaac Collins & sons, [1805]), 337–38. The building trade was the major battleground over this issue in the 1820s and 1830s when Boston and Philadelphia workmen struggled to gain the ten-hour day, and their New York City brothers fought to keep it. See David R. Roediger and Philip S. Foner, *Our Own Time: A History of American Labor and the Working Day* (New York: Verso, 1989), 10–12, 24–25, 30–34.

31. Virtually every issue of the *Mechanic's Free Press* in the late 1820s contains an ongoing discussion among workingmen about cooperation. For a sample, see the articles reprinted in *Doc. Hist.* 5:124–37. Theorists and scholars have generally failed to give cooperative activity its proper emphasis. Saposs, for example, discussed only the cooperatives of early carpenters and cordwainers in John R. Commons, David J. Saposs, Helen L. Sumner, E. B. Mittelmann, H. E. Hoagland, John B. Andrews, and Selig Perlman, *History of Labour in the United States*, 2nd ed., 4 vols. (New York: MacMillan Co., 1946), 2:127–30. Also in error is Ian Quimby's description of early cooperation as "a measure of the ineffectiveness of the attempt to form union." "The Cordwainers Protest: A Crisis in Labor Relations," *Winterthur Portfolio* 3 (1967): 91. Cooperatives in the early national period developed as adjuncts to struggles over wages, working conditions and hours; rather than "a measure of the ineffectiveness of the attempt to form unions," these formed a component of what effectiveness the unions had. For some of the theory that such efforts later inspired abroad, see Pierre-Joseph Proudhon, *Selected Writings of Proudhon*, ed. Stewart Edwards (Garden City, N.Y.: Anchor Books, 1969), 124, 133. "Labor must be paid for only by labor and the raw material must be free," argued Proudhon, 129. Karl Marx and Friederich Engels continually disparaged such utopian advocacy of such measures, but they were among the few early labor theorists who recognized that cooperative activity emerged from the material conditions and strivings of workers rather than from any abstract theories, arguing that workers "repeatedly set up collective enterprises which, however, always perished because they were unable to compete" against the ever larger and more well financed capitalist

enterprises. *The German Ideology,* in *Collected Works,* Vol. 5, Marx and Engels: 1845–1847 (Moscow: Progress Publishers, 1976), 371.

32. For the cabinetmakers, see below for Philadelphia, and for New York; *American Citizen,* December 8, 1802; for their employers' response, *New York Evening Post,* December 28, 1802, and January 5, 1803; for the journeymen's rebuttal, *New York Evening Post,* January 5, 7, 1803; *American Citizen,* April 16, 1803; and the *New York Gazette and General Advertiser,* April 26, 1803. For those of the carpenters: *Independent Journal; or, General Advertiser,* September 21, 1785; *Dunlap's American Daily Advertiser,* May 11, 1791, in *The Faith,* 334; and *American Citizen,* May 23, 1810. A Journeymen Carpenters Association may have pioneered cooperative ventures of this sort decades earlier. *New York Gazette,* November 18, 1771, cited in Morris, *Government and Labor,* 199. For those of the cordwainers: Baltimore *Daily Intelligencer,* June 28, 1795; "Brutus" in the *Commercial Advertiser,* April 20, 1801; *Aurora,* April 26, 28, 1806; New York *Evening Post,* February 4, 1815, and January 30, February 14, 1813; and Steffens, 176–77. For those of the tailors, see the Baltimore *American and Daily Advertiser,* June 5, 1799. Significantly, workers had formed such a house of call as early as 1768 in response to a "late Reduction of [the] Wages of journeymen Taylors" in the city. *New York Journal,* April 7, 1768, cited in Morris, *Government and Labor,* 196.

33. Asbridge, 21–22.

34. Scharf and Westcott, 2:987. The "five alls" of contemporary rural Britain included a king, a bishop, a lawyer, and a poor countryman, the lawyer claiming "I plead for all." See "Alls" in Francis Gose, *1811 Dictionary of the Vulgar Tongue: A Dictionary of Buckish Slang, University Wit, and Pickpocket Eloquence,* foreward by Robert Cromie (Northfield, Illinois: Digest Books, 1971).

35. *Trial of the Boot & Shoemakers of Philadelphia,* 61, 59; "Historical Sketch of the Philadelphia Typographical Society," 195; and PTS, December 16, 14, 1803, January 7, 11, 1804.

36. *Federal Gazette,* May 17, 1791; *American Citizen,* June 2, 1810; *New York Evening Post,* November 24, 1804; and letter to Building Committee of the New York City Hall, n.d., John McComb MS, New York Historical Society, discussed in Rock, 284–85.

37. NYTS, February 24, March 3, 24, 31, 1810; partially reprinted in Barnett, 357–58. The location of the general meeting of March 3 was specifically identified as Harmony Hall—the carpenters' meeting place as well. The veteran Philadelphia freethinker, Edward Thompson, mentioned the tavern, which in 1825 hosted a celebration of Paine's birthday. George E. McDonald quotes him in *Fifty Years of Freethought,* 2 vols. (New York: Truth Seeker Co., 1929 and 1931), 2:576. The cordwainers apparently wanted financial help from other societies to enable them to appeal the case to a higher court.

38. *The Philadelphia Cabinet and Chair-Makers Book of Prices* (Philadelphia: n.p., 1794), of which no copy has survived, but for which copyright information remains, as does an announcement of its availability. *Pennsylvania Gazette*, May 28, 1794. *The Journeymen Cabinet and Chair-Makers' Book of Prices* (Philadelphia: printed by Ormrod & Conrad, 1795), 3; and *Pennsylvania Packet*, July 16, 1795.

39. *Aurora, and General Advertiser*, April 7, 1796.

40. *Ibid; Pennsylvania Packet*, February 17, 1796.

41. *Pennsylvania Packet*, February 17, 1796.

42. *Aurora, and General Advertiser*, April 7, 1796.

43. *Ibid.* On the Federal Society of Journeymen Cordwainers, see *Trial of the Boot & Shoemakers of Philadelphia*, 93–94.

44. The actual destiny of the Federal Society of Journeymen Cabinet and Chair-Makers remains uncertain, but it may have survived for another decade, when a new organization appeared that may have only been the result of a reorganization of the existing union in an attempt to avoid the danger of criminal prosecution. Eighteen hundred six was, after all, the year of the cordwainers' trial. *The Constitution of the Pennsylvania Society of Journeymen Cabinet-Makers of the City of Philadelphia. Instituted November 8, 1806—Incorporated May 20, 1825. Revised October 10, 1829* (Philadelphia: printed by Garden and Thompson, 1829).

45. "Address to the Journeymen Cordwainers L.B. of Philadelphia," in *American Labor Songs of the Nineteenth Century*, ed. Philip S. Foner (Urbana and Chicago: University of Illinois Press, 1974), 11, 12. McIlvaine was probably then about twenty years of age. He died in August, 1836, at the age of fifty-seven. See Barker, 515, cited above, Prologue, note 19.

46. Quoted by Lynd, *Intellectual Origins of American Radicalism*, 21–22.

47. Quoted by Lynd, "The Mechanics in New York Politics," 21–22; *Maryland Gazette*, February 29, 1788; *Pennsylvania Packet*, November 5, 1776; *Independent Chronicle*, September 8, 1791; *Aurora*, April 28, 1806. Between "the aristocracy and democracy, that is the rich and the poor there is constant warfare." *Maryland Gazette*, February 29, 1788. These are quoted in Main's *Social Structure*, 226, 229–30, 236–38; Lance Banning, *The Jeffersonian Persuassion: Evolution of a Party Ideology* (Ithaca, New York: Cornell University Press, 1978), 158–59; and Morris, "Labor and Mercantilism," 132.

48. Manning, *The Key of Libberty, Shewing the Causes Why a Free Government has Always Failed, and a Remidy Against It*, comp. Samuel Eliot Morison (Billerica, Massachusetts: Manning Association, 1922), 5, 15; and "Seditious Writings," in *The Faith*, 46. Manning felt that he offered "no new docterin if I may judge from the many scraps of history I have Seen of antiant Republicks." Nevertheless, the Fed-

eralist passage of the Sedition Law in 1798 seems to have made the publication of his work unadvisable for a cautious editor. Manning, 5, ix–xi. For the curious tale of David Brown, who collided directly with the Federal crusade against sedition, see James Morton Smith, *Freedom's Fetters: the Alien and Sedition Laws and American Civil Liberties,* 2d ed. (Ithaca, New York: Cornell University Press, 1956), 257–70. Although Federal prosecution brought to light Brown's speeches and poetry, their confiscation by the government resulted in their destruction. Fortunately, the prosecution used extensive quotations from them in the indictment, which provided Irving Mark and Eugene L. Schwaab with their short selection of Brown's writings in their 1952 anthology. Unfortunately, however, the original indictment has since disappeared from the Federal Archives and Records Center at Waltham Massachusetts. Letters to the author, November 12, 22, 1974.

Brown, who claimed to have visited eighty Massachusetts towns in the course of his activities, probably had occasion to pass the "Old Manse," Manning's home "on the main road between the seacoast and the upper Merrimac Valley," posing the interesting possibility that the two knew each other and perhaps influenced the development of each other's thinking. Manning, v.

49. Eaton, 74, 7–8.

50. *Ibid,* 8, 27, and for the figures he lampooned, 35–38, 42–44, 48–49, 66–67. See also, "The Auctioneer," "The Modern Merchant," and "The Grocers," on 31–33, 33–35, and 52–56.

51. Manning, 16–17; *Massachusetts Mercury,* May 26, 1799, or *Salem Gazette,* March 29, 1799; and Brown in *The Faith,* 45, 46. Note Brown's striking anticipation of William Heighton's concern as to whether "the sacred sounds of LIBERTY and EQUALITY have any actual existence among us, or are, in reality, more than mere empty sounds?" Heighton concluded that "real liberty and equality, have never yet been attained, even by American citizens. . . ." *The Principles of Aristocratic Legislation, Developed in an Address, Delivered to the Working People of the District of Southwark . . . ,* (Philadelphia: John Coates, Jr., Printer, 1828), 6.

52. Eaton, 56–57.

53. Paine, *Rights of Man, Part Second,* and *Agrarian Justice,* in *The Life and Major Writings of Thomas Paine,* ed. Philip S. Foner, 2d ed. (Secaucus, New Jersey: Citadel Press, 1974), 425–31, 433–39, 610, 611.

54. In general, see Mark A. Lause, "The 'Unwashed Infidelity': Thomas Paine and Early New York City Labor History," *Labor History* 27 (Summer 1986): 385–409. On Bruce, see "Reminiscences of Thomas Paine." On Ming, see Gilbert Vale, *The Life of Thomas Paine* (New York: Gilbert Vale, 1841), 159; and Hugins, 90. One John McLaughlin, apparently the man of that name who later became a member of the Columbia Typographical Society, also printed an edition of *The*

Rights of Man (Nashville, Tennessee: John McLaughlin, 1799); and, on his membership, see Constitution of the Columbia Typographical Union. A striker of 1786, Richard Folwell printed *Agrarian Justice* (Philadelphia: R. Folwell, for B. F. Bache, 1797). On Christian, see Francis, 136; Conway, 301; and Evans, "A Brief Sketch of the Life of Thomas Paine," x–xi. Christian later applied his rationalist mind to the task of organizing the early city. See his *A Brief Treatise, on the Police of the City of New-York. By a Citizen.* (New York: printed by Southwick & Pelsue, 1812); and his *Notes on the Police of the City of New-York. . . .* (New York: J. Seymour, 1813), issued in a second edition by Seymour in 1818.

55. Eaton, 9–10; and *Proposal by J. W. Scott, for publishing by subscription. The Moment: a poem, addressed to the American people and other poems By J. McCoy* (broadside; Philadelphia: n.p., 1809). For Paine's proposal that republican governments give the equivalent of fifteen pounds to each young person arriving at twenty-one years of age, see his *Agrarian Justice,* in the *The Life and Major Writings of Thomas Paine,* 612–13, 618. Along similar lines, Benjamin Franklin, in his will, provided a fund from which young tradesmen could draw loans. Van Doren, *Benjamin Franklin,* 762–64.

EPILOGUE. To Digest a Plan

1. NYTS, May 26, 1810; [Cornelius Camden Blatchly,] *An Essay on Common Wealths* (New York: New-York Society for Promoting Communities, 1822), 3–4; Stevens, 107.

2. "The Address of the Working Shoemakers of Philadelphia, to the Public," *Aurora, and General Advertiser,* November 28, 1805; in *The Faith,* 336; and *Trial of the Boot & Shoemakers of Philadelphia,* 111. The *Aurora* took its stance the day before the union addressed the public. "Among the blessings which were promised to mankind by the American revolution," argued its editorial, "was the emancipation of industry from fetters forged by luxury, laziness, aristocracy and fraud." Should the masters have the right to "say to another, contrary to the will of him who labors, what shall be the price of his labor," the Federal Constitution would be "a farce" and the Bill of Rights "only a satire upon human credulity." November 27, 1805.

3. Labor historians have tended to view the acquittal of unionists in the 1842 appeal of the *Commonwealth v. Hunt* as the final blow to the use of common law to prosecute labor organizations, but Marjorie Turner found an additional twenty-seven such labor trials between 1843 and 1890. Later judges, it seems, acknowledged *Commonwealth v. Hunt* as establishing workers' legal right to have unions, but nevertheless convicted unionists for the "criminal," "unlawful," "mischievous," "oppressive" or other "bad purposes" their organiza-

tions pursued. As officially applied, the law upheld the employers' right to hire private armies to break labor organizations and use the police, militia, and regular army to demobilize unionists. Similarly, the politicians and the courts showed very little interest in the way civic, social, and business associations of employers engaged in concerted actions of all sorts, even as they acted against labor organizations that used tactics like the boycott of unfair employers; Turner, 58–72. Turner also argues, on 71–72, that common law may again be used to prosecute labor organizations. See also Raymond L. Hogler's discussion in "Labor History and Criminal Labor Law: An Interdisciplinary Approach," *Labor History* 30 (Spring 1989): 171–74.

4. Significantly, labor prosecutions involved men of both Republican and federalist persuasions. For example, while one faction of the Democratic-Republicans defended the Philadelphia cordwainers, another faction prosecuted it. Certainly, in that case, the defendants had an able and dedicated advocate in Caesar Rodney, a prominent Jeffersonian later to serve as U.S. Attorney General under President James Madison, but their peers in Baltimore found an advocate in Luther Martin, the Federalist lawyer who had frustrated Jefferson with his defense of Aaron Burr a few years earlier. Employing shoemakers and tanners met upon the generally common ground of their Republican political affiliations to undermine the sources of leather for a journeymen's cooperative workshop; the Republican tanners backed their political cothinkers among employing shoemakers seeking to impose a new rule requiring any applicant for employment in the craft to carry a "discharge in writing" from his previous employer. Quimby, 83. William Duane's editorial on behalf of the right of the Federal Society of Journeymen Cordwainers to organize is in the *Aurora,* May 26, 1806. See also: Walter Nelles, "The First American Labor Case," *Yale Law Journal* 41 (1931): 170–73; Paul S. Clarkson and R. Samuel Jett, *Luther Martin of Maryland* (Baltimore and London: Johns Hopkins Press, 1970), 277–78. Charles Steffen acknowledges Martin's defense but still implied that the workingmen tended to be Republican. 223; and *Commercial Advertiser,* April 20, 18, 1801; and Rock, 65. See, too, the Union Society of Journeymen Cordwainers, September 19, October 19, 1808, and the *New York Evening Post,* October 24, 1808. The failure of the local newspapers to reprint this union renunciation of the act—and there would have been little point in issuing a renunciation had it not sent copies to the local press—and the failure of the New York City editor to clearly label the events it described as taking place in Baltimore caused some confusion. Rock ascribed the act to the New York Society, p. 280, while Steffen, without a copy of the disassociation from the act, overemphasized the intensity of working-class Republicanism in Baltimore, 196–98. On the New York printers, see Guersey, 1:260–61, 262. Baptis Irvine, who, as the Republican editor of the *Baltimore Whig,* encouraged

the 1812 riot against the *Federal Republican,* had infuriated the Philadelphia Typographical Society by working below scale in that city as a non-union printer. Brigham, 1436; and PTS, May 16, 1807. Bartholomew Graves, who left the society in 1803, became both a locally prominent Republican and an anti-union master printer, issuing the *Trial of the Boot & Shoemakers of Philadelphia* with its admonition that "It is better that the law be known and certain, than that it be right," p. 59.

5. See the *American Citizen,* March 22, 1810, and the *Examiner,* January 1, 1814, both quoted and discussed in Rock, 127, 94–95. Like David Brown, "Poor Mechanic" wrote, in words anticipating William Heighton's, "When we can become united like a band of brothers in claiming our equal rights, oppression will begin to totter on its throne, and extortion tremble on its rotten seat." *An Address Delivered before the Mechanics and Working Classes Generally, of the City and County of Philadelphia at the Universalist Church, in Callowhill Street, on Wednesday Evening, November 12, 1827. By the "Unlettered Mechanic."* (Philadelphia: published by request of the Mechanics' Gazette, 1829), 14.

6. Commons, 1:125.

7. E. Stewart, 892.

8. Stevens, 107–09; and E. Stewart, 896–97.

9. On Willis, "Boston printers' Festival," *The Printer* 2 (June 1859): 26. On Reins, "New York Typographical Society," *The Printer* 2 (July 1859): 49; the previously cited obituary on "The Death of David H. Reins," which took place on March 23, 1862, at West Farms, now part of the Bronx; and Stevens, 81–82. A veteran of the still older Franklin Typographical Association maintained an active interest in the craft until his death in 1866, some sixty years after setting up shop in the old printing office of the Tory publisher James Rivington. "George Bruce," 178. For an untitled but lengthy sketch of David Bruce, see *The Printer* 1 (March 1859): 257–59. Thomas G. Woodward, too, retained his ties to the craft until his death of consumption at Bellevue in 1872. *Printers' Circular* 7 (March 1870): 19. Charles McDevitt, who joined the New York Typographical Society shortly before its rejection of regulatory activities, remained active well into the 1870s, dying in 1876. On McDevitt, see the piece on the "New York Typographical Society," cited above; *The Printer* 5 (February 1864): 51–52; his "Extract from 'Typographical Reminiscences,' Read at the Celebration of Franklin's Birthday, January 17, 1865," in *The Printer* 6 (February 1865): 21–22; accounts of his activities in *The Printers' Circular* 2 (February 1868): 391–92, 7 (August 1873): 212, and 11 (September 1876): 188; and *Tribute to the Memory of Charles McDevitt who was nearly Sixty Years a member of the New York Typographical Society* (New York: F. Hart & Co., state printers, 1877). For William Wood, possibly the early

unionist of the same name, see the *Printers' Circular* 12 (May 1877): 64.

10. A small circle of Ricardian socialists began to work for the establishment of a city-wide organization. By the end of the following year, they had constructed the Mechanics' Union. Among them was the apparent target of John McIlvaine's "Address to the Journeymen Cordwainers L.B.," in *American Labor Songs of the Nineteenth Century*, 11 and 12. John J. Dubois, the shoemaker, also worked periodically as a scrivener, hence plausibly inspiring McIlvaine's granting of the "L.B." *The Philadelphia Directory for 1797.* Dubois had apparently completed his apprenticeship around 1794, the year of both his marriage and his initial participation in the organizing drive among local shoemakers from which the Federal Society emerged. For his marriage to Juliana Miller on February 27, 1794, at St. Paul's, see "Pennsylvania Marriages Prior to 1810," in *Pennsylvania Archives*, 2d ser. 9:492; and for involvement in the early union, *Trial of the Boot & Shoemakers of Philadelphia*. For listings of Dubois as a shoemaker, see *The Philadelphia Directory for 1800. By Cornelius William Stafford* (Philadelphia: printed by William W. Woodward, 1800); and James Robinson, *Philadelphia Directory* for 1802, 1803, 1805, 1806, 1808, and 1809. If his advocacy of caution and moderation during the disputes of 1804–05 were symptomatic of an earlier attitude, he may well have been skeptical of proposals like those of the printer McIlvaine or the cabinetmaker Christian. In any case, as a leader of that union, he had managed its strikes of 1799, 1804, and 1805, had faced trial and conviction on its behalf in the course of its prosecution in 1806.

In an age when workers were particularly transient and short-lived, Dubois had seen many of his former union brothers come and go. George Keimer, the secretary of the society and Dubois' codefendant in 1806 turned up, eight years later, in distant St. Louis, selling shoes made in Philadelphia. *Missouri Gazette*, July 16, 1814, in Frederic L. Billon, *Annals of St. Louis* (New York: Arno Press, 1971; originally published 1888), 129. James Geoghegan, the organizer of the union's defense during the trial, died in 1825. *Index of Wills and Administrative Records: Philadelphia, Pennsylvania, 1692–1850,* comp. Robert T. and Mildred C. Williams, 4 vols. (Danboro, Pennsylvania: Richard T. and Mildred T. Williams, 1971–72), 3 (1811–1831): 63. On this circle, see Louis Arkey's "The Mechanics Union of Trade Associations and the Formation of the Philadelphia Workingmen's Movement," *Pennsylvania Magazine of History and Biography* 76 (April 1952): 144–48 and 172. See also Heighton's statement that "the present efforts of the Working People" of the area had "originally developed in part, in the fall of 1826, in a Trade Society," that of his and Dubois's craft. *The Principles of Aristocratic Legislation*, 4. Heighton delivered an important and convincing plea for a city-central body of the local labor organizations in April, 1827, and another in November. In the following month, the Mechanics' Union of Trade Associations formed. In addition to *An Address, Delivered Before the Mechanics and Working Classes Generally,* see *An Address to the Members of Trade Societies, and to the Working Classes Generally: Being an Exposition . . . Together with a Suggestion and Outlines of a Plan, . . .* (Philadelphia: Office of the Mechanics' Gazette, 1827). See also David Harris, *Socialist Orgins in the United States: the American Forerunners of Marx, 1817–1832* (Assen, 1966), 82–90. The spring of 1828 saw his exposé of *The Principles of Aristocratic Legislation,* urging the Mechanics' Union to turn to political action in the upcoming local elections. Dubois sat on the committee to oversee its publication. He also later chaired a distinct meeting of the new Workingmen's Party which elected him a delegate to the party's general convention. In the next year, 1829, Dubois ran for county coroner on the labor ticket. *Mechanics' Free Press,* August 9, 1828, September 19, 26, October 3, 10, 17, 1829.

11. For the New York City party, see Hugins and Wilentz. By 1828, when the Philadelphia party organized, some New York City workingmen battled alongside local merchants and manufacturers against auctioneers bringing cheaper imported British goods into the local market. Murray N. Rothbard, *The Panic of 1819: Reaction and Policies* (New York: Columbia University Press, 1962), 179–80; and Horace Secrist, "The Anti-Auction Movement and the New York City Workingmen's Party of 1829," *Transactions of the Wisconsin Academy of Science, Arts, and Letters,* vol. 17, part 1, no. 2 (1911): 149–66. Ephraim Conrad published a tract by "A Loaf Bread Maker," probably Jonas Humbert, a political leader of the local bakers for at least twenty years. Charles Sotheran, *Horace Greeley and Other Pioneers of American Socialism,* 2d ed. (New York: McMillan Co., 1915), 102–03; and Rock, 144n.11, 190–91, 196–97. Like Conrad, Huestis, an associate of John Windt and other freethinkers and Owenites, would have supported the *Daily Sentinel* faction, while the former also chaired a meeting in the Fourth Ward. *New York Daily Sentinel,* July 31, 1830. One of the candidates also supported by Humbert, Ming, and the Agrarians was George Bruce, who many years before had helped to organize and lead the Franklin Typographical Society. As the reformed party drifted closer to the Jacksonian Democrats in early 1830, a section of the party aligned with the *Evening Journal* took an orientation friendly to the Whigs; active on its behalf was Robert Townsend, who twenty years before had presided over meetings of his fellow journeymen carpenters. Clearly Hugins, 44, 45, 70–72, 75, judges Townsend too harshly as an outsider dabbling in labor politics; Townsend's presence also undermines the charge, first leveled by its former allies in the *Sentinel* faction and reinforced by later historians, that this faction was simply composed of opportunistic politicians as opposed to the center grouping

of the party, which allegedly enjoyed the backing of the genuine work-ingmen as well as Owenite intellectuals.

12. On Fanshaw, see "Meeting of the Independent Democrats at the Chinese Building," *New York Daily Tribune*, August 7, 1852; John Jentz, "Artisans, Evangelicals, and the City: A Social History of Abolition and Labor Reform in Jacksonian New York" (PhD diss., City University of New York, 1977), 365, 374, 424, 438; and material on his will in the Undated folder, New York Typographical Society Papers, 1816–1885, Manuscript Room, New York City Public Library. On Williams see *The Printers' Circular* 13 (July 1878): 106. Not all surviving early union-ists took this sort of a course. Some who had found success in the interim had little interest in labor. In addition to Chandler, a former Boston unionist, C. C. Hazewell lived long enough to publish a denun-ciation of "Agrarianism" in the *Atlantic Monthly* 3 (April 1859), accord-ing to Arthur M. Schlesinger, Jr., *The Age of Jackson* (New York: Little, Brown & Co., 1945), 506–07.

13. George Henry Evans, "Of the Origins and Progress of the Work-ing Men's Party in New York," in *The Radical* 3 (February 1842): 18.

14. Churchill, 8.

APPENDIX A. Clandestine Labor Organizations

1. Lipset, Trow and Coleman, 38–39.

2. McNeill, 71; Frank Carlton, *The History and Problems of Organ-ized Labor* (Boston: D. C. Heath & Company, 1911), 17. The Boston local celebrated its centennial in 1906. See Charles Jacob Stowell, "The Journeymen Tailors' Union of America: A Study in Trade Union Policy," as *University of Illinois Studies in the Social Sciences* 7 (December 1918): 9.

3. A. Aspinall, *Early English Trade Unions* (London: Batchworth Press, 1949), 33–35, 35n.–36n.

4. *Selected Documents Illustrating the History of Trade Unionism*, vol. 1, *The Tailoring Trade*, ed. Frank W. Galton (London, New York: Longmans, Green, and Co., 1896), 97; Aspinall, 231–33, 233n.

5. *Trial of Twenty-Four Journeymen Tailors*, 177, 169–70, 241, 212–13, 133, 171, 158, 264. The success of this labor organization in thwart-ing their prosecution had a direct impact on the development of the city-wide movement of labor that year. See Arky, 157–58.

6. *Ibid*, 156, 158. See also, for the presence of a different, unin-corporated society alongside the "benevolent" club, 134; and for their meeting places, 124–25, 132–33, 139.

7. Commons, 2:25n., 243; Foner, 567. This tradition among the local tailors was, of course, fed continually by immigrant craftsmen like Wilhelm Weitling.

8. McNeill, 71; and Aspinall, 233. Two associations are listed in *The Philadelphia Directory* for 1811.

9. An informer on their British contemporaries wrote, "Shoemakers and other mechanics adopt similar plans to form unions, but I am given to understand their method is not so well arranged" as those of the tailors or hatters. Aspinall, 232. Reports of shop meetings, elections of delegates, the fining of delegates for revealing the location of their delegated meetings to the unelected, and efforts to regulate the trade in secret found their way to the Home Office. 272–73. Constitution and By Laws of the Union Society of Journeymen Cordwainers of the City and Precents of Baltimore, September 21, 1807; and for further communications from the Philadelphia union, July 10, 17, 1809. See also Article 21 of the Constitution of the Baltimore union, and Report of the Trial of the Journeymen Cordwainers, 30–31. In addition to the sources cited on the shoemakers' trials, see the records of Baltimore prosecution in *Doc. Hist.* 3:249–50, and the original documents in the July, 1809, Session, Criminal Dockets and Minutes of the Court of Oyer and Terminer, Baltimore City Criminal Court, Maryland Hall of Records, Annapolis, Maryland, a source used extensively and well by Steffens.

10. E. Stewart, 880.

Sources

Early American Labor History

Many of the primary sources used in this study have remained largely neglected and merit some further discussion. Readers interested in specific citations should consult the appropriate references in the text.

Early in this century, George E. Barnett worked on "The Printers: A Study in American Trade Unionism," *American Economics Association Quarterly*, 3d ser., 10 (October 1909): 435–759. In the process, he had copied the invaluable minutes of the Philadelphia Typographical Society for 1802–04 and 1806–10, and of the New York Typographical Society for 1809–18. Both of these are now in the Special Collections of the Milton S. Eisenhower Library at Johns Hopkins University in Baltimore. Also useful are the New York Typographical Society Papers, 1816–85 in the Manuscript Collections of the New York City Public Library.

A number of publications have information on wages, working conditions, and organizational patterns. They include *Constitution of the Franklin Society (Printers) of the City of Philadelphia, Instituted March 8, 1788* (Philadelphia: printed by Stewart & Cochran, 1792); *Scale of Prices, Established October 28, 1809. By the New-York Typographical Society*, broadside (New York: n.p., n.d.); *Constitution of the New-York Typographical*

Society, passed July, 1809. (New York: C. S. Van Winkle, 1810); and *Scale of Prices, Established January 7th, 1815, by the Albany Typographical Society,* broadside (Albany: n.p., 1815).

Over time, scholars have reprinted invaluable sources. Ethelbert Stewart also published many old records in his "A Documentary History of Early Organizations of Printers," United States Department of Commerce and Labor *Bulletin* 11 (November 1905): 857–1033. The New York Typographical Society's circular "To the Master Printers of the City of New-York" [December 30, 1809] is included on pp. 37–39 of *The Faith of Our Fathers: An Anthology Expressing the Aspirations of the Common Man, 1790–1850,* ed. Irving Mark and Eugene L. Schwaab (New York: Alfred A. Knopf, 1952), a neglected collection that includes other material on early labor as well. John McIlvaine's remarkable *An Address to the Journeymen Cordwainers L.B. of Philadelphia,* broadside (Philadelphia: n.p., printed at Johnson's Cheap Card and Job Office, [ca. 1796]) is in *American Labor Songs of the Nineteenth Century,* comp. Philip S. Foner (Urbana: University of Illinois Press, 1974): 11, with a facsimile reproduction on 12.

The addresses by union printers are also revealing. Four by New York City journeymen survive from these years: John Clough, *An Address, Delivered on the Fourth of July, 1801. Before the Franklin Typographical Society of New-York, and a Select Company* (New York: George F. Hopkins, 1801); Thomas Ringwood, *An Address Delivered before the Franklin Typographical Association of New-York, and a Select Company; on the Fifth of July, 1802: In Commemoration of the Twenty-Seventh Anniversary of American Independence, and of the Third of the Association* (New York: Southwick and Crooker, 1802); George Asbridge, *An Oration, Delivered before the New-York Typographical Society at Their Second Anniversary, on the Fourth of July, 1811* (New York: C. S. Van Winkle, 1811); and Ebeneezer Mack, *An Oration, Delivered before the New-York Typographical Society, on the Fifth of July, 1813, in Celebration of the Thirty-Seventh Anniversary of American Independence, and Fourth of the Society* (New York: S. Woodworth and Co., 1813). Two from elsewhere offer similar insights: William

Burdick, *An Oration on the Nature and Effects of the Art of Printing. Delivered in Franklin-Hall, July 5, 1802, before the Boston Franklin Association* (Boston: Munroe and Francis, 1802); and George Churchill, *An Address, Pronounced before the Albany Typographical Society, November 6, 1813; on the Advantages Resulting to Mankind from the Invention of Printing* (Albany: n.p., 1813). The address that Joseph Gleason read before the New York union in 1810 was probably Joseph Perkin, *An Oration on Eloquence. Pronounced at the Anniversary Commencement of Harvard University in Cambridge, July 16, 1794* (Boston: Ezra W. Weld and William Greenough, 1794).

Some autobiographical writings are important, if exceptional: *Recollections of the Life of John Binns: Twenty-Nine Years in Europe and Fifty-Three in the United States. Written by Himself, with Anecdotes, Political Historical and Miscellaneous* (Philadelphia: printed by Parry and M'Millan, 1854); and *Autobiography of Thurlow Weed*, ed. Harriet A. Weed (Boston: Houghton, Mifflin and Co., 1883); and Thurlow Weed Barnes compiled a supplemental *Memoir of Thurlow Weed* (Boston: Houghton, Mifflin and Co., 1884). See also the various reminiscences of Charles McDevitt, John Wakefield Frances, and Walt Whitman cited in the notes. Tragedies have robbed us of other sources. According to *The History of Madison County Illinois. With Biographical Sketches of Many Prominent Men and Pioneers* (Edwardsville, Illinois: W. R. Brink & Co., 1882) 85, George Churchill left voluminous writings and reminiscences to the Chicago Historical Society just in time to be destroyed by an 1871 fire that gutted much of its archival material.

Early unionists also issued a wide variety of their own works; Peter Force compiled the most famous of these, *American Archives: Consisting of a Collection of authentick records . . . a documentary history of the origins and progress of the North American colonies. . . .* (Washington: U.S. Congress, 1837–53). Other titles include Joseph Gleason, *An Oration pronounced on the thirtieth Anniversary of American Independence July 4, 1806* (Boston: Oliver & Munroe, 1806); Jacob M. Berriman and Frances Wrigley, *The History of America, abridged for the use of Children of All Denominations* (Philadelphia: printed by Wrigley and Berriman, 1795); *The Following is copied from the journal kept by Mr. Jacob M. Berriman, during his tour to the westward of Fort Recovery . . .*, broadside (Suffield, Connecticut: printed by Edward Gray, 1799); Ira Jones, *A New Treatise on the Consumption Containing an Attempt to Investigate its Real Nature. . . .* (Newfield, Connecticut: printed by Lazarus Beach, 1796); and his *A Present to the Unprejudiced. Being an Attempt to Prove that the Soul and Body of Man Cannot Be Seperated. . . .* (Newfield: printed by Beach and Jones, 1795); John H. Sherman, *A General Account of the Miranda Expedition, Including the Trial and Execution of Ten of his Officers. . . .* (New York: McFarlane & Long, 1808); John W. Scott, *An Historical Sketch of the Pine Street, or Third Presbyterian Church in the City of Philadelphia* (Philadelphia: Bailey, 1837); *A Discourse before the Provident Society, April 3d, 1811, the Eighteenth Anniversary of the Institution* (Philadelphia: n.p., 1811); and *Proposal by J. W. Scott, for Publishing by Subscription, the Moment: a poem, addressed to the American People and other poems By J. McCoy*, broadside (Philadelphia: n.p., 1809); and, possibly, John I. Johnson, *Reflections on Political Society, An Oration . . . Before the Tammany Society* (New York: Freneau and Minuet, 1797). Particularly noteworthy are several collections of poetry, including *The Poetical Recreations of John W. Scott* (Philadelphia: n.p., 1809); David Bruce, *Poems chiefly in the Scottish Dialect* (Washington, Pennsylvania: printed by John Colerick, 1801); and Theophilus Eaton, *Review of New-York, or Rambles Through the City. Original Poems. Moral, Religious, Sarcastic, Descriptive* (New York: printed by John Low, 1813), and its second edition (New York: John Low, 1814).

Later union printers themselves compiled and wrote much of their own history, often using documentary material, some since lost. A series of such sketches appeared regularly in their trade journals, *The Printer* of New York and *The Printers' Circular* of Philadelphia. The latter serialized the "Historical Sketch of the Philadelphia Typographical Society," with installments relative to the years before 1830 in the numbers from March through August 1867; and A. T. Cavis and E. MacMurray, "History of the Columbia Typographical Society" from October

1868 through March 1870. This union also compiled and published lists of former members and officers along with new wage scales; for this study, I used the *Constitution of the Columbia Typographical Society . . . Together with Lists of Officers, Honorary members, and Members of the Society . . .* (Washington, D.C.: Columbia Typographical Union, 1866).

Other relevant compilations include *Leaves of History from the Archives of the Boston Typographical Union No. 13: From the Foundation of the Boston Typographical Society to the Diamond Jubilee of Its Successors* (Boston: Boston Typographical Union, 1923); *Half-Century Souvenir and First Historical Year-Book of the Albany Typographical Union Number Four*, ed. Charles H. Whittemore, et al. (Albany: J. B. Lyons Co., 1905); and *Tribute to the Memory of Charles McDevitt, who was nearly Sixty Years a Member of the New York Typographical Society* (New York: F. Hart & Co., 1877).

Printers' interest in the history of unionism in their craft is also evident in George Stevens, *New York Typographical Union No. 6: Study of a Modern Trade Union and Its Predecessors* (Albany: J. B. Lyon Company, 1913); and George A. Tracy, *The History of the Typographical Union* (Indianapolis, International Typographical Union, 1913). This legacy persisted faintly into our own time, as is evident in such offical accounts as *A Study of the History of the International Typographical Union*, 2 vols. (Colorado Springs: Executive Committee of the I.T.U., 1964, 1967), 1:27–58, or such unofficial work as Douglas McMurtrie's extensive writings on the spread of printing in the U.S. and the late Henry P. Rosemont's "Benjamin Franklin and the Philadelphia Typographical Strikers of 1786," *Labor History* 22 (Summer 1981): 398–429.

Printers in general wrote much of the small library available on various aspects of the craft's history. Isaiah Thomas, *The History of Printing in America, with a Biography of Printers*, 2 vols. (Worcester, Massachusetts: printed by Isaac Sturtevant for Isaiah Thomas, 1810) has gone through various printings, including what was, for the years under discussion, the informatively annotated and revised 1874 edition by Albany printer Joel Munsell, who issued his own *Typographical Miscellany* in 1850.

For other supplementing sources, see "William McCulloch's Additions to Thomas' History of Printing," edited by Clarence S. Brigham in the *American Antiquarian Society Proceedings*, n.s., 31 (1921): 89–247; and "[William] Goddard's Contributions to Thomas' 'History of Printing,'" in Brigham, *Journals and Journeymen: A Contribution to the History of Early American Newspapers* (Philadelphia: University of Pennsylvania Press, 1950). A unique source for the first half of the nineteenth century is "The Printers of Philadelphia," serialized for over two years of the *Printers' Circular* from January 1868. The best recent scholarly guide to the trade in the early national period is Rollo G. Silver, *The American Printer, 1787–1825* (Charlottesville, Virginia: University Press of Virginia, 1967), with a particularly informative discussion of unionism, 13–27.

Rich antiquarian and bibliographical compilations provide important information on early American printed matter and printers. A starting point is Charles Evans, *American Bibliography: A Chronological Dictionary of All Books, Pamphlets, and Periodical Publications Printed in the United States of America from the Genesis of Printing in 1639 Down to and including the Year 1920. With Bibliographical and Biographical Notes*, 14 vols. (Chicago: printed by Blakely Press, 1903–59). Ralph P. Shaw and Richard Shoemaker—and later Gayle Cooker, Carol Rinder Knight, and Scott Buntjen—carried forward Evans's project with *American Bibliography: A Preliminary Checklist through 1834*, 34 vols., plus indices (New York: Scarecrow Press, 1958–82). For the volumes by Evans, Roger Bristol compiled a very useful *Index of Printers, Publishers and Booksellers Indicated by Charles Evans in American Bibliography* (Charlottesville, Virginia: Bibliographical Society of America, 1961); and, for the later volumes, see Knight's and Bunjen's index, *American Bibliography: A Preliminary Checklist* (Methuen, New Jersey: Scarecrow Press, 1983). For the early periodical press: Clarence S. Brigham, *History and Bibliography of American Newspapers*, 2 vols. (Worcester: American Antiquarian Society, 1947), which gives the locations of extant copies and contains a useful index of newspaper printers, and Benjamin M. Lewis, *A Register of Editors, Printers, and Publishers of American*

Magazines, 1741–1810 (New York: New York Public Library, 1957).
The appendix to Donald H. Stewart's *The Oppositionist Press
in the Federalist Period* (Albany: State University of New York
Press, 1969) gives the politics of many of these publications.

A number of well-indexed collections provide guides to advertisements, statements, and articles appearing in contemporary
newspapers and city directories. Further, the Printers' File and
Printers' Authorities File at the American Antiquarian Society,
Worcester, Massachusetts, provide some important information about some of the individual printers who built the first
American trade unions, based on both primary and secondary
sources.

Some published guides cover only materials for specific places.
For Philadelphia, see *The Arts and Crafts in Philadelphia,
Maryland, and South Carolina, 1786–1800, 2d ser., Gleanings
from Newspapers,* collected by Alfred Coxe Prime (n.p.: Walpole
Society, 1932); and Margaret Woodbury, *Public Opinion in
Philadelphia, 1789–1801* (Northampton, Massachusetts: Depart-
ment of History, Smith College, 1920). Useful clippings and list-
ings from the city directories may be found in Harry Glenn
Brown, "Philadelphia's Contribution to the Book Arts and Book
Trade, 1796–1810" in *Papers of the Bibliographic Society of
America* 37 (1943): 275–92. He and Maude O. Brown compiled
"A Directory of the Book Arts and Book Trade in Philadelphia
to 1820, including Painters and Engravers," *Bulletin of the New
York Public Library* 52 (1949): 211–26, 290–98, 339–47, 387–401,
447–58, 492–503, 564–73, 615–22; and 54:25–37, 89–92, 123–45.
Equivalent titles for New York City: *The Arts and Crafts in
New York, 1777–1799: Advertisements and News Items from
New York City Newspapers,* and *The Arts and Crafts in New
York, 1800–1804: Advertisements and News Items from New
York City Newspapers,* both comp. Ruth Suswein Gottesman
(New York: New York Historical Society, 1948 and 1949); and *A
Register of Artists, Engravers, Booksellers, Bookbinders, Print-
ers and Publishers in New York City, 1633–1820,* comp. George
Leslie McKay (New York: New York Public Library, 1942), upon
which Harry A. Weiss based *The Number of Persons and Firms
Connected with the Graphic Arts in New York City, 1633–1820*

(New York: New York Public Library, 1946). See, too, *Boston Printers, Publishers, and Booksellers: 1640–1800*, ed. Benjamin Franklin V (Boston: G. K. Hall & Co., 1980). Also revelant are three compilations by Rollo G. Silver: *The Boston Book Trade, 1800–1825* (New York: New York Public Library, 1949); "The Baltimore Book Trade, 1800–1825," *Bulletin of the New York Public Library* 57 (January 1957): 114–25, 187–201, 248–51, 297–305, 349–57; and "The Book Trade and the Protective Tariff: 1800–1804," *Papers of the Bibliographical Society of America* 46 (1952): 33–44.

Students of unionism in trades other than printing will find the aforementioned indices and extracts invaluable. Evans's *American Bibliography*, for example, is the only source for publication of the *Constitution of the Mutual Benefit Society of Cordwainers of the City of New York, Instituted March, 1806* (New York: John E. Scoper Co., 1808), and *The Philadelphia Cabinet and Chair-Makers' Book of Prices* (Philadelphia: n.p., 1794). No copies have been located.

Shoemakers began unionizing in the early national period and left an immense amount of information. Much can be gleaned from the accounts of their trials for conspiracy from 1806 into 1842, reprinted in *A Documentary History of American Industrial Society*, ed. John R. Commons, et al, 2d ed., 10 vols. (New York: Russell and Russell, 1958). For the Baltimore society and its trial, see the MS Criminal Dockets and Minutes of the Court of Oyer and Terminer, July, 1809 Sessions, Baltimore City Criminal Court; and the apparently confiscated MS Constitution and By Laws of the Union Society of Journeymen Cordwainers of the City and Precents of Baltimore [includes Minutes, 1806–1809], both in the Maryland Hall of Records, Annapolis.

Furniture workers established such militant and stable organizations that one cannot help but wonder how much what museum curators and private collectors treasure today was the product of union labor, or, indeed, how any could prize the craftsmanship while being indifferent to the unionist standards that protected it. In addition to the newspaper accounts of their activities, see *The Journeymen Cabinet and Chair-Maker's Book of Prices* (Philadelphia: printed by Ormrod & Conrad, 1795); *The*

Cabinet-Makers' Philadelphia and London Book of Prices
(Philadelphia: Snowden and McCorkle, 1796); *The Constitution of the Pennsylvania Society of Journeymen Cabinet-Makers of the City of Philadelphia. Instituted November 8, 1806— Incorporated May 20, 1825. Revised October 10, 1829* (Philadelphia: printed by Garden and Thompson, 1829), a typed copy of which is in the Labor Collections of the Wisconsin Historical Society at Madison; and *The Journeymen Cabinet and Chair-Makers of New York Book of Prices* (New York: n.p., 1796).

Finally, the New York union in the shipbuilding trades left some notable sources. *The Constitution of the New-York Journeymen Shipwrights Society* (New York: n.p., 1804) represented an early organization that had collapsed by 1815. The Manuscripts Room of the New York Public Library has a marvelous collection on its successor, including its Constitution/Members, 1815–16 [includes Minutes, 1815–16]; Roll of Members, 1815–18; Account Book, 1818–27; Bank Book, 1823–28; and Rolls of Members, 1818.

Index